J.S. MILL
ON LIBERTY

This volume brings together in a convenient form J.S. Mill's *On Liberty* and a selection of important essays by a number of eminent Mill scholars, including Isaiah Berlin, Alan Ryan, John Rees, C.L. Ten and Richard Wollheim. As well as providing authoritative commentary upon *On Liberty*, the essays also reflect a broader debate about the philosophical foundations of Mill's liberalism, particularly the question of the connection between Mill's professed utilitarianism and his commitment to individual liberty. In a substantial introduction the editors survey the debate and conclude that the outcome has profound and disturbing implications, both for our understanding of Mill's classic defence of individual freedom and more generally for the style of liberal argument with which Mill is typically identified.

The book will be of interest to students of Mill, to ethical and political philosophers and to anyone interested in the contemporary status of liberalism.

John Gray is a Fellow of Jesus College, Oxford
G.W. Smith is Lecturer in Politics at the University of Lancaster

ROUTLEDGE PHILOSOPHERS
IN FOCUS SERIES
Series editor: Stanley Tweyman
York University, Toronto

GODEL: *THEOREM* IN FOCUS
Edited by S. G. Shanker

DAVID HUME: *DIALOGUES CONCERNING
NATURAL RELIGION* IN FOCUS
Edited by Stanley Tweyman

CIVIL DISOBEDIENCE IN FOCUS
Edited by Hugo Adam Bedau

JOHN LOCKE: *LETTER CONCERNING
TOLERATION* IN FOCUS
*Edited by John Horton and
Susan Mendus*

ARISTOTLE: *DE ANIMA* IN FOCUS
Edited by Michael Durrant

RENÉ DESCARTES: *MEDITATIONS* IN FOCUS
Edited by Stanley Tweyman

PLATO: *MENO* IN FOCUS
Edited by Jane M. Day

J.S. MILL
ON LIBERTY
in focus

Edited by
John Gray
and
G.W. Smith

London and New York

First published 1991
by Routledge
11 New Fetter Lane, London EC4P 4EE

Simultaneously published in the USA and Canada
by Routledge
29 West 35th Street, New York, NY 10001

Reprinted 1996

Typeset in 10/12 pt Bembo by
Florencetype Ltd, Kewstoke, Avon
Printed in Great Britain by
T. J. Press (Padstow) Ltd, Padstow, Cornwall

British Library Cataloguing in Publication Data
Mill, John Stuart 1806–1873
J. S. Mill's 'On liberty' in focus. – (Routledge
philosophers in focus series).
1. Liberty. Mill, John Stuart, 1806–1873. On liberty
I. Title   II. Gray, John   III. Smith, G. W.
323.44

Library of Congress Cataloguing in Publication Data
J. S. Mill's On liberty in focus
edited by John Gray and G. W. Smith.
p.   cm. – (Routledge philosophers in focus series)
Includes bibliographical references and index.
1. Mill, John Stuart, 1806–1873. On Liberty. 2. Liberty.
I. Gray, John. II. Smith, G. W. III. Series.
JC585.M75 1991
323.44 – dc20   91–40793

ISBN 0–415–01000–4 (hbk)
ISBN 0–415–01001–2 (pbk)

CONTENTS

CONTENTS

ACKNOWLEDGEMENTS

The editors and the publishers would like to thank the following copyright holders for permission to reprint material: Oxford University Press for 'John Stuart Mill and the ends of life' by Sir Isaiah Berlin from his *Four Essays on Liberty* (1969); Richard Wollheim for 'John Stuart Mill and Isaiah Berlin: the ends of life and the preliminaries of morality'; *The Listener* for 'John Stuart Mill's art of living' by Alan Ryan (74: 1965); Basil Blackwell for 'A re-reading of Mill on liberty' by John Rees (*Political Studies* 1960); Athlone Press for extracts from 'J.S. Mill on freedom' by G.W. Smith, originally published in Zbigniew Pelczynski and John Gray, eds, *Conceptions of Liberty in Political Philosophy* (1984).

INTRODUCTION

John Gray and G.W. Smith

In recent years, much interpretation and criticism of John Stuart Mill's *On Liberty* has focused on the dialogue between traditional and revisionary schools of Mill scholarship.[1] The traditional school of interpretation has a distinguished pedigree in the received version of nineteenth-century British intellectual history. According to this view, there is to be found in the works of Jeremy Bentham and James Mill a systematic moral doctrine which animates the practical politics and reformist projects of the Philosophic Radicals. It is widely agreed that the Philosophic Radicals had a significant impact on policy and government in Britain in the middle decades of the nineteenth century, altering, often for the better, much in central and local government and in the law.[2] These reformist projects were inspired by the doctrines of classical utilitarianism, encapsulated in the principle that only pleasure has intrinsic value and right conduct is that which maximizes pleasure, or best promotes general welfare, where this is conceived as the sum of all pleasures. Classical utilitarianism, expounded by Bentham and his disciple James Mill, is thus a theory at once hedonistic and consequentialist, affirming that only pleasure is good and that rightness consists in the production of those consequences that are best in terms of the pleasure they contain. It is this simple doctrine, crude perhaps, but coherent enough, which the classical utilitarians propagated, and which informed their reformist activities.

According to the traditional school of Mill interpretation and criticism, John Stuart Mill was brought to recognize the limitations of classical utilitarianism but was nevertheless unable entirely to emancipate himself from the influence of his father and Bentham, with the result that he remained an inconsistent and merely eclectic thinker in whose work no coherent doctrine can be found.

1

Undoubtedly, the most eloquent and influential exponent of this view is Isaiah Berlin. Berlin presents his reading of Mill in the seminal paper which constitutes the first critical contribution appended to Mill's celebrated essay in this volume. But it is perhaps worth remarking that Berlin is by no means alone amongst contemporary scholars in taking the line first struck by Mill's great Victorian critic, James Fitzjames Stephen.[3] Indeed, apart from Fitzjames Stephen's vigorous broadside, arguably the most radical and uncompromising traditionalist attack is that mounted by Gertrude Himmelfarb.[4] It may be useful briefly to consider Himmelfarb's interpretation of Mill as a point of fairly acute contrast with that of Berlin. Himmelfarb maintains that it is quite pointless for us to seek for a logical connection between the philosophy of utilitarianism and On Liberty because Mill manifestly simply gave up on attempting any systematic link between freedom and utility. True, he describes the essay as a 'kind of philosophic textbook of a single truth'.[5] But the 'truth' in question is not the Principle of Utility, that is to say, the precept which directs us to pursue the greatest happiness of the greatest number; it is rather the celebrated 'one very simple principle' of the first chapter of On Liberty, according to which 'the sole end for which mankind are warranted, individually or collectively, in interfering with the liberty of action of any of their number, is self-protection' (p. 30). Mill's 'single truth' is thus the celebrated Principle of Liberty (or Harm Principle), which he presents as being 'entitled to govern absolutely the dealings of society with the individual in the way of compulsion and control, whether the means used be physical force in the form of legal penalties, or the moral coercion of public opinion' (p. 30). Himmelfarb contends that Mill invokes the Principle of Liberty as an 'absolute' defence of individual freedom against utility-based considerations, and that he does so precisely because he perceives the tendency of the latter to justify social encroachments upon individual liberty in the name of maximizing the general happiness.[6] In an arresting corollary she maintains that this stance in no way involves Mill in abandoning utilitarianism as such. It is not that Mill changes his mind over a period of years in the course of extricating himself from Benthamism, finally to reveal himself in On Liberty as a thoroughly reconstructed liberal. It is rather that Mill's mind remains in a profound tension between strictly incompatible principles, a tension exhibited *inter alia* in the fact that although On Liberty and *Utilitarianism* were prepared for

2

press pretty well contemporaneously by Mill he proceeds in each upon quite distinct and incommensurable premises – freedom in the one book, utility in the other.[7] The traditional interpretation could scarcely be put in a sharper fashion.

Himmelfarb's reading, however, rests heavily upon a questionable interpretation of what Mill means by the Principle of Liberty's governing social interference with individual freedom 'absolutely'. She maintains that Mill means by this that the Principle is primary and underived and thus in conflict with a logically independent Principle of Utility. The difficulties with this are twofold. First, Mill certainly never saw himself as being torn between contending principles. Thus, recording the stages of his intellectual career in his *Autobiography*, he stresses his concern for consistency: 'I found the fabric of my old and taught opinions giving way in many fresh places, but was incessantly occupied with weaving it anew.'[8] Second, even within the ambit of the argument of *On Liberty* Himmelfarb's interpretation is somewhat forced. For the natural reading of Mill here is that he is simply claiming that considerations of 'self-protection' are 'absolute' in the sense of being the sole or the exclusive consideration to be held to be relevant in respect of 'the dealings of society with the individual in the way of compulsion or control'. That is to say, he intends the term to refer to the application, rather than to the derivation, of the Principle. Moreover, whereas the effect of Himmelfarb's reading is abruptly to foreclose further discussion of Mill's philosophical consistency, the advantage of this alternative is to leave the question of whether Mill can (or wishes) to derive the Principle of Liberty from a superordinate Principle of Utility an open one, and hence whether or to what degree he succeeds as a consistent thinker. It thus enables us to address what otherwise is in danger of being neglected, namely the need for a careful examination of Mill's distinctive and original treatment of key concepts such as 'liberty of action', 'self-protection', and 'harm' in the context of his very much modified and revised understanding of his inherited classical utilitarian inheritance.[9] Mill claims that the fabric of his thought is all of a piece; we owe it to him to take the claim seriously.

What has perhaps made Berlin's version of the traditional interpretation the primary focus of much succeeding Mill scholarship is his recognition that Mill's mind is both capable of great complexity and susceptible to deep ambivalence. In his immensely influential contribution to this volume Berlin vividly depicts the extent and depth of Mill's dilemmas and concludes that Mill never was able successfully to surmount his difficulties and to reconcile his continuing endorsement of utilitarian theory with his actual moral and political commitments.[10] In particular, and above all, he ultimately fails to square his theoretical commitment to an aggregative and welfarist utilitarianism, in which individual liberty has only an instrumental value, with his substantive view that human choice, autonomy, individuality, and freedom of action have moral importance in themselves, independently of their contribution to general welfare. Since no utilitarian argument can possibly show that liberty has intrinsic value and should be given priority over the claims of general welfare, the project Mill attempts in *On Liberty* is thus doomed from the start. Whereas consistent utilitarians such as Bentham or James Fitzjames Stephen treat liberty as a neutral means to overall welfare, Mill evidently regards diversity, individuality, and 'experiments in living' as valuable for their own sakes. The enterprise he thus undertakes in *On Liberty* is the heroic but ultimately vain one of trying to demonstrate that giving priority to liberty over other goods, and even over the claims of general welfare, will over the long haul best promote the general welfare.

Berlin's classic criticism of Mill suggests that Mill, like Berlin himself (but without explicitly theorizing the insight, and indeed while resisting its implications for ethical theory), recognizes an ultimate diversity of values that are often in conflict, rarely fully combinable and lack any overarching standard in terms of which trade-offs between them can be arbitrated. This value-pluralist position is, of course, wholly at variance with the explicit monism of Mill's official ethical theory. In Berlin's view, then, Mill's mind is divided against itself, not only in virtue of his conflicting commitments to the maximization of general welfare and the protection of individual liberty, but also, more deeply, in his conception of the relations between moral theory and moral judgement. For, whereas Mill's official view, like that of the classical utilitarians, is that theory should prevail over intuition, in practice Mill's moral and political judgements are often impossible to justify in classical utilitarian terms. Mill's reweaving of utilitarian theory is an attempt to bring theory and intuition into equilibrium, but such a project, Berlin agrees, is bound to end in failure.

However, although he regards *On Liberty* as being fatally flawed

in respect of philosophical consistency and rigour, Berlin nevertheless celebrates it as a passionate and inspiring call-to-arms in the
cause of individual liberty. With immense sympathy, and with an
eloquence perhaps rivalled only by Mill himself, Berlin depicts Mill
as a thinker animated, indeed even enthused, by a distinctive and
profound vision of human living. His vision of humankind is not at
all the narrow and sterile view of official Benthamism, according to
which human beings are merely pleasure-seeking and pain-avoiding
machines, but rather of human beings as uniquely individual
personalities, endowed with priceless potentialities and capacities
for moral choice and spiritual growth; a vision the social corollary
of which is a society at once caring and tolerant, displaying a
commitment to a profound respect for persons in the common
cultivation of freedom and individuality. For Berlin, then, the
permanent value of *On Liberty* is to be found in the passion and the
eloquence with which Mill attempts to persuade us to share his
vision. And it would indeed be fatuous to deny or belittle the
interest and importance of the literary or rhetorical dimensions of
Mill's essay to which Berlin alerts us, aspects which have perhaps
been unduly neglected by Mill scholars.[11] Nevertheless, Berlin's
seminal essay has primarily had the effect of stimulating further
analytical work upon the argument of *On Liberty*, in the form of a
renewed discussion of the traditional interpretation, a discussion in
which Berlin's central claim, that Mill's mind is essentially self-
divided and that there is no coherent doctrine to be found in his
writings, has come increasingly to be questioned. It is this debate
which we shall pursue. The three chapters following that of Berlin,
by Alan Ryan, John Rees, and John Gray in different ways take up
this revisionary theme.

Alan Ryan's original and penetrating interpretation of Mill, in
terms of the centrality of Mill's conception of the 'Art of Life',
initiated a new era in Mill studies. In the convenient summary
presented in this volume, Ryan argues that, contrary to the
traditional view, Mill's work can be shown to contain a coherent
and unitary theory, of which *On Liberty* is a consistent application.[12]
The nub of this theory, as Ryan interprets it, is a radically
innovative development of the utilitarian theory of practical
reasoning in which several distinct spheres or departments are
recognized within practical life. Mill's terminology is not entirely
consistent, but Ryan maintains that Mill's intention is clear, and it
is primarily to distinguish the sphere of Morality from those of

Prudence and Excellence (which he sometimes calls Nobility). Thus, according to Mill's theory of the Art of Life, which he sets forth in the later chapters of his *System of Logic*, all these spheres of practical reasoning are governed by the sovereign Principle of Utility which affirms that only pleasure, or happiness, has ultimate value. Of the three departments Mill distinguishes, however, only that of Morality generates obligations, and none specifies an obligation to promote general welfare. What is of particular interest in Mill's account as Ryan construes it is that he identifies the sphere of Morality with enforceability and harm-prevention. That is to say, the subject matter of morality, in Mill's revisionary conception of it, is precisely that of enforceable obligations about harm-prevention. Hence Mill's position is that both Prudence (the concern for one's own interests) and Excellence (the pursuit of beauty or nobility in character) are inherently outside the sphere of enforcement and, therefore, of morality. The import of this for the argument of *On Liberty* is that prudence and ideals of character belong to the self-regarding sphere, the sphere of liberty. The 'one very simple principle' can then be seen as the dominant principle in Mill's revisionary or critical morality. In excluding both paternalist restraint on liberty intended to prevent harm to self, and moralist or perfectionist limitations of liberty aimed at promoting virtue or worthiness in character, the Principle of Liberty is revealed as a theorem, or at least as a plausible application, of the doctrine of the Art of Life itself.

The effect of Ryan's revolutionary interpretation of Mill's thought is to bridge the supposed logical hiatus asserted by the traditionalists between utility and freedom, *On Liberty* now figuring as a fragment of a larger philosophical project of which *Utilitarianism* is a further component. For, in *Utilitarianism*, Mill seeks to distinguish within morality its most stringent and essential element, namely, claims of justice; these latter, being entirely negative, having strictly to do with the prevention of injury to the vital interests of others. It is, then, as a principle of justice, and not merely of morality, that the Principle of Liberty should properly be interpreted. The various consequential arguments of *On Liberty*, such as the argument from the fallibility of opinions, and the argument for individuality as an ingredient in human well-being, then emerge as arguments in support of the claim that it is the Principle of Liberty, and not some other moral principle, that is best suited as the fundamental maxim of justice. And, underlying this specific argument, is the general argument of the theory of the Art of Life, according to which the utilitarian objective of maximizing pleasure or happiness is best promoted, not directly, but by acting in accordance with the maxims of the various departments of the Art of Life. Ryan's sympathetic and fruitful reading has undoubtedly done much to correct the standard view of Mill as a confused and unsystematic thinker and of *On Liberty* as a muddle-headed attempt to marry liberal and utilitarian values that was doomed from the start. The upshot of Ryan's reinterpretation is that Millian liberal utilitarianism, whatever its ultimate defensibility, cannot simply be written off as incoherent.

This is not to say, however, that Mill's position is without difficulties. A traditional objection to Mill's doctrine in *On Liberty* is that the Principle of Liberty it seeks to defend is thoroughly indeterminate in its meaning and application. If restraint of liberty can be justified only on condition that it prevents harm to others, what is to count as harming others? Can offence to the feelings of others be accounted a harm to them? And can the nature and severity of harms be established without recourse to moral judgements that might prove intractably controversial? Thus, Ryan refers to the celebrated controversy concerning the Wolfenden Committee Report on Homosexuality and Prostitution, and, in particular, to the strictures of Lord Justice Devlin upon the apparently Millian assumptions of the Committee, and he does so in a way which serves to raise precisely these questions.[13] The Committee had advocated a relaxation in some respects of the English laws against homosexuality and prostitution, and they had done so on the grounds that 'there must remain a realm of private morality and immorality, which is, in brief and crude terms, not the law's business' (p. 162). Devlin's response is that where there is immorality there is, or is likely to be (Devlin is unclear here), social harm. And, since the law's business is with protecting society from harm, it cannot possibly recognize a private realm of action in principle beyond its reach. Ryan argues that both parties to the debate misconstrue Mill's depiction of the private sphere and hence his understanding of morality: in so far as the Committee's concerns are with relations between consenting adults the issue cannot be one of other-regarding morality in any form, as such relations must, on Millian principles, fall within the self-regarding sphere of Prudence or, possibly, Aesthetics. Undoubtedly, Ryan's distinctions clarify what the issue is, and serve to eliminate what, at least from a Millian point of view, must be regarded as spurious red-herrings. But identifying whose harm is properly in question does not of itself solve the essential problem which divided the parties, namely whether, or in what respects, such activities might harm non-consenting third parties, or society at large.

It is in order to answer questions of this sort that John Rees seeks, in the justly celebrated paper which follows that of Ryan, to interpret Mill's Principle of Liberty as referring to harm to others' interests.[14] On Rees's reading the self-regarding area becomes, not the sphere of conduct that affects no one else, which would surely be virtually empty, but instead the area in which the interests of others are not affected injuriously. This construal of Mill's conception of harm as meaning a set-back to an interest has considerable textual support in *On Liberty*, and it provides a way of avoiding at least some of the problems generated by the vagueness of the notion of harm. For if a conception of interests can be fleshed out in such a way as to enable us to identify and weigh them without recourse to disputed and question-begging value-judgements, the Harm Principle might be invested with some genuine action-guiding force and the self-regarding area, or sphere of liberty, endowed with a determinate content. That Rees's interpretation has merit is suggested by much recent work in the Millian tradition, most particularly by that of Joel Feinberg, the first volume of whose magisterial *The Moral Limits of the Criminal Law* is devoted to a systematic and persuasive development of Mill's conception of harm as a set-back to interests, which plausibly resolves many of the difficult and puzzling cases such an account creates.[15] At the very least, Rees's chapter provides the intellectual resources required to resist the standard claim made by many critics since Fitzjames Stephen that, since all acts may affect others, the sphere is necessarily empty. For, in making 'interests' rather than 'effects' the crucial term in Mill's Principle, Rees opens the way for an interpretation of that principle in which it can serve at least some of the purposes Mill has in mind for it. Along with that of Ryan, Rees's rereading of Mill can claim credit for reviving Mill studies by developing a powerful new model of his thought which is resistant to the traditional criticisms of its manifest inconsistency, muddle-headedness or vacuity.

In John Gray's chapter, the project undertaken is that of weaving together in a coherent pattern the principal elements of the revisionary interpretations of Ryan, Rees, and others, and of setting out a new account of Mill's view of happiness and individuality.[16] In part, Gray's interpretation is a development of that of Rees, in that he accepts that harm for Mill means injury to interests and goes on to maintain that Mill has an account of vital human interests – namely, interests in security and autonomy – which resembles Rawls's theory of the primary goods but which is derivable from his utilitarianism. In his account of Mill's utilitarianism, Gray is indebted to Ryan's work on Mill's doctrine of the Art of Life, and to the interpretation put forward by Berger of Mill's utilitarianism as being hierarchical and pluralistic.[17] Gray, however, goes further than either Ryan or Berger might wish in arguing that Mill's is a distinctive species of indirect utilitarianism. This variety of utilitarianism is distinctive in that in it the Principle of Utility functions as an axiological rather than as an action-guiding principle, specifying that only happiness has intrinsic value. Its bearing on action is thus indirect, inasmuch as it serves as a standard of assessment for motives, dispositions, rules, and entire codes of conduct (and not only for moral codes). It is in its claim that the Principle of Utility functions as a standard of assessment for the whole of practical life, and not just for rules of conduct, that indirect utilitarianism is to be distinguished from rule-utilitarianism. The Principle of Utility thus constitutes a standard of criticism and reform for all branches of practice, and it issues, not in specific injunctions to action, but in the *axiomata media*, or guiding maxims, of the various departments of the Art of Life.

The substantive claims of Gray's contribution to this volume concern the application of Mill's indirect utilitarianism to the project undertaken in *On Liberty*. He argues that Mill supports his argument for the Principle of Liberty by way of a theory of the vital human interests in security and autonomy. Mill's argument for the status of security as a vital interest is given in the last chapter of *Utilitarianism*, which was written before *On Liberty* but published after it, and which may be interpreted as a sort of prolegomenon to the later work. The argument for the role of autonomy as a vital interest is found mainly in *On Liberty* itself, and most particularly in chapter 3, where Mill presents 'individuality' as a vital ingredient in human well-being. In Gray's revisionary interpretation, Mill's conception of happiness differs markedly from that of classical utilitarianism, and in ways that tend to support Mill's argument for the importance of liberty. For, according to this reading, human happiness is connected inseparably with successful activity in which each person's generic and specific powers are realized. This is to say that, with Aristotle, Mill conceives human happiness as a mode of flourishing in which the powers distinctive of the human species find full expression: it represents the completion of human nature. Against Aristotle, but along with von Humboldt, he holds that happiness for a human being consists in the realization, not only of the powers and capacities he has in common with the species as a whole, but also of the nature that is peculiarly his own – of his individuality. Believing that each person possesses a nature peculiar to himself, as well as the nature common to his species, Mill is able to represent individuality as a constitutive ingredient, and not just a necessary condition, of human happiness.

Gray's interpretation of Mill's understanding of happiness helps the argument of *On Liberty* in several ways. In the first place, it confirms the pluralistic character of Mill's utilitarianism by maintaining that happiness will have a different, and indeed a peculiar and unique, content for each person. Second, Mill argues that, given the indefinite diversity of the content and conditions of human happiness, it is best promoted by according individuals the maximum freedom in which to try out 'experiments in living'. And Mill's conception of happiness supports the argument in yet a third way, through his claim that the happiness achieved when a man realizes the demands of his unique nature is co-extensive with the higher pleasure discussed in *Utilitarianism*. This last is a claim never made explicitly by Mill, but it is latent in much of *On Liberty*, again especially in the chapter on individuality. In so far as the higher pleasures are autonomously chosen activities and, moreover, activities which express each person's unique individuality, the human happiness of which individuality is an essential ingredient must contain as a constituent autonomy and, therefore, freedom. Hence, *On Liberty* may be understood as an argument for the status of autonomy as a vital human interest, as an essential part of the 'permanent interests of man as a progressive being' (p. 31). The overall strategy of Mill's argument in *On Liberty* is thus to forge conceptual links between liberty and human happiness, in terms of which the claim that the promotion of happiness requires the protection of liberty, even at apparent cost to happiness, loses its aspect of paradox and becomes plausible and defensible in the broader context of his indirect utilitarianism.

In C.L. Ten's chapter, the traditional interpretation and criticism of Mill is given a distinguished restatement in the context of a critique of recent work by Gray, Rees, Honderich, Berger, Hoag, and others.[18] The upshot of Ten's critique is that none of the reformulations of Mill's argument in *On Liberty* advanced by these writers succeeds in reconciling Mill's utilitarian and liberal commitments. In different ways each of these revisionist writers tries to show how excluding certain consequences (for example, feelings of offence) from the utilitarian calculus as other-regarding grounds for limiting liberty can be justified in utilitarian terms. Their strategy of argument is to show how the self-regarding area can be given a definite and non-trivial content by restricting the range of effects on others that come under the scope of the Harm Principle. In part, Ten's critique builds on earlier criticisms of some aspects of the revisionary interpretations. Thus Honderich and Wollheim argue persuasively that Rees fails to show in Mill any satisfactory account of interests.[19] Certainly, interests cannot be constituted by social recognition, since this would render the application of the Harm Principle unacceptably conservative and relativistic. Nor does Rees's interpretation contain any clear account of the relations between interests, even essential interests, and moral rights. Ten finds analogous difficulties in Dworkin's ingenious attempt to exclude illiberal or non-utilitarian preferences from the utilitarian calculus – a move attempted also by Wollheim.[20] No good reason exists, he concludes, for not weighing all preferences in the utilitarian calculus – a procedure which must tend to undermine the Principle of Liberty. He goes on incisively to criticize Gray's reinterpretation of *On Liberty* as an exercise in indirect utilitarianism. His first criticism is that even an indirect utilitarian argument could not support the absolute (or at least quasi-absolute) status Mill wishes to confer on the Principle of Liberty. This illustrates a general, and perhaps fatal, difficulty of indirect utilitarianism, namely, that the critical and the practical levels of moral thought cannot, either in practice or consistently with utilitarian ethics, be sealed off hermetically from one another. Ten's second, and no less effective, line of criticism is that Mill's indirect utilitarian argument for liberty, even if it were formally coherent, would fail because it depends on premises that are doubtful or false. As Gray himself admits, Mill gives no evidence for the claim that those who have experienced the pleasures of liberty will never renounce them; indeed Mill explicitly rejects the thesis of the irreversibility of liberty needed to support his Principle of Liberty. For he is clear that, even if (implausibly enough) people who have once tasted the benefits of liberty will never give them up in their own case, they are unlikely to show any similar concern for the liberty of others. This is to say that Gray's defence of Mill, like the others considered by Ten, founders on the fact of deep and widespread illiberal preferences to which a consistent utilitarian is bound to give weight at both the critical and the practical levels of moral thinking. Ten's conclusion may be stated in another, more specific, fashion. Liberal political morality requires that rights to freedom and autonomy be conferred equally on all. No utilitarian theory, however, not even the complex, pluralistic, and hierarchical indirect utilitarianism attributed to Mill by Gray, can from its aggregative maximizing premises derive a distributive principle such as Mill's Principle of Liberty. Such principles act as constraints on the promotion of happiness even as Mill conceives it. The traditional view appears, then, to be vindicated: in attempting to derive from the Principle of Utility a principle that constrains the pursuit of general welfare (by reference to the value of liberty) Mill is engaged in a strictly impossible enterprise.

Mill employs the phrase 'liberty of action' to characterize the kind of freedom he has in mind as qualifying for protection by the Principle of Liberty (p. 30). In his chapter G.W. Smith shifts the focus of attention from the question of the derivation of the principle, and from whether Mill can give a satisfactory account of what is to count as 'harming others', to ask a number of questions about Mill's understanding of freedom itself. What is his conception of the attributes of the free agent, that is to say, of the agent who is considered to have freedom to lose and hence who requires, and benefits from, the protection of the Principle of Liberty? How broadly, or narrowly, is the protective net of liberty thus spread? Indeed, is it possible to identify any clear and determinate boundaries in respect of Mill's understanding of freedom, or is his thinking here as essentially indeterminate as it appears to be in respect of harm itself? And, finally, is Mill's handling of the concept of freedom such that we can accept Berlin's picture of Mill as, if not a consistent utilitarian, at least an exemplary exponent of fundamental liberal values?

Smith argues that although Mill regards the absence of coercion, whether 'physical' or 'moral', as a necessary condition of freedom, he by no means takes it to be sufficient. Thus, animals free from chains or intimidation would still fail to enjoy 'freedom of action', in the sense of the phrase implied in Mill's Principle of Liberty; for

Berlin is surely correct when he says that Mill's understanding of freedom reflects his understanding of human nature, and that what for Mill ultimately distinguishes humankind from animals is their capacity for choice (p. 135). Gray makes substantially the same point in his identification of the close logical connection established by Mill between freedom, autonomy, and that distinctively human form of happiness to be found in the development and exercise of individuality (pp. 194–207). It may be replied to this that although choice is crucial to Mill's conception of the free agent, freedom of choice and individuality stand at some logical distance from one another, and that Mill regards choice as essentially a 'negative' matter of absence of impediments upon a range of opportunities whereas individuality involves the 'positive' achievement of a particular and valued kind of activity: indeed, that the former is a necessary, but logically distinct, condition of the latter. Smith contends, however, that Mill evolves a conception of free agency in which the one is elided into the other, with complicating, indeed for the liberal, ominous, implications for the Principle of Liberty.

Smith claims to find the roots of Mill's conception of freedom in On Liberty in his discussion of liberty in the System of Logic, where Mill attempts to tackle the traditional philosophical problem of freedom and determinism, particularly in the form of the doctrine of the social determination of character propagated with such missionary zeal by the early socialist Robert Owen. According to Owen we cannot be free because we are all merely products of our social circumstances; as he puts it, in a phrase repeated by Mill, 'our characters are made for us and not by us'. Mill, of course, feels bound to reject what amounts to an argument for the inevitability of universal social conformism and he responds by evolving a modification of Humean compatibilism, according to which human freedom is essentially bound up with agents' ability causally to intervene in the social process of character formation by taking a hand in amending themselves. Clearly with his own experience of extricating himself from the consequences of his father's efforts to mould the perfect Utilitarian in mind, Mill argues that Owen is mistaken and that we can alter our character, but only if we have the requisite desire to do so. As a professed empiricist and determinist Mill cannot of course make any appeal to a contra-casual act of will to explain the actual occurrence of the desire for self-change; if it occurs it must be socially produced. Hence the vital necessity for individuals to live in societies marked by a 'variety of situations' and multifarious 'experiments in living'. For only under these circumstances may we expect the crucial desire for self-change to be stimulated and individuals to engage in the exercise and development of the uniquely human capacities which they enjoy as 'progressive beings'. Irrespective of its metaphysical status as a solution to the problem of freedom and determinism, or of its philosophical standing as an account of human autonomy, the effect of Mill's innovations, Smith argues, is to point him in a very fruitful direction as far as his strictly social theory is concerned. For the 'self-amendment' of the *System of Logic* evolves naturally into the 'individuality' of *On Liberty*, and the logical form of the conception of freedom Mill hammers out in response to Owen proves ideally suited to identify and resist what he considers to be the greatest threat in modern 'democratic' society, namely, the growth of an insidious pall of deadening social uniformity of manners and beliefs, the effect of which is to prevent people from even aspiring to do what they could do if they tried.

The 'liberty of action' of the Principle of Liberty is thus best understood as being intended by Mill primarily to delimit a self-regarding sphere in which individuals may exhibit a very specific and indeed exacting kind of free agency: specific in that its sense is heavily theoretical and must be elicited from Mill's metaphysics (in this respect, at least, Mill is impressively consistent); and exacting in that the full fruition of this very distinctive conception of freedom represents an achievement on the part of agents who must not only actually conceive a desire for character self-change but must also strive successfully against present habits, inclinations, and the variety of social pressures to realize their ideals of personality. It is this latter consideration in particular which, Smith maintains, in effect elides the distinction between 'negative' and 'positive' freedom and injects a significant element of illiberalism into Mill's position. The difficulty is that Mill is by no means either particularly consistent or particularly liberal in his views as to the distribution of these vital powers and capacities in the population at large. He is clear, however, that they are by no means universal. Thus, in the *System of Logic* he identifies those who suffer from 'inveterate habits', or experience 'intractable compulsions', as failing to qualify as free agents *tout court*. In *Utilitarianism* he goes much further in expressing an intense pessimism about the prospects for many young persons developing any 'capacity for the nobler feelings', a capacity intimately associated in Mill's mind with choice and with the exercise of the particularly 'human faculties of perception, judgement, discriminative feeling, mental activity, and even moral preference', and consequently with his conception of autonomy and free agency (p. 74). In *On Liberty*, in contrast, the prevailing tone is optimistic. Children, young persons and the manifestly mentally incapable apart, Mill professes himself confident in the ability of most people in a modern society to respond positively to the influence of education and example, and, if necessary, exhortation and criticism; and the protective net of the Principle of Liberty is cast correspondingly widely. But even here Mill lapses, placing entire populations in 'backward' societies beyond the pale of liberty. Smith concludes that the scope of principle is therefore radically indeterminate, expanding and contracting according to Mill's fluctuating opinions as to the prospects of the majority aspiring to, and becoming capable of, genuine 'liberty of action'. In so far as Smith's contribution reveals further incoherencies in Mill's position it supports the generally sceptical view of Mill propounded by the traditional school of interpretation headed by Berlin, but it also goes a step further. For Berlin represents Mill as paying the price of philosophical consistency for his liberalism, whereas, according to Smith, his liberalism is itself neither particularly consistent nor, given its constituent assumptions, particularly liberal.

In Richard Wollheim's contribution, a powerful attempt is made to defend Mill from the classical statement of the traditional view by Isaiah Berlin with which we began. Wollheim ascribes to Mill a species of utilitarianism which is complex but non-hierarchical. Its complexity is roughly the pluralism stressed in other revisionary interpretations: the conditions and content of happiness vary for different people and there are diverse elements that go to make up the happiness of any one person. Wollheim goes further than these, perhaps unexceptionable, claims when he maintains that utility itself is complex for Mill in that (once a certain level of civilization has been achieved) every person will have their own conception of their utility in the form of their personal conception of the good or plan of life. Like other, similar interpretations, Wollheim attributes an hierarchical character to Mill's utilitarianism inasmuch as a form of 'preliminary utilitarianism' applies until people achieve the capacities needed to form their own conceptions of the good. After that point, however, according to Wollheim, Mill's utilitarianism has a non-hierarchical character in that the Principle of Utility no longer dominates personal conceptions of utility as it does in classical utilitarianism, in which utility stands to secondary principles in a straightforwardly instrumental, means–end relation. In Millian complex utilitarianism, by contrast, secondary principles become partly constitutive of utility in virtue of their role as elements in personal conceptions of utility or the good. In other words, while the relationship between preliminary and complex utilitarianism is hierarchical in the sense that complex utilitarianism comes into play only when the demands of preliminary utilitarianism are satisfied, complex utilitarianism is not itself hierarchical, since utility is then to be found only in the diverse conceptions people form of their own utilities. Complex utilitarianism undergirds Mill's argument for liberty, in Wollheim's interpretation, because liberty is a condition of both the formation and the practical actualization of personal conceptions of utility. At the level of complex utility, at least, liberty and utility are inseparable, and a conflict between them of the sort represented in the traditional interpretations cannot occur. Indeed, because of the role of choice in forming personal conceptions of utility, liberty and utility have a mutually constitutive relation. Mill's complex utilitarianism and his liberalism are not then competitive but are rather aspects of each other. On this view, Berlin is mistaken, and Mill's project in *On Liberty* is a success.

What are we to make of Wollheim's challenge to Berlin, and of the other revisionary interpretations of Mill's *On Liberty*? A powerful objection to Wollheim's defence of Mill is that it neglects the possibility of conflict between preliminary and complex utilitarianism. The difficulty is akin to that which confronts Mill's account of the higher pleasures in *Utilitarianism*: what are we to do if promoting the higher pleasures conflicts with promoting the lower? What sort of trade-off is to be made between the higher and the lower pleasures? Could less of a higher pleasure count for more in the utilitarian calculations than more of a lower pleasure? Such a lexical ordering of the higher over the lower pleasures, according to which the higher pleasures have an infinite weight over the lower, is surely incompatible with any plausible version of the utilitarian calculus. The analogous difficulty with Wollheim's argument is that it fails to recognize the possibility of conflict between preliminary and complex utilitarianism and so gives no guidance as to how such conflict is to be resolved. It is hard to see how, in such a case, complex utilitarianism, and with it the privileged place of liberty, could prevail in any systematic fashion.

The indirect utilitarianism attributed to Mill by Gray, and the theory of the Art of Life on which it is based, face no less serious difficulties. As to the Art of Life, Mill's theory contains no recognition of conflict between the various spheres or areas of practice. Where conflict does occur, say between the demands of Prudence and Morality, it is difficult to see how recourse to the Principles of Utility can be avoided. In that case, the maxims of Morality, including the Principle of Liberty, could well be defeated by the claims of utility. This suggests a doubt about the viability of indirect utilitarianism itself. The status of the Principle of Utility as a purely axiological principle with no direct implication for conduct is thus ultimately problematic, and the idea that the critical and the practical levels of moral thought can be altogether separated might be thought to lack credibility. This is only to say, in particular connection with the argument of *On Liberty*, that even an indirect utilitarian argument cannot support the quasi-absolute status of the Principle of Liberty, or prohibit its abridgement when general welfare is thereby promoted.

If we take Mill's claims about the utilitarian foundation of his Principle of Liberty as seriously as he apparently did, doubts must therefore arise as to its credentials as part of any tenable liberal political morality. Moreover, the principle as Mill states it specifies only a necessary condition of justified restraint of liberty; it tells us when we may restrict liberty, not when we ought to do so. Nor does it tell us anything about how much liberty may justifiably be sacrificed for how much harm-prevention. These questions are answerable, in the terms of Mill's doctrine, only by recourse to the sovereign Principle of Utility. At that point, however, the maximizing momentum of utilitarianism re-enters Mill's doctrine, with results that must be troubling for any liberal. For, clearly enough, a restraint of liberty that is felicifically optimal in terms of harm-prevention may at the same time be highly inequitable in terms of the resultant distribution of liberty. In other words, despite the apparently distributive role of the Principle of Liberty, Mill's theory lacks the resources to protect the equal distribution of liberty that is surely an essential element of any liberal morality. This, in turn, is only to restate the most traditional criticism of Millian liberal utilitarianism, namely that it founders on the impossibility of deriving from aggregative maximizing premises a stringent distributive principle, even an inadequate one such as Mill's. It is also to say that, despite the efforts of Rees and others to give the Principle of Liberty a decent measure of determinacy, the very structure of Mill's doctrine prevents it from protecting any definite sphere of liberty.

We have already dealt with the ambiguities and difficulties in Mill's conception of freedom, difficulties which also point in the direction of radical indeterminancy in the sense and scope of the Principle of Liberty. But, perhaps the most fundamental objection to the argument of *On Liberty* concerns, not the conception of agent freedom that it deploys, nor even the attempt to give the priority of liberty a utilitarian foundation, but, instead, the conception of happiness or utility contained therein. The nub of the problem is that even the complex and pluralistic account of happiness fails to do justice to radical conflicts among its various ingredients, that is to say, to their frequent uncombinability and incommensurability. It is as true of any one person as it is of any society of persons that some forms of happiness or flourishing, some forms of excellence or of virtue, are liable to exclude or to drive out others, and that sometimes there is no rational means of arbitrating this conflict. In Mill's case, he fails to see the conflicts likely to arise amongst the practical demands made by conflicting or contradictory elements even in a single individual's complex nature. Nor does he appreciate that a liberal society of the sort he envisaged would necessarily crowd out forms of life and flourishing that an autonomous Millian individual might nevertheless wish to adopt. (For example, Gauguin was perhaps able to fulfil the demands of his unique nature only by moving into the arcadian culture of Tahiti, but he could not have done so had Tahiti been inhabited by autonomous individuals such as himself.) In making the bold and imaginative move of disaggregating happiness or utility into its diverse embodiments in personal plans and conceptions of life, Mill fails to recognize either the latent conflicts within the natures and forms of happiness of human beings or the incommensurabilities revealed when the complexity and plurality of human happiness are fully perceived. The fundamental incommensurability of basic values (perhaps most systematically and impressively explored by Joseph Raz in his *The Morality of Freedom*) constitutes a major challenge to all theories of practical reasoning.[21] But it is especially damaging to utilitarianism, even – indeed, especially – to the utilitarianism of John Stuart Mill, in which this truth is half-recognized in the interests of

18

liberalism but then suppressed for the sake of his official utilitarian commitments.

The upshot of our survey of the traditional and revisionary interpretations of the essay collected with this edition of *On Liberty* is therefore a sceptical one. Despite all the resourcefulness of the revisionary views, the traditional critique of Mill on liberty still retains considerable force. This is to say that, even if (as seems likely) the revisionist interpreters are often on strong ground in strictly exegetical terms, the reinterpreted argument of *On Liberty* remains vulnerable to most of the traditional criticisms. The new wave of interpretation has, for these reasons, done little to diminish the force of the sympathetic but devastating assessment of Mill found in the seminal paper by Isaiah Berlin with which we began.

It is a tribute to the perennial interest of Mill's essay that it should still provoke reflection on some of the most fundamental questions in moral and political philosophy. For that reason alone *On Liberty* deserves our continuing and serious study. It merits our continued examination, again, if only because later foundational work in liberal theory, such as John Rawls' *A Theory of Justice*, has been little more successful in giving liberal political morality a privileged claim on reason.[22] The failure of Mill's project in *On Liberty* is surely deeply instructive for us even today, when perhaps few would defend utilitarianism. For, if Berlin is right in his insistence on the ultimate incommensurability of basic values, then there are insuperable limits to the scope and authority of moral and political philosophy in virtue of parallel limits on the theorizability of moral and political life itself. It is an irony of intellectual history that the study of *On Liberty* should have this result, so chastening to the ambitions of philosophers, and so subversive of the certainties of liberalism.

NOTES

['CW' refers to *The Collected Works of John Stuart Mill* (ed. J.M. Robson) (Toronto and London, Toronto University Press and Routledge, 1963).]

1 For a list of traditional and revisionary interpretations of Mill see J. Gray, *Mill on Liberty: a Defence* (London, Routledge & Kegan Paul, 1983), 131.

2 See e.g. R. Pearson and G. Williams, *Political Thought and Public Policy in the Nineteenth Century: an Introduction* (London, Longman, 1984), ch.1; S. Conway, 'Bentham and the nineteenth-century revolution in government', in R. Bellamy, ed., *Victorian Liberalism: Nineteenth-Century Thought and Practice* (London, Routledge, 1990), 71–90.

3 J.F. Stephen, *Liberty, Equality, Fraternity*, ed., R.J. White (Cambridge,

Cambridge University Press, 1967).

4 See Himmelfarb's edition of Mill's *Essays on Politics and Culture* (New York, Doubleday, 1962); the Introduction to *On Liberty* (Harmondsworth, Penguin, 1974); and *On Liberty and Liberalism: the case of John Stuart Mill* (New York, Knopf, 1974), passim.

5 Mill, *CW*, 1:259.

6 Himmelfarb, Introduction, *On Liberty*, 30; *On Liberty and Liberalism*, ch. 1.

7 Whereas '[t]he primary goods in *Utilitarianism* were morality and a sense of unity; the primary goods in *On Liberty* were liberty and individuality'. *On Liberty and Liberalism*, 107.

8 Mill, *CW*, 1:163.

9 For criticism of Himmelfarb's interpretation of Mill see J.C. Rees, *John Stuart Mill's On Liberty*, ed. G.L. Williams (Oxford, Clarendon Press, 1985), ch. 4, and C.L. Ten *Mill on Liberty* (Oxford, Clarendon Press, 1980), ch. 9, sect. 3.

10 Berlin's interpretation of Mill, and of liberalism generally, is also elaborated in his classic 'Two concepts of liberty', in *Four Essays on Liberty* (London, Oxford University Press, 1969); see also his introduction to the same volume; and 'On the pursuit of the ideal' in Henry Havely (ed.), *The Crooked Timber of Humanity: Chapters in the History of Ideas* (London, John Murray, 1990).

11 See M. Canovan, 'The eloquence of John Stuart Mill', *History of Political Thought* 8 (1987), 506–20.

12 Alan Ryan elaborates his interpretation of Mill in *John Stuart Mill* (New York, Pantheon Books, 1970); 2nd edn. (London, Macmillan, 1987).

13 For the debate on the 'enforcement of morality' see H.L.A. Hart, *Law, Liberty and Morality* (London, Oxford University Press, 1963) and P. Devlin, *The Enforcement of Morals* (London, Oxford University Press, 1965).

14 John Rees's later work on Mill has been brought together posthumously in the volume referred to in note 9.

15 Joel Feinberg, *The Moral Limits of the Criminal Law*, vols. 1–4 (London, Oxford University Press, 1984–8).

16 Gray's interpretation of Mill is to be found in Gray, *Mill on Liberty: a Defence*.

17 Fred Berger, *Happiness, Justice and Freedom: the Moral and Political Philosophy of John Stuart Mill* (Berkeley, University of California Press, 1984).

18 T. Honderich, ' "On Liberty' " and morality dependent harms', *Political Studies* 30 (1982), 504–14; R.W. Hoag, 'Happiness and freedom: recent work on John Stuart Mill', *Philosophy and Public Affairs* 15 (1986), 188–99.

19 R. Wollheim, 'John Stuart Mill and the limits of state action', *Social Research* 40 (1973), 1–30; and Honderich *op. cit.*

20 R. Dworkin, 'Do we have a right to pornography?' in R. Dworkin, *A Matter of Principle* (London, Harvard University Press, 1985).

21 Joseph Raz, *The Morality of Freedom* (London, Oxford University Press, 1986).

22 John Rawls, *A Theory of Justice* (London, Oxford University Press, 1971).

ON LIBERTY

John Stuart Mill

The grand, leading principle, towards which every argument
unfolded in these pages directly converges, is the absolute
and essential importance of human development in its
richest diversity.

> Wilhelm Von Humboldt:
> *Sphere and Duties of Government*

To the beloved and deplored memory of her who was the inspirer, and in part the author, of all that is best in my writings – the friend and wife whose exalted sense of truth and right was my strongest incitement, and whose approbation was my chief reward – I dedicate this volume. Like all that I have written for many years, it belongs as much to her as to me; but the work as it stands has had, in a very insufficient degree, the inestimable advantage of her revision; some of the most important portions having been reserved for a more careful re-examination, which they are now never destined to receive. Were I but capable of interpreting to the world one half the great thoughts and noble feelings which are buried in her grave, I should be the medium of a greater benefit to it, than is ever likely to arise from anything that I can write, unprompted and unassisted by her all but unrivalled wisdom.

1 INTRODUCTORY

The subject of this Essay is not the so-called Liberty of the Will, so unfortunately opposed to the misnamed doctrine of Philosophical Necessity; but Civil, or Social Liberty: the nature and limits of the power which can be legitimately exercised by society over the individual. A question seldom stated, and hardly ever discussed, in general terms, but which profoundly influences the practical controversies of the age by its latent presence, and is likely soon to make itself recognized as the vital question of the future. It is so far from being new, that, in a certain sense, it has divided mankind, almost from the remotest ages; but in the stage of progress into which the more civilized portions of the species have now entered, it presents itself under new conditions, and requires a different and more fundamental treatment.

The struggle between Liberty and Authority is the most conspic-uous feature in the portions of history with which we are earliest familiar, particularly in that of Greece, Rome, and England. But in old times this contest was between subjects, or some classes of subjects, and the Government. By liberty, was meant protection against the tyranny of the political rulers. The rulers were conceived (except in some of the popular governments of Greece) as in a necessarily antagonistic position to the people whom thë ruled. They consisted of a governing One, or a governing tribe or caste, who derived their authority from inheritance or conquest, who, at all events, did not hold it at the pleasure of the governed, and whose supremacy men did not venture, perhaps did not desire, to contest, whatever precautions might be taken against its oppressive exercise. Their power was regarded as necessary, but also as highly dangerous; as a weapon which they would attempt to use against their subjects, no less than against external enemies. To prevent the weaker members of the community from being preyed upon by innumerable vultures, it was needful that there should be an animal of prey stronger than the rest, commissioned to keep them down. But as the king of the vultures would be no less bent upon preying on the flock than any of the minor harpies, it was indispensable to be in a perpetual attitude of defence against his beak and claws. The aim, therefore, of patriots was to set limits to the power which the ruler should be suffered to exercise over the community; and this limitation was what they meant by liberty. It was attempted in two ways. First, by obtaining a recognition of certain immunities, called political liberties or rights, which it was to be regarded as a breach of duty in the ruler to infringe, and which, if he did infringe, specific resistance, or general rebellion, was held to be justifiable. A second, and generally a later expedient, was the establishment of constitutional checks, by which the consent of the community, or of a body of some sort, supposed to represent its interests, was made a necessary condition to some of the more important acts of the governing power. To the first of these modes of limitation, the ruling power, in most European countries, was compelled, more or less, to submit. It was not so with the second; and, to attain this, or when already in some degree possessed, to attain it more completely, became everywhere the principal object of the lovers of liberty. And so long as mankind were content to combat one enemy by another, and to be ruled by a master, on condition of being guaranteed more or less efficaciously against his tyranny, they did not carry their aspirations beyond this point.

A time, however, came, in the progress of human affairs, when men ceased to think it a necessity of nature that their governors should be an independent power, opposed in interest to themselves. It appeared to them much better that the various magistrates of the State should be their tenants or delegates, revocable at their pleasure. In that way alone, it seemed, could they have complete security that the powers of government would never be abused to their disadvantage. By degrees this new demand for elective and temporary rulers became the prominent object of the exertions of the popular party, wherever any such party existed; and superseded, to a considerable extent, the previous efforts to limit the power of rulers. As the struggle proceeded for making the ruling power emanate from the periodical choice of the ruled, some persons began to think that too much importance had been attached to the limitation of the power itself. *That* (it might seem) was a resource against rulers whose interests were habitually opposed to those of the people. What was now wanted was, that the rulers should be identified with the people; that their interest and will should be the interest and will of the nation. The nation did not need to be protected against its own will. There was no fear of its tyrannizing over itself. Let the rulers be effectually responsible to it, promptly removable by it, and it could afford to trust them with power of which it could itself dictate the use to be made. Their power was but the nation's own power, concentrated, and in a form convenient for exercise. This mode of thought, or rather perhaps of feeling, was common among the last generation of European liberalism, in the Continental section of which it still apparently predominates. Those who admit any limit to what a government may do, except in the case of such governments as they think ought not to exist, stand out as brilliant exceptions among the political thinkers of the Continent. A similar tone of sentiment might by this time have been prevalent in our own country, if the circumstances which for a time encouraged it, had continued unaltered.

But, in political and philosophical theories, as well as in persons, success discloses faults and infirmities which failure might have concealed from observation. The notion, that the people have no need to limit their power over themselves, might seem axiomatic, when popular government was a thing only dreamed about, or read of as having existed at some distant period of the past. Neither was that notion necessarily disturbed by such temporary aberrations as those of the French Revolution, the worst of which were the work of an usurping few, and which, in any case, belonged, not to the permanent working of popular institutions, but to a sudden and convulsive outbreak against monarchical and aristocratic despotism. In time, however, a democratic republic came to occupy a large portion of the earth's surface, and made itself felt as one of the most powerful members of the community of nations; and elective and responsible government became subject to the observations and criticisms which wait upon a great existing fact. It was now perceived that such phrases as 'self-government', and 'the power of the people over themselves', do not express the true state of the case. The 'people' who exercise the power are not always the same people with those over whom it is exercised; and the 'self-government' spoken of is not the government of each by himself, but of each by all the rest. The will of the people, moreover, practically means the will of the most numerous or the most active *part* of the people; the majority, or those who succeed in making themselves accepted as the majority; the people, consequently, *may* desire to oppress a part of their number; and precautions are as much needed against this as against any other abuse of power. The limitation, therefore, of the power of government over individuals loses none of its importance when the holders of power are regularly accountable to the community, that is, to the strongest party therein. This view of things, recommending itself equally to the intelligence of thinkers and to the inclination of those important classes in European society to whose real or supposed interests democracy is adverse, has had no difficulty in establishing itself; and in political speculations 'the tyranny of the majority' is now generally included among the evils against which society requires to be on its guard.

Like other tyrannies, the tyranny of the majority was at first, and is still vulgarly, held in dread, chiefly as operating through the acts of the public authorities. But reflecting persons perceived that when society is itself the tyrant – society collectively, over the separate individuals who compose it – its means of tyrannizing are not restricted to the acts which it may do by the hands of its political functionaries. Society can and does execute its own mandates: and if it issues wrong mandates instead of right, or any mandates at all in things with which it ought not to meddle, it practises a social tyranny more formidable than many kinds of political oppression, since, though not usually upheld by such extreme penalties, it leaves fewer means of escape, penetrating much more deeply into the details of life, and enslaving the soul itself. Protection, therefore, against the tyranny of the magistrate is not enough: there needs protection also against the tyranny of the prevailing opinion and feeling; against the tendency of society to impose, by other means than civil penalties, its own ideas and practices as rules of conduct on those who dissent from them; to fetter the development, and, if possible, prevent the formation, of any individuality not in harmony with its ways, and compel all characters to fashion themselves upon the model of its own. There is a limit to the legitimate interference of collective opinion with individual independence: and to find that limit, and maintain it against encroachment, is as indispensable to a good condition of human affairs, as protection against political despotism.

But though this proposition is not likely to be contested in general terms, the practical question, where to place the limit – how to make the fitting adjustment between individual independence and social control – is a subject on which nearly everything remains to be done. All that makes existence valuable to any one, depends on the enforcement of restraints upon the actions of other people. Some rules of conduct, therefore, must be imposed, by law in the first place, and by opinion on many things which are not fit subjects for the operation of law. What these rules should be, is the principal question in human affairs; but if we except a few of the most obvious cases, it is one of those which least progress has been made in resolving. No two ages, and scarcely any two countries, have decided it alike; and the decision of one age or country is a wonder to another. Yet the people of any given age and country no more suspect any difficulty in it, than if it were a subject on which mankind had always been agreed. The rules which obtain among themselves appear to them self-evident and self-justifying. This all but universal illusion is one of the examples of the magical influence of custom, which is not only, as the proverb says, a second nature, but is continually mistaken for the first. The effect of custom, in preventing any misgiving respecting the rules of conduct which mankind impose on one another, is all the more complete because the subject is one on which it is not generally considered necessary that reasons should be given, either by one person to others, or by each to himself. People are accustomed to believe, and have been encouraged in the belief by some who aspire to the character of philosophers, that their feelings, on subjects of this nature, are better than reasons, and render reasons unnecessary. The practical principle which guides them to their opinions on the regulation of human conduct, is the feeling in each person's mind that everybody should be required to act as he, and those with whom he sympathizes, would like them to act. No one, indeed, acknowledges to himself that his standard of judgement is his own liking; but an opinion on a point of conduct, not supported by reasons, can only count as one person's preference; and if the reasons, when given, are a mere appeal to a similar preference felt by other people, it is still only many people's liking instead of one. To an ordinary man, however, his own preference, thus supported, is not only a perfectly satisfactory reason, but the only one he generally has for any of his notions of morality, taste, or propriety, which are not expressly written in his religious creed; and his chief guide in the interpretation even of that. Men's opinions, accordingly, on what is laudable or blameable, are affected by all the multifarious causes which influence their wishes in regard to the conduct of others, and which are as numerous as those which determine their wishes on any other subject. Sometimes their reason – at other times their prejudices or superstitions: often their social affections, not seldom their antisocial ones, their envy or jealousy, their arrogance or contemptuousness: but most commonly, their desires or fears for themselves – their legitimate or illegitimate self-interest. Wherever there is an ascendant class, a large portion of the morality of the country emanates from its class interests, and its feelings of class superiority. The morality between Spartans and Helots, between planters and negroes, between princes and subjects, between nobles and roturiers, between men and women, has been for the most part the creation of these class interests and feelings: and the sentiments thus generated, react in turn upon the moral feelings of the members of the ascendant class, in their relations among themselves. Where, on the other hand, a class, formerly ascendant, has lost its ascendancy, or where its ascendancy is unpopular, the prevailing moral sentiments frequently bear the impress of an impatient dislike of superiority. Another grand determining principle of the rules of conduct, both in act and forbearance, which have been enforced by law or opinion, has been the servility of mankind towards the supposed preferences or aversions of their temporal masters, or of their gods. This servility, though essentially selfish, is not hypocrisy; it gives rise to perfectly genuine sentiments of abhorrence; it made men burn magicians and heretics. Among so many baser influences, the general and obvious interests of society have of course had a share, and a large one, in the direction of the moral sentiments: less, however, as a matter of reason, and on their own account, than as a consequence of the sympathies and anti-pathies which grew out of them: and sympathies and antipathies which had little or nothing to do with the interests of society, have made themselves felt in the establishment of moralities with quite as great force.

The likings and dislikings of society, or of some powerful portion of it, are thus the main thing which has practically determined the rules laid down for general observance, under the penalties of law or opinion. And in general, those who have been in advance of society in thought and feeling, have left this condition of things unassailed in principle, however they may have come into conflict with it in some of its details. They have occupied themselves rather in inquiring what things society ought to like or dislike, than in questioning whether its likings or dislikings should be a law to individuals. They preferred endeavouring to alter the feelings of mankind on the particular points on which they were themselves heretical, rather than make common cause in defence of freedom, with heretics generally. The only case in which the higher ground has been taken on principle and maintained with consistency, by any but an individual here and there, is that of religious belief: a case instructive in many ways, and not least so as forming a most striking instance of the fallibility of what is called the moral sense: for the *odium theologicum*, in a sincere bigot, is one of the most unequivocal cases of moral feeling. Those who first broke the yoke of what called itself the Universal Church, were in general as little willing to permit difference of religious opinion as that church itself. But when the heat of the conflict was over, without giving a complete victory to any party, and each church or sect was reduced to limit its hopes to retaining possession of the ground it already occupied; minorities, seeing that they had no chance of becoming majorities, were under the necessity of pleading to those whom they could not convert, for permission to differ. It is accordingly on this battle-field, almost solely, that the rights of the individual against society have been asserted on broad grounds of principle, and the claim of society to exercise authority over dissentients, openly controverted. The great writers to whom the world owes what religious liberty it possesses, have mostly asserted freedom of conscience as an indefeasible right, and denied absolutely that a human being is accountable to others for his religious belief. Yet so natural to mankind is intolerance in whatever they really care about, that religious freedom has hardly anywhere been practically realized, except where religious indifference, which dislikes to have its peace disturbed by theological quarrels, has added its weight to the scale. In the minds of almost all religious persons, even in the most tolerant countries, the duty of toleration is admitted with tacit reserves. One person will bear with dissent in matters of church government, but not of dogma; another can tolerate everybody, short of a Papist or a Unitarian; another, every one who believes in revealed religion; a few extend their charity a little further, but stop at the belief in a God and in a future state. Wherever the sentiment of the majority is still genuine and intense, it is found to have abated little of its claim to be obeyed.

In England, from the peculiar circumstances of our political history, though the yoke of opinion is perhaps heavier, that of law is lighter, than in most other countries of Europe; and there is considerable jealousy of direct interference, by the legislative or the executive power, with private conduct; not so much from any just regard for the independence of the individual, as from the still subsisting habit of looking on the government as representing an opposite interest to the public. The majority have not yet learnt to feel the power of the government their power, or its opinions their opinions. When they do so, individual liberty will probably be as much exposed to invasion from the government, as it already is from public opinion. But, as yet, there is a considerable amount of feeling ready to be called forth against any attempt of the law to control individuals in things which they have not hitherto been accustomed to be controlled by it; and this with very little discrimination as to whether the matter is, or is not, within the legitimate sphere of legal control; insomuch that the feeling, highly salutary on the whole, is perhaps quite as often misplaced as well grounded in the particular instances of its application. There is, in fact, no recognized principle by which the propriety or impropriety of government interference is customarily tested. People decide according to their personal preferences. Some, whenever they see any good to be done, or evil to be remedied, would willingly instigate the government to undertake the business; while others prefer to bear almost any amount of social evil, rather than add one to the departments of human interests amenable to governmental control. And men range themselves on one or the other side in any particular case, according to this general direction of their sentiments; or according to the degree of interest which they feel in the particular thing which it is proposed that the government should do, or according to the belief they entertain that the government would, or would not, do it in the manner they prefer; but very rarely on account of any opinion to which they consistently adhere, as to what things are fit to be done by a government. And it seems to me that in consequence of this absence of rule or principle, one side is at present as often wrong as the other; the interference of government is, with about equal frequency, improperly invoked and improperly condemned.

The object of this Essay is to assert one very simple principle, as entitled to govern absolutely the dealings of society with the individual in the way of compulsion and control, whether the means used be physical force in the form of legal penalties, or the moral coercion of public opinion. That principle is, that the sole end for which mankind are warranted, individually or collectively, in interfering with the liberty of action of any of their number, is self-protection. That the only purpose for which power can be rightfully exercised over any member of a civilized community, against his will, is to prevent harm to others. His own good, either physical or moral, is not a sufficient warrant. He cannot rightfully be compelled to do or forbear because it will be better for him to do so, because it will make him happier, because, in the opinions of others, to do so would be wise, or even right. These are good reasons for remonstrating with him, or reasoning with him, or persuading him, or entreating him, but not for compelling him, or visiting him with any evil in case he do otherwise. To justify that, the conduct from which it is desired to deter him, must be calculated to produce evil to some one else. The only part of the conduct of any one, for which he is amenable to society, is that which concerns others. In the part which merely concerns himself, his independence is, of right, absolute. Over himself, over his own body and mind, the individual is sovereign.

It is, perhaps, hardly necessary to say that this doctrine is meant to apply only to human beings in the maturity of their faculties. We are not speaking of children, or of young persons below the age which the law may fix as that of manhood or womanhood. Those who are still in a state to require being taken care of by others, must be protected against their own actions as well as against external injury. For the same reason, we may leave out of consideration those backward states of society in which the race itself may be considered as in its nonage. The early difficulties in the way of spontaneous progress are so great, that there is seldom any choice of means for overcoming them; and a ruler full of the spirit of improvement is warranted in the use of any expedients that will attain an end, perhaps otherwise unattainable. Despotism is a legitimate mode of government in dealing with barbarians, provided the end be their improvement, and the means justified by actually effecting that end. Liberty, as a principle, has no application to any state of things anterior to the time when mankind have become capable of being improved by free and equal discussion. Until then, there is nothing for them but implicit obedience to an Akbar or a Charlemagne, if they are so fortunate as to find one. But as soon as mankind have attained the capacity of being guided to their own improvement by conviction or persuasion (a period long since reached in all nations with whom we need here concern ourselves), compulsion, either in the direct form or in that of pains and penalties for non-compliance, is no longer admissible as a means to their own good, and justifiable only for the security of others.

It is proper to state that I forgo any advantage which could be derived to my argument from the idea of abstract right, as a thing independent of utility. I regard utility as the ultimate appeal on all ethical questions; but it must be utility in the largest sense, grounded on the permanent interests of man as a progressive being. Those interests, I contend, authorize the subjection of individual spontaneity to external control, only in respect to those actions of each, which concern the interest of other people. If any one does an act hurtful to others, there is a prima facie case for punishing him, by law, or, where legal penalties are not safely applicable, by general disapprobation. There are also many positive acts for the benefit of others, which he may rightfully be compelled to perform; such as, to give evidence in a court of justice; to bear his fair share in the common defence, or in any other joint work necessary to the interest of the society of which he enjoys the protection; and to perform certain acts of individual beneficence, such as saving a fellow creature's life, or interposing to protect the defenceless against ill-usage, things which whenever it is obviously a man's duty to do, he may rightfully be made responsible to society for not doing. A person may cause evil to others not only by his actions but by his inaction, and in either case he is justly accountable to them for the injury. The latter case, it is true, requires a much more cautious exercise of compulsion than the former. To make any one anwerable for doing evil to others, is the rule; to make him answerable for not preventing evil, is, comparatively speaking, the exception. Yet there are many cases clear enough and grave enough to justify that exception. In all things which regard the external relations of the individual, he is *de jure* amenable to those whose interests are concerned, and if need be, to society as their protector. There are often good reasons for not holding him to the responsibility; but these reasons must arise from the special expediencies of the case: either because it is a kind of case in which he is on the whole likely to act better, when left to his own discretion, than when controlled in any way in which society have it in their power to control him; or because the attempt to exercise control would produce other evils, greater than those which it would prevent. When such reasons as these preclude the enforcement of responsibility, the conscience of the agent himself should step into the vacant judgement-seat, and protect those interests of others which have no external protection; judging himself all the more rigidly, because the case does not admit of his being made accountable to the judgement of his fellow creatures.

But there is a sphere of action in which society, as distinguished from the individual, has, if any, only an indirect interest; comprehending all that portion of a person's life and conduct which affects only himself, or if it also affects others, only with their free, voluntary, and undeceived consent and participation. When I say only himself, I mean directly, and in the first instance: for whatever affects himself, may affect others through himself; and the objection which may be grounded on this contingency will receive consideration in the sequel. This, then, is the appropriate region of human liberty. It comprises, first, the inward domain of consciousness; demanding liberty of conscience, in the most comprehensive sense; liberty of thought and feeling; absolute freedom of opinion and sentiment on all subjects, practical or speculative, scientific, moral or theological. The liberty of expressing and publishing opinions may seem to fall under a different principle, since it belongs to that part of the conduct of an individual which concerns other people; but, being almost of as much importance as the liberty of thought itself, and resting in great part on the same reasons, is practically inseparable from it. Secondly, the principle requires liberty of tastes and pursuits; of framing the plan of our life to suit our own character; of doing as we like, subject to such consequences as may follow: without impediment from our fellow creatures, so long as what we do does not harm them, even though they should think our conduct foolish, perverse, or wrong. Thirdly, from this liberty of each individual, follows the liberty, within the same limits, of combination among individuals; freedom to unite, for any purpose not involving harm to others: the persons combining being supposed to be of full age, and not forced or deceived.

No society in which these liberties are not, on the whole, respected, is free, whatever may be its form of government; and none is completely free in which they do not exist absolute and unqualified. The only freedom which deserves the name, is that of pursuing our own good in our own way, so long as we do not attempt to deprive others of theirs, or impede their efforts to obtain it. Each is the proper guardian of his own health, whether bodily, or mental and spiritual. Mankind are greater gainers by suffering each other to live as seems good to themselves, than by compelling each to live as seems good to the rest.

Though this doctrine is anything but new, and, to some persons, may have the air of a truism, there is no doctrine which stands more directly opposed to the general tendency of existing opinion and practice. Society has expended fully as much effort in the attempt (according to its lights) to compel people to conform to its notions of personal, as of social excellence. The ancient commonwealths thought themselves entitled to practise, and the ancient philosophers countenanced, the regulation of every part of private conduct by public authority, on the ground that the State had a deep interest in the whole bodily and mental discipline of every one of its citizens; a mode of thinking which may have been admissible in small republics surrounded by powerful enemies, in constant peril of being subverted by foreign attack or internal commotion, and to which even a short interval of relaxed energy and self-command might so easily be fatal, that they could not afford to wait for the salutary permanent effects of freedom. In the modern world, the greater size of political communities, and, above all, the separation between spiritual and temporal authority (which placed the direction of men's consciences in other hands than those which controlled their worldly affairs), prevented so great an interference by law in the details of private life; but the engines of moral repression have been wielded more strenuously against divergence from the reigning opinion in self-regarding, than even in social matters; religion, the most powerful of the elements which have entered into the formation of moral feeling, having almost always been governed either by the ambition of a hierarchy, seeking control over every department of human conduct, or by the spirit of Puritanism. And some of those modern reformers who have placed themselves in strongest opposition to the religions of the past, have been no way behind either churches or sects in their assertion of the right of spiritual domination: M. Comte, in particular, whose social system, as unfolded in his *Système de Politique Positive*, aims at establishing (though by moral more than by legal appliances) a despotism of society over the individual, surpassing anything contemplated in the political ideal of the most rigid disciplinarian among the ancient philosophers.

Apart from the peculiar tenets of individual thinkers, there is also in the world at large an increasing inclination to stretch unduly the powers of society over the individual, both by the force of opinion and even by that of legislation: and as the tendency of all the changes taking place in the world is to strengthen society, and diminish the power of the individual, this encroachment is not one of the evils which tend spontaneously to disappear, but, on the contrary, to grow more and more formidable. The disposition of mankind, whether as rulers or as fellow citizens, to impose their own opinions and inclinations as a rule of conduct on others, is so energetically supported by some of the best and by some of the worst feelings incident to human nature, that it is hardly ever kept under restraint by anything but want of power; and as the power is not declining, but growing, unless a strong barrier of moral conviction can be raised against the mischief, we must expect, in the present circumstances of the world, to see it increase.

It will be convenient for the argument, if, instead of at once entering upon the general thesis, we confine ourselves in the first instance to a single branch of it, on which the principle here stated is, if not fully, yet to a certain point, recognized by the current opinions. This one branch is the Liberty of Thought: from which it is impossible to separate the cognate liberty of speaking and of writing. Although these liberties, to some considerable amount, form part of the political morality of all countries which profess religious toleration and free institutions, the grounds, both philosophical and practical, on which they rest, are perhaps not so familiar to the general mind, nor so thoroughly appreciated by many even of the leaders of opinion, as might have been expected. Those grounds, when rightly understood, are of much wider application than to only one division of the subject, and a thorough consideration of this part of the question will be found the best introduction to the remainder. Those to whom nothing which I am about to say will be new, may therefore, I hope, excuse me, if on a subject which for now three centuries has been so often discussed, I venture on one discussion more.

2 OF THE LIBERTY OF
THOUGHT AND DISCUSSION

The time, it is to be hoped, is gone by, when any defence would be necessary of the 'liberty of the press' as one of the securities against corrupt or tyrannical government. No argument, we may suppose, can now be needed, against permitting a legislature or an executive, not identified in interest with the people, to prescribe opinions to them, and determine what doctrines or what arguments they shall be allowed to hear. This aspect of the question, besides, has been so often and so triumphantly enforced by preceding writers, that it needs not be specially insisted on in this place. Though the law of England, on the subject of the press, is as servile to this day as it was in the time of the Tudors, there is little danger of its being actually put in force against political discussion, except during some temporary panic, when fear of insurrection drives ministers and judges from their propriety;[1] and, speaking generally, it is not, in constitutional countries, to be apprehended, that the government, whether completely responsible to the people or not, will often attempt to control the expression of opinion, except when in doing

---

1   These words had scarcely been written, when, as if to give them an emphatic contradiction, occurred the Government Press Prosecutions of 1858. That ill-judged interference with the liberty of public discussion has not, however, induced me to alter a single word in the text, nor has it at all weakened my conviction that, moments of panic excepted, the era of pains and penalties for political discussion has, in our own country, passed away. For, in the first place, the prosecutions were not persisted in; and, in the second, they were never, properly speaking, political prosecutions. The offence charged was not that of criticizing institutions, or the acts or persons of rulers, but of circulating what was deemed an immoral doctrine, the lawfulness of Tyrannicide.

    If the arguments of the present chapter are of any validity, there ought to exist the fullest liberty of professing and discussing, as a matter of ethical conviction, any doctrine, however immoral it may be considered. It would, therefore, be irrelevant and out of place to examine here, whether the doctrine of Tyrannicide deserves that title. I shall content myself with saying that the subject has been at all times one of the open questions of morals; that the act of a private citizen in striking down a criminal, who, by raising himself above the law, has placed himself beyond the reach of legal punishment or control, has been accounted by whole nations, and by some of the best and wisest of men, not a crime, but an act of exalted virtue; and that, right or wrong, it is not of the nature of assassination, but of civil war. As such, I hold that the instigation to it, in a specific case, may be a proper subject of punishment, but only if an overt act has followed, and at least a probable connexion can be established between the act and the instigation. Even then, it is not a foreign government, but the very government assailed, which alone, in the exercise of self-defence, can legitimately punish attacks directed against its own existence.

so it makes itself the organ of the general intolerance of the public. Let us suppose, therefore, that the government is entirely at one with the people, and never thinks of exerting any power of coercion unless in agreement with what it conceives to be their voice. But I deny the right of the people to exercise such coercion, either by themselves or by their government. The power itself if illegitimate. The best government has no more title to it than the worst. It is as noxious, or more noxious, when exerted in accordance with public opinion, than when in opposition to it. If all mankind minus one, were of one opinion, and only one person were of the contrary opinion, mankind would be no more justified in silencing that one person, than he, if he had the power, would be justified in silencing mankind. Were an opinion a personal possession of no value except to the owner; if to be obstructed in the enjoyment of it were simply a private injury, it would make some difference whether the injury was inflicted only on a few persons or on many. But the peculiar evil of silencing the expression of an opinion is, that it is robbing the human race; posterity as well as the existing generation; those who dissent from the opinion, still more than those who hold it. If the opinion is right, they are deprived of the opportunity of exchanging error for truth: if wrong, they lose, what is almost as great a benefit, the clearer perception and livelier impression of truth, produced by its collision with error.

It is necessary to consider separately these two hypotheses, each of which has a distinct branch of the argument corresponding to it. We can never be sure that the opinion we are endeavouring to stifle is a false opinion; and if we were sure, stifling it would be an evil still.

First: the opinion which it is attempted to suppress by authority may possibly be true. Those who desire to suppress it, of course deny its truth; but they are not infallible. They have no authority to decide the question for all mankind, and exclude every other person from the means of judging. To refuse a hearing to an opinion, because they are sure that it is false, is to assume that *their* certainty is the same thing as *absolute* certainty. All silencing of discussion is an assumption of infallibility. Its condemnation may be allowed to rest on this common argument, not the worse for being common.

Unfortunately for the good sense of mankind, the fact of their fallibility is far from carrying the weight in their practical judgement, which is always allowed to it in theory; for while every one well knows himself to be fallible, few think it necessary to take any precautions against their own fallibility, or admit the supposition that any opinion, of which they feel very certain, may be one of the examples of the error to which they acknowledge themselves to be liable. Absolute princes, or others who are accustomed to unlimited deference, usually feel this complete confidence in their own opinions on nearly all subjects. People more happily situated, who sometimes hear their opinions disputed, and are not wholly unused to be set right when they are wrong, place the same unbounded reliance only on such of their opinions as are shared by all who surround them, or to whom they habitually defer: for in proportion to a man's want of confidence in his own solitary judgement, does he usually repose, with implicit trust, on the infallibility of 'the world' in general. And the world, to each individual, means the part of it with which he comes in contact; his party, his sect, his church, his class of society: the man may be called, by comparison, almost liberal and large-minded to whom it means anything so comprehensive as his own country or his own age. Nor is his faith in this collective authority at all shaken by his being aware that other ages, countries, sects, churches, classes, and parties have thought, and even now think, the exact reverse. He devolves upon his own world the responsibility of being in the right against the dissentient worlds of other people; and it never troubles him that mere accident has decided which of these numerous worlds is the object of his reliance, and that the same causes which make him a Churchman in London, would have made him a Buddhist or a Confucian in Pekin. Yet it is as evident in itself, as any amount of argument can make it, that ages are no more infallible than individuals; every age having held many opinions which subsequent ages have deemed not only false but absurd; and it is as certain that many opinions, now general, will be rejected by future ages, as it is that many, once general, are rejected by the present.

The objection likely to be made to this argument would probably take some such form as the following. There is no greater assumption of infallibility in forbidding the propagation of error, than in any other thing which is done by public authority on its own judgement and responsibility. Judgement is given to men that they may use it. Because it may be used erroneously, are men to be told that they ought not to use it at all? To prohibit what they think pernicious, is not claiming exemption from error, but fulfilling the duty incumbent on them, although fallible, of acting on their conscientious conviction. If we were never to act on our opinions, because those opinions may be wrong, we should leave all our interests uncared for, and all our duties unperformed. An objection which applies to all conduct, can be no valid objection to any conduct in particular. It is the duty of governments, and of individuals, to form the truest opinions they can; to form them carefully, and never impose them upon others unless they are quite sure of being right. But when they are sure (such reasoners may say), it is not conscientiousness but cowardice to shrink from acting on their opinions, and allow doctrines which they honestly think dangerous to the welfare of mankind, either in this life or in another, to be scattered abroad without restraint, because other people, in less enlightened times, have persecuted opinions now believed to be true. Let us take care, it may be said, not to make the same mistake: but governments and nations have made mistakes in other things, which are not denied to be fit subjects for the exercise of authority: they have laid on bad taxes, made unjust wars. Ought we therefore to lay on no taxes, and, under whatever provocation, make no wars? Men, and governments, must act to the best of their ability. There is no such thing as absolute certainty, but there is assurance sufficient for the purposes of human life. We may, and must, assume our opinion to be true for the guidance of our own conduct: and it is assuming no more when we forbid bad men to pervert society by the propagation of opinions which we regard as false and pernicious.

I answer, that it is assuming very much more. There is the greatest difference between presuming an opinion to be true, because, with every opportunity for contesting it, it has not been refuted, and assuming its truth for the purpose of not permitting its refutation. Complete liberty of contradicting and disproving our opinion, is the very condition which justifies us in assuming its truth for purposes of action; and on no other terms can a being with human faculties have any rational assurance of being right.

When we consider either the history of opinion, or the ordinary conduct of human life, to what is it to be ascribed that the one and the other are no worse than they are? Not certainly to the inherent force of the human understanding; for, on any matter not self-evident, there are ninety-nine persons totally incapable of judging of it, for one who is capable; and the capacity of the hundredth person is only comparative; for the majority of the eminent men of every past generation held many opinions now known to be erroneous, and did or approved numerous things which no one will now justify. Why is it, then, that there is on the whole a preponderance among mankind of rational opinions and rational conduct? If there really is this preponderance – which there must be unless human affairs are, and have always been, in an almost desperate state – it is owing to a quality of the human mind, the source of everything respectable in man either as an intellectual or as a moral being, namely, that his errors are corrigible. He is capable of rectifying his mistakes, by discussion and experience. Not by experience alone. There must be discussion, to show how experience is to be interpreted. Wrong opinions and practices gradually yield to fact and argument: but facts and arguments, to produce any effect on the mind, must be brought before it. Very few facts are able to tell their own story, without comments to bring out their meaning. The whole strength and value, then, of human judgement, depending on the one property, that it can be set right when it is wrong, reliance can be placed on it only when the means of setting it right are kept constantly at hand. In the case of any person whose judgement is really deserving of confidence, how has it become so? Because he has kept his mind open to criticism of his opinions and conduct. Because it has been his practice to listen to all that could be said against him; to profit by as much of it as was just, and expound to himself, and upon occasion to others, the fallacy of what was fallacious. Because he has felt, that the only way in which a human being can make some approach to knowing the whole of a subject, is by hearing what can be said about it by persons of every variety of opinion, and studying all modes in which it can be looked at by every character of mind. No wise man ever acquired his wisdom in any mode but this; nor is it in the nature of human intellect to become wise in any other manner. The steady habit of correcting and completing his own opinion by collating it with those of others, so far from causing doubt and hesitation in carrying it into practice, is the only stable foundation for a just reliance on it: for, being cognizant of all that can, at least obviously, be said against him, and having taken up his position against all gainsayers – knowing that he has sought for objections and difficulties, instead of avoiding them, and has shut out no light which can be thrown upon the subject from any quarter – he has a right to think his judgement better than that of any person, or any multitude, who have not gone through a similar process.

It is not too much to require that what the wisest of mankind, those who are best entitled to trust their own judgement, find necessary to warrant their relying on it, should be submitted to by that miscellaneous collection of a few wise and many foolish individuals, called the public. The most intolerant of churches, the Roman Catholic Church, even at the canonization of a saint, admits, and listens patiently to, a 'devil's advocate'. The holiest of men, it appears, cannot be admitted to posthumous honours, until all that the devil could say against him is known and weighed. If even the Newtonian philosophy were not permitted to be questioned, mankind could not feel as complete assurance of its truth as they now do. The beliefs which we have most warrant for, have no safeguard to rest on, but a standing invitation to the whole world to prove them unfounded. If the challenge is not accepted, or is accepted and the attempt fails, we are far enough from certainty still; but we have done the best that the existing state of human reason admits of; we have neglected nothing that could give the truth a chance of reaching us: if the lists are kept open, we may hope that if there be a better truth, it will be found when the human mind is capable of receiving it; and in the meantime we may rely on having attained such approach to truth, as is possible in our own day. This is the amount of certainty attainable by a fallible being, and this the sole way of attaining it.

Strange it is, that men should admit the validity of the arguments for free discussion, but object to their being 'pushed to an extreme'; not seeing that unless the reasons are good for an extreme case, they are not good for any case. Strange that they should imagine that they are not assuming infallibility, when they acknowledge that there should be free discussion on all subjects which can possibly be *doubtful*, but think that some particular principle or doctrine should be forbidden to be questioned because it is so *certain*, that is, because *they are certain* that it is certain. To call any proposition certain, while there is any one who would deny its certainty if permitted, but who is not permitted, is to assume that we ourselves, and those who agree with us, are the judges of certainty, and judges without hearing the other side.

In the present age – which has been described as 'destitute of faith, but terrified at scepticism' – in which people feel sure, not so much that their opinions are true, as that they should not know what to do without them – the claims of an opinion to be protected from public attack are rested not so much on its truth, as on its

41

importance to society. There are, it is alleged, certain beliefs, so useful, not to say indispensable to well-being, that it is as much the duty of governments to uphold those beliefs, as to protect any other of the interests of society. In a case of such necessity, and so directly in the line of their duty, something less than infallibility may, it is maintained, warrant, and even bind, governments, to act on their own opinion, confirmed by the general opinion of mankind. It is also often argued, and still oftener thought, that none but bad men would desire to weaken these salutary beliefs; and there can be nothing wrong, it is thought, in restraining bad men, and prohibiting what only such men would wish to practise. This mode of thinking makes the justification of restraints on discussion not a question of the truth of doctrines, but of their usefulness; and flatters itself by that means to escape the responsibility of claiming to be an infallible judge of opinions. But those who thus satisfy themselves, do not perceive that the assumption of infallibility is merely shifted from one point to another. The usefulness of an opinion is itself matter of opinion: as disputable, as open to discussion, and requiring discussion as much, as the opinion itself. There is the same need of an infallible judge of opinions to decide an opinion to be noxious, as to decide it to be false, unless the opinion condemned has full opportunity of defending itself. And it will not do to say that the heretic may be allowed to maintain the utility or harmlessness of his opinion, though forbidden to maintain its truth. The truth of an opinion is part of its utility. If we would know whether or not it is desirable that a proposition should be believed, is it possible to exclude the consideration of whether or not it is true? In the opinion, not of bad men, but of the best men, no belief which is contrary to truth can be really useful: and can you prevent such men from urging that plea, when they are charged with culpability for denying some doctrine which they are told is useful, but which they believe to be false? Those who are on the side of received opinions, never fail to take all possible advantage of this plea; you do not find *them* handling the question of utility as if it could be completely abstracted from that of truth: on the contrary, it is, above all, because their doctrine is the 'truth', that the knowledge or the belief of it is held to be so indispensable. There can be no fair discussion of the question of usefulness, when an argument so vital may be employed on one side, but not on the other. And in point of fact, when law or public feeling do not permit the truth of an opinion to be disputed, they are just as little tolerant of a denial of its usefulness. The utmost they allow is an extenuation of its absolute necessity, or of the positive guilt of rejecting it.

In order more fully to illustrate the mischief of denying a hearing to opinions because we, in our own judgement, have condemned them, it will be desirable to fix down the discussion to a concrete case; and I choose, by preference, the cases which are least favourable to me – in which the argument against freedom of opinion, both on the score of truth and on that of utility, is considered the strongest. Let the opinions impugned be the belief in a God and in a future state, or any of the commonly received doctrines of morality. To fight the battle on such ground, gives a great advantage to an unfair antagonist; since he will be sure to say (and many who have no desire to be unfair will say it internally), Are these the doctrines which you do not deem sufficiently certain to be taken under the protection of law? Is the belief in a God one of the opinions, to feel sure of which, you hold to be assuming infallibility? But I must be permitted to observe, that it is not the feeling sure of a doctrine (be it what it may) which I call an assumption of infallibility. It is the undertaking to decide that question *for others*, without allowing them to hear what can be said on the contrary side. And I denounce and reprobate this pretension not the less, if put forth on the side of my most solemn convictions. However positive any one's persuasion may be, not only of the falsity but of the pernicious consequences – not only of the pernicious consequences, but (to adopt expressions which I altogether condemn) the immorality and impiety of an opinion; yet if, in pursuance of that private judgement, though backed by the public judgement of his country or his cotemporaries, he prevents the opinion from being heard in its defence, he assumes infallibility. And so far from the assumption being less objectionable or less dangerous because the opinion is called immoral or impious, this is the case of all others in which it is most fatal. These are exactly the occasions on which the men of one generation commit those dreadful mistakes, which excite the astonishment and horror of posterity. It is among such that we find the instances memorable in history, when the arm of the law has been employed to root out the best men and the noblest doctrines; with deplorable success as to the men, though some of the doctrines have survived to be (as if in mockery) invoked, in defence of similar conduct towards those who dissent from *them*, or from their received interpretation.

Mankind can hardly be too often reminded, that there was once a man named Socrates, between whom and the legal authorities and public opinion of his time, there took place a memorable collision. Born in an age and country abounding in individual greatness, this man has been handed down to us by those who best knew both him and the age, as the most virtuous man in it; while *we* know him as the head and prototype of all subsequent teachers of virtue, the source equally of the lofty inspiration of Plato and the judicious utilitarianism of Aristotle, '*i maëstri di color che sanno*', the two headsprings of ethical as of all other philosophy. This acknowledged master of all the eminent thinkers who have since lived – whose fame, still growing after more than two thousand years, all but outweighs the whole remainder of the names which make his native city illustrious – was put to death by his countrymen, after a judicial conviction, for impiety and immorality. Impiety, in denying the gods recognized by the State; indeed his accuser asserted (see the *Apologia*) that he believed in no gods at all. Immorality, in being, by his doctrines and instructions, a 'corruptor of youth'. Of these charges the tribunal, there is every ground for believing, honestly found him guilty, and condemned the man who probably of all then born had deserved best of mankind, to be put to death as a criminal.

To pass from this to the only other instance of judicial iniquity, the mention of which, after the condemnation of Socrates, would not be an anti-climax: the event which took place on Calvary rather more than eighteen hundred years ago. The man who left on the memory of those who witnessed his life and conversation, such an impression of his moral grandeur, that eighteen subsequent centuries have done homage to him as the Almighty in person, was ignominiously put to death, as what? As a blasphemer. Men did not merely mistake their benefactor; they mistook him for the exact contrary of what he was, and treated him as that prodigy of impiety, which they themselves are now held to be, for their treatment of him. The feelings with which mankind now regard these lamentable transactions, especially the later of the two, render them extremely unjust in their judgement of the unhappy actors. These were, to all appearance, not bad men – not worse than men commonly are, but rather the contrary; men who possessed in a full, or somewhat more than a full measure, the religious, moral, and patriotic feelings of their time and people: the very kind of men who, in all times, our own included, have every chance of passing through life blameless and respected. The high-priest who rent his garments when the words were pronounced, which, according to all the ideas of his country, constituted the blackest guilt, was in all probability quite as sincere in his horror and indignation, as the generality of respectable and pious men now are in the religious and moral sentiments they profess; and most of those who now shudder at his conduct, if they had lived in his time, and been born Jews, would have acted precisely as he did. Orthodox Christians who are tempted to think that those who stoned to death the first martyrs must have been worse men than they themselves are, ought to remember that one of those persecutors was Saint Paul.

Let us add one more example, the most striking of all, if the impressiveness of an error is measured by the wisdom and virtue of him who falls into it. If ever any one, possessed of power, had grounds for thinking himself the best and most enlightened among his cotemporaries, it was the Emperor Marcus Aurelius. Absolute monarch of the whole civilized world, he preserved through life not only the most unblemished justice, but what was less to be expected from his Stoical breeding, the tenderest heart. The few failings which are attributed to him, were all on the side of indulgence: while his writings, the highest ethical product of the ancient mind, differ scarcely perceptibly, if they differ at all, from the most characteristic teachings of Christ. This man, a better Christian in all but the dogmatic sense of the word, than almost any of the ostensibly Christian sovereigns who have since reigned, persecuted Christianity. Placed at the summit of all the previous attainments of humanity, with an open, unfettered intellect, and a character which led him of himself to embody in his moral writings the Christian ideal, he yet failed to see that Christianity was to be a good and not an evil to the world, with his duties to which he was so deeply penetrated. Existing society he knew to be in a deplorable state. But such as it was, he saw, or thought he saw, that it was held together, and prevented from being worse, by belief and reverence of the received divinities. As a ruler of mankind, he deemed it his duty not to suffer society to fall in pieces; and saw not how, if its existing ties were removed, any others could be formed which could again knit it together. The new religion openly aimed at dissolving these ties: unless, therefore, it was his duty to adopt that religion, it seemed to be his duty to put it down. Inasmuch then as the theology of Christianity did not appear to him true or of divine origin; inasmuch as this strange history of a crucified God was not credible to him, and a system which purported to rest entirely upon a foundation to him so wholly unbelievable, could not be foreseen by him to be that renovating agency which, after all abatements, it has in fact proved to be; the gentlest and most amiable of philosophers and rulers, under a solemn sense of duty, authorized the persecution of Christianity. To my mind this is one of the most tragical facts in all history. It is a bitter thought, how different a thing the Christianity of the world might have been, if the Christian faith had been adopted as the religion of the empire under the auspices of Marcus Aurelius instead of those of Constantine. But it would be equally unjust to him and false to truth, to deny, that no one plea which can be urged for punishing anti-Christian teaching, was wanting to Marcus Aurelius for punishing, as he did, the propagation of Christianity. No Christian more firmly believes that Atheism is false, and tends to the dissolution of society, than Marcus Aurelius believed the same things of Christianity; he who, of all men then living, might have been thought the most capable of appreciating it. Unless any one who approves of punishment for the promulgation of opinions, flatters himself that he is a wiser and better man than Marcus Aurelius – more deeply versed in the wisdom of his time, more elevated in his intellect above it – more earnest in his search for truth, or more single-minded in his devotion to it when found; – let him abstain from that assumption of the joint infallibility of himself and the multitude, which the great Antoninus made with so unfortunate a result.

Aware of the impossibility of defending the use of punishment for restraining irreligious opinions, by any argument which will not justify Marcus Antoninus, the enemies of religious freedom, when hard pressed, occasionally accept this consequence, and say, with Dr Johnson, that the persecutors of Christianity were in the right; that persecution is an ordeal through which truth ought to pass, and always passes successfully, legal penalties being, in the end, powerless against truth, though sometimes beneficially effective against mischievous errors. This is a form of the argument for religious intolerance, sufficiently remarkable not to be passed without notice.

A theory which maintains that truth may justifiably be persecuted because persecution cannot possibly do it any harm, cannot be charged with being intentionally hostile to the reception of new truths; but we cannot commend the generosity of its dealing with the persons to whom mankind are indebted for them. To discover to the world something which deeply concerns it, and of which it was previously ignorant; to prove to it that it had been mistaken on some vital point of temporal or spiritual interest, is as important a service as a human being can render to his fellow creatures, and in certain cases, as in those of the early Christians and of the Reformers, those who think with Dr Johnson believe it to have been the most precious gift which could be bestowed on mankind. That the authors of such splendid benefits should be requited by martyrdom, that their reward should be to be dealt with as the vilest of criminals, is not, upon this theory, a deplorable error and misfortune, for which humanity should mourn in sackcloth and ashes, but the normal and justifiable state of things. The propounder of a new truth, according to this doctrine, should stand, as stood, in the legislation of the Locrians, the proposer of a new law, with a halter round his neck, to be instantly tightened if the public assembly did not, on hearing his reasons, then and there adopt his proposition. People who defend this mode of treating benefactors, cannot be supposed to set much value on the benefit; and I believe this view of the subject is mostly confined to the sort of persons who think that new truths may have been desirable once, but that we have had enough of them now.

But, indeed, the dictum that truth always triumphs over persecution, is one of those pleasant falsehoods which men repeat after one another till they pass into commonplaces, but which all experience refutes. History teems with instances of truth put down by persecution. If not supressed for ever, it may be thrown back for centuries. To speak only of religious opinions: the Reformation broke out at least twenty times before Luther, and was put down. Arnold of Brescia was put down. Fra Dolcino was put down. Savonarola was put down. The Albigeois were put down. The Vaudois were put down. The Lollards were put down. The Hussites were put down. Even after the era of Luther, wherever persecution was persisted in, it was successful. In Spain, Italy, Flanders, the Austrian empire, Protestantism was rooted out; and, most likely, would have been so in England, had Queen Mary lived, or Queen Elizabeth died. Persecution has always succeeded, save where the heretics were too strong a party to be effectually persecuted. No reasonable person can doubt that Christianity might have been extirpated in the Roman Empire. It spread, and became predominant, because the persecutions were only occasional, lasting but a short time, and separated by long intervals of almost undisturbed propagandism. It is a piece of idle sentimentality that truth, merely as truth, has any inherent power denied to error, of prevailing against the dungeon and the stake. Men are not more zealous for truth than they often are for error, and a sufficient application of legal or even of social penalties will generally succeed in stopping the propagation of either. The real advantage which truth has, consists in this, that when an opinion is true, it may be extinguished once, twice, or many times, but in the course of ages there will generally be found persons to rediscover it, until some one of its reappearances falls on a time when from favourable circumstances it escapes persecution until it has made such head as to withstand all subsequent attempts to suppress it.

It will be said, that we do not now put to death the introducers of new opinions: we are not like our fathers who slew the prophets, we even build sepulchres to them. It is true we no longer put heretics to death; and the amount of penal infliction which modern feeling would probably tolerate, even against the most obnoxious opinions, is not sufficient to extirpate them. But let us not flatter ourselves that we are yet free from the stain even of legal persecution. Penalties for opinion, or at least for its expression, still exist by law; and their enforcement is not, even in these times, so unexampled as to make it at all incredible that they may some day be revived in full force. In the year 1857, at the summer assizes of the county of Cornwall, an unfortunate man,[2] said to be of unexceptionable conduct in all relations of life, was sentenced to twenty-one months' imprisonment, for uttering, and writing on a gate, some offensive words concerning Christianity. Within a month of the same time, at the Old Bailey, two persons, on two separate occasions,[3] were rejected as jurymen, and one of them grossly insulted by the judge and by one of the counsel, because they honestly declared that they had no theological belief; and a third, a foreigner,[4] for the same reason, was denied justice against a thief. This refusal of redress took place in virtue of the legal doctrine, that no person can be allowed to give evidence in a court of justice, who does not profess belief in a God (any god is sufficient) and in a future state; which is equivalent to declaring such persons to be

---

2   Thomas Pooley, Bodmin Assizes, 31 July 1857. In December following, he received a free pardon from the Crown.
3   George Jacob Holyoake, 17 August 1857; Edward Truelove, July 1857.
4   Baron de Gleichen, Marlborough-street Police Court, 4 August 1857.

outlaws, excluded from the protection of the tribunals; who may not only be robbed or assaulted with impunity, if no one but themselves, or persons of similar opinions, be present, but any one else may be robbed or assaulted with impunity, if the proof of the fact depends on their evidence. The assumption on which this is grounded is that the oath is worthless, of a person who does not believe in a future state; a proposition which betokens much ignorance of history in those who assent to it (since it is historically true that a large proportion of infidels in all ages have been persons of distinguished integrity and honour); and would be maintained by no one who had the smallest conception how many of the persons in greatest repute with the world, both for virtues and for attainments, are well known, at least to their intimates, to be unbelievers. The rule, besides, is suicidal, and cuts away its own foundation. Under pretence that atheists must be liars, it admits the testimony of all atheists who are willing to lie, and rejects only those who brave the obloquy of publicly confessing a 'detested creed rather than affirm a falsehood. A rule thus self-convicted of absurdity so far as regards its professed purpose, can be kept in force only as a badge of hatred, a relic of persecution; a persecution, too, having the peculiarity, that the qualification for undergoing it, is the being clearly proved not to deserve it. The rule, and the theory it implies, are hardly less insulting to believers than to infidels. For if he who does not believe in a future state, necessarily lies, it follows that they who do believe are only prevented from lying, if prevented they are, by the fear of hell. We will not do the authors and abettors of the rule the injury of supposing, that the conception which they have formed of Christian virtue is drawn from their own consciousness.

These, indeed, are but rags and remnants of persecution, and may be thought to be not so much an indication of the wish to persecute, as an example of that very frequent infirmity of English minds, which makes them take a preposterous pleasure in the assertion of a bad principle, when they are no longer bad enough to desire to carry it really into practice. But unhappily there is no security in the state of the public mind, that the suspension of worse forms of legal persecution, which has lasted for about the space of a generation, will continue. In this age the quiet surface of routine is as often ruffled by attempts to resuscitate past evils, as to introduce new benefits. What is boasted of at the present time as the revival of religion, is always, in narrow and uncultivated minds, at least as much the revival of bigotry; and where there is the strong permanent leaven of intolerance in the feelings of a people, which at all times abides in the middle classes of this country, it needs but little to provoke them into actively persecuting those whom they have never ceased to think proper objects of persecution.[5] For it is this – it is the opinions men entertain, and the feelings they cherish, respecting those who disown the beliefs they deem important, which makes this country not a place of mental freedom. For a long time past, the chief mischief of the legal penalties is that they strengthen the social stigma. It is that stigma which is really effective, and so effective is it, that the profession of opinions which are under the ban of society is much less common in England, than is, in many other countries, the avowal of those which incur risk of judicial punishment. In respect to all persons but those whose pecuniary circumstances make them independent of the goodwill of other people, opinion, on this subject, is as efficacious as law; men might as well be imprisoned, as excluded from the means of earning their bread. Those whose bread is already secured, and who desire no favours from men in power, or from bodies of men, or from the public, have nothing to fear from the open avowal of any opinions, but to be ill-thought of and ill-spoken of, and this it ought not to require a very heroic mould to

5   Ample warning may be drawn from the large infusion of the passions of a persecutor, which mingled with the general display of the worst parts of our national character on the occasion of the Sepoy insurrection. The ravings of fanatics or charlatans from the pulpit may be unworthy of notice; but the heads of the Evangelical party have announced as their principle for the government of Hindoos and Mohammedans, that no schools be supported by public money in which the Bible is not taught, and by necessary consequence that no public employment be given to any but real or pretended Christians. An under-Secretary of State, in a speech delivered to his constituents on November 12, 1857, is reported to have said: 'Toleration of their faith' (the faith of a hundred millions of British subjects), 'the superstition which they called religion, by the British Government, had had the effect of retarding the ascendancy of the British name, and preventing the salutary growth of Christianity. . . . Toleration was the great corner-stone of the religious liberties of this country; but do not let them abuse that precious word toleration. As he understood it, it meant the complete liberty to all, freedom of worship, *among Christians, who worshipped upon the same foundation.* It meant toleration of all sects and denominations of *Christians who believed in the one mediation.*' I desire to call attention to the fact, that a man who has been deemed fit to fill a high office in the government of this country, under a liberal Ministry, maintains the doctrine that all who do not believe in the divinity of Christ are beyond the pale of toleration. Who, after this imbecile display, can indulge the illusion that religious persecution has passed away, never to return?

enable them to bear. There is no room for any appeal *ad misericordiam* in behalf of such persons. But though we do not now inflict so much evil on those who think differently from us, as it was formerly our custom to do, it may be that we do ourselves as much evil as ever by our treatment of them. Socrates was put to death, but the Socratic philosophy rose like the sun in heaven, and spread its illumination over the whole intellectual firmament. Christians were cast to the lions, but the Christian church grew up a stately and spreading tree, overtopping the older and less vigorous growths, and stifling them by its shade. Our merely social intolerance kills no one, roots out no opinions, but induces men to disguise them, or to abstain from any active effort for their diffusion. With us, heretical opinions do not perceptibly gain, or even lose, ground in each decade or generation; they never blaze out far and wide, but continue to smoulder in the narrow circles of thinking and studious persons among whom they originate, without ever lighting up the general affairs of mankind with either a true or a deceptive light. And thus is kept up a state of things very satisfactory to some minds, because, without the unpleasant process of fining or imprisoning anybody, it maintains all prevailing opinions outwardly undisturbed, while it does not absolutely interdict the exercise of reason by dissentients afflicted with the malady of thought. A convenient plan for having peace in the intellectual world, and keeping all things going on therein very much as they do already. But the price paid for this sort of intellectual pacification, is the sacrifice of the entire moral courage of the human mind. A state of things in which a large portion of the most active and inquiring intellects find it advisable to keep the general principles and grounds of their convictions within their own breasts, and attempt, in what they address to the public, to fit as much as they can of their own conclusions to premises which they have internally renounced, cannot send forth the open, fearless characters, and logical, consist-ent intellects who once adorned the thinking world. The sort of men who can be looked for under it, are either mere conformers to commonplace, or time-servers for truth, whose arguments on all great subjects are meant for their hearers, and are not those which have convinced themselves. Those who avoid this alternative, do so by narrowing their thoughts and interest to things which can be spoken of without venturing within the region of principles, that is, to small practical matters, which would come right of them-selves, if but the minds of mankind were strengthened and enlarged, and which will never be made effectually right until then: while that which would strengthen and enlarge men's minds, free and daring speculation on the highest subjects, is abandoned.

Those in whose eyes this reticence on the part of heretics is no evil, should consider in the first place, that in consequence of it there is never any fair and thorough discussion of heretical opinions; and that such of them as could not stand such a discussion, though they may be prevented from spreading, do not disappear. But it is not the minds of heretics that are deteriorated most, by the ban placed on all inquiry which does not end in the orthodox conclusions. The greatest harm done is to those who are not heretics, and whose whole mental development is cramped, and their reason cowed, by the fear of heresy. Who can compute what the world loses in the multitude of promising intellects combined with timid characters, who dare not follow out any bold, vigorous, independent train of thought, lest it should land them in something which would admit of being considered irreligious or immoral? Among them we may occasionally see some man of deep conscientiousness, and subtle and refined understanding, who spends a life in sophisticating with an intellect which he cannot silence, and exhausts the resources of ingenuity in attempting to reconcile the promptings of his conscience and reason with orthodoxy, which yet he does not, perhaps, to the end succeed in doing. No one can be a great thinker who does not recognize, that as a thinker it is his first duty to follow his intellect to whatever conclusions it may lead. Truth gains more even by the errors of one who, with due study and preparation, thinks for himself, than by the true opinions of those who only hold them because they do not suffer themselves to think. Not that it is solely, or chiefly, to form great thinkers, that freedom of thinking is required. On the contrary, it is as much and even more indispensable, to enable average human beings to attain the mental stature which they are capable of. There have been, and may again be, great individual thinkers, in a general atmosphere of mental slavery. But there never has been, nor ever will be, in that atmosphere, an intellectually active people. When any people has made a temporary approach to such a character, it has been because the dread of heterodox speculation was for a time suspended. Where there is a tacit convention that principles are not to be disputed; where the discussion of the greatest questions which can occupy humanity is considered to be closed, we cannot hope to find that generally high scale of mental activity which has made some periods of history so remarkable. Never when controversy avoided the subjects which are large and important enough to kindle enthusiasm, was the mind of a people stirred up from its foundations, and the impulse given which raised even persons of the most ordinary intellect to something of the dignity of thinking beings. Of such we have had an example in the condition of Europe during the times immediately following the Reformation; another, though limited to the Continent and to a more cultivated class, in the speculative movement of the latter half of the eighteenth century; and a third, of still briefer duration, in the intellectual fermentation of Germany during the Goethian and Fichtean period. These periods differed widely in the particular opinions which they developed; but were alike in this, that during all three the yoke of authority was broken. In each, an old mental despotism had been thrown off, and no new one had yet taken its place. The impulse given at these three periods has made Europe what it now is. Every single improvement which has taken place either in the human mind or in institutions, may be traced distinctly to one or other of them. Appearances have for some time indicated that all three impulses are wellnigh spent; and we can expect no fresh start, until we again assert our mental freedom.

Let us now pass to the second division of the argument, and dismissing the supposition that any of the received opinions may be false, let us assume them to be true, and examine into the worth of the manner in which they are likely to be held, when their truth is not freely and openly canvassed. However unwillingly a person who has a strong opinion may admit the possibility that his opinion may be false, he ought to be moved by the consideration that however true it may be, if it is not fully, frequently, and fearlessly discussed, it will be held as a dead dogma, not a living truth.

There is a class of persons (happily not quite so numerous as formerly) who think it enough if a person assents undoubtingly to what they think true, though he has no knowledge whatever of the grounds of the opinion, and could not make a tenable defence of it against the most superficial objections. Such persons, if they can once get their creed taught from authority, naturally think that no good, and some harm, comes of it being allowed to be questioned. Where their influence prevails, they make it nearly impossible for the received opinion to be rejected wisely and considerately, though it may still be rejected rashly and ignorantly; for to shut out discussion entirely is seldom possible, and when it once gets in, beliefs not grounded on conviction are apt to give way before the slightest semblance of an argument. Waiving, however, this possibility – assuming that the true opinion abides in the mind, but abides as a prejudice, a belief independent of, and proof against, argument – this is not the way in which truth ought to be held by a rational being. This is not knowing the truth. Truth, thus held, is but one superstition the more, accidentally clinging to the words which enunciate a truth.

If the intellect and judgement of mankind ought to be cultivated, a thing which Protestants at least do not deny, on what can these faculties be more appropriately exercised by any one, than on the things which concern him so much that it is considered necessary for him to hold opinions on them? If the cultivation of the understanding consists in one thing more than in another, it is surely in learning the grounds of one's own opinions. Whatever people believe, on subjects on which it is of the first importance to believe rightly, they ought to be able to defend against at least the common objections. But, some one may say, 'Let them be *taught* the grounds of their opinions. It does not follow that opinions must be merely parroted because they are never heard controverted. Persons who learn geometry do not simply commit the theorems to memory, but understand and learn likewise the demonstrations; and it would be absurd to say that they remain ignorant of the grounds of geometrical truths, because they never hear any one deny, and attempt to disprove them.' Undoubtedly: and such teaching suffices on a subject like mathematics, where there is nothing at all to be said on the wrong side of the question. The peculiarity of the evidence of mathematical truths is, that all the argument is on one side. There are no objections, and no answers to objections. But on every subject on which difference of opinion is possible, the truth depends on a balance to be struck between two sets of conflicting reasons. Even in natural philosophy, there is always some other explanation possible of the same facts; some geocentric theory instead of heliocentric, some phlogiston instead of oxygen; and it has to be shown why that other theory cannot be the true one; and until this is shown, and until we know how it is shown, we do not understand the grounds of our opinion. But when we turn to subjects infinitely more complicated, to morals, religion, politics, social relations, and the business of life, three-fourths of the arguments for every disputed opinion consist in dispelling the appearances which favour some opinion different from it. The greatest orator, save one, of antiquity, has left it on record that he always studied his adversary's case with as great, if not with still greater, intensity than even his own. What Cicero practised as the means of forensic success, requires to be imitated by all who study any subject in order to arrive at the truth. He who knows only his own side of the case, knows little of that. His reasons may be good, and no one may have been able to refute them. But if he is equally unable to refute the reasons on the opposite side; if he does not so much as know what they are, he has no ground for preferring either opinion. The rational position for him would be suspension of judgement, and unless he contents himself with that, he is either led by authority, or adopts, like the generality of the world, the side to which he feels most inclination. Nor is it enough that he should hear the arguments of adversaries from his own teachers, presented as they state them, and accompanied by what they offer as refutations. That is not the way to do justice to the arguments, or bring them into real contact with his own mind. He must be able to hear them from persons who actually believe them; who defend them in earnest, and do their very utmost for them. He must know them in their most plausible and persuasive form; he must feel the whole force of the difficulty which the true view of the subject has to encounter and dispose of; else he will never really possess himself of the portion of truth which meets and removes that difficulty. Ninety-nine in a hundred of what are called educated men are in this condition; even of those who can argue fluently for their opinions. Their conclusion may be true, but it might be false for anything they know: they have never thrown themselves into the mental position of those who think differently from them, and considered what such persons may have to say; and consequently they do not, in any proper sense of the word, know the doctrine which they themselves profess. They do not know those parts of it which explain and justify the remainder; the considerations which show that a fact which seemingly conflicts with another is reconcilable with it, or that, of two apparently strong reasons, one and not the other ought to be preferred. All that part of the truth which turns the scale, and decides the judgement of a completely informed mind, they are strangers to; nor is it ever really known, but to those who have attended equally and impartially to both sides, and endeavoured to see the reasons of both in the strongest light. So essential is this discipline to a real understanding of moral and human subjects, that if opponents of all important truths do not exist, it is indispensable to imagine them, and supply them with the strongest arguments which the most skilful devil's advocate can conjure up.

To abate the force of these considerations, an enemy of free discussion may be supposed to say, that there is no necessity for mankind in general to know and understand all that can be said against or for their opinions by philosophers and theologians. That it is not needful for common men to be able to expose all the misstatements or fallacies of an ingenious opponent. That it is enough if there is always somebody capable of answering them, so that nothing likely to mislead uninstructed persons remains unrefuted. That simple minds, having been taught the obvious grounds of the truths inculcated on them, may trust to authority for the rest, and being aware that they have neither knowledge or talent to resolve every difficulty which can be raised, may repose in the assurance that all those which have been raised have been or can be answered, by those who are specially trained to the task.

Conceding to this view of the subject the utmost that can be claimed for it by those most easily satisfied with the amount of understanding of truth which ought to accompany the belief of it; even so, the argument for free discussion is no way weakened. For even this doctrine acknowledges that mankind ought to have a rational assurance that all objections have been satisfactorily answered; and how are they to be answered if that which requires to be answered is not spoken? or how can the answer be known to be satisfactory, if the objectors have no opportunity of showing that it is unsatisfactory? If not the public, at least the philosophers and theologians who are to resolve the difficulties, must make themselves familiar with those difficulties in their most puzzling form; and this cannot be accomplished unless they are freely stated, and placed in the most advantageous light which they admit of. The Catholic Church has its own way of dealing with this embarrassing problem. It makes a broad separation between those who can be permitted to receive its doctrines on conviction, and those who must accept them on trust. Neither, indeed, are allowed any choice as to what they will accept; but the clergy, such at least as can be fully confided in, may admissibly and meritoriously make themselves acquainted with the arguments of opponents, in order to answer them, and may, therefore, read heretical books; the laity, not unless by special permission, hard to be obtained. This discipline recognizes a knowledge of the enemy's case as beneficial to the teachers, but finds means, consistent with this, of denying it to the rest of the world: thus giving to the *élite* more mental culture, though not more mental freedom, than it allows to the mass. By this device it succeeds in obtaining the kind of mental superiority which its purposes require; for though culture without freedom never made a large and liberal mind, it can make a clever *nisi prius* advocate of a cause. But in countries professing Protestantism, this resource is denied; since Protestants hold, at least in theory, that the responsibility for the choice of a religion must be borne by each for himself, and cannot be thrown off upon teachers. Besides, in the present state of the world, it is practically impossible that writings which are read by the instructed can be kept from the uninstructed. If the teachers of mankind are to be cognizant of all that they ought to know, everything must be free to be written and published without restraint.

If, however, the mischievous operation of the absence of free discussion, when the received opinions are true, were confined to leaving men ignorant of the grounds of those opinions, it might be thought that this, if an intellectual, is no moral evil, and does not affect the worth of the opinions, regarded in their influence on the character. The fact, however, is, that not only the grounds of the opinion are forgotten in the absence of discussion, but too often the meaning of the opinion itself. The words which convey it, cease to suggest ideas, or suggest only a small portion of those they were originally employed to communicate. Instead of a vivid conception and a living belief, there remain only a few phrases retained by rote; or, if any part, the shell and husk only of the meaning is retained, the finer essence being lost. The great chapter in human history which this fact occupies and fills, cannot be too earnestly studied and meditated on.

It is illustrated in the experience of almost all ethical doctrines and religious creeds. They are all full of meaning and vitality to those who originate them, and to the direct disciples of the originators. Their meaning continues to be felt in undiminished strength, and is perhaps brought out into even fuller consciousness, so long as the struggle lasts to give the doctrine or creed an ascendancy over other creeds. At last it either prevails, and becomes the general opinion, or its progress stops; it keeps possession of the ground it has gained, but ceases to spread further. When either of these results has become apparent, controversy on the subject flags, and gradually dies away. The doctrine has taken its place, if not as a received opinion, as one of the admitted sects or divisions of opinion: those who hold it have generally inherited, not adopted it; and conversion from one of these doctrines to another, being now an exceptional fact, occupies little place in the thoughts of their professors. Instead of being, as at first, constantly on the alert either to defend themselves against the world, or to bring the world over to them, they have subsided into acquiescence, and neither listen, when they can help it, to arguments against their creed, nor trouble dissentients (if there be such) with arguments in its favour. From this time may usually be dated the decline in the living power of the doctrine. We often hear the teachers of all creeds lamenting the difficulty of keeping up in the minds of believers a lively apprehension of the truth which they nominally recognize, so that it may penetrate the feelings, and acquire a real mastery over the conduct. No such difficulty is complained of while the creed is still fighting for its existence: even the weaker combatants then know and feel what they are fighting for, and the difference between it and other doctrines; and in that period of every creed's existence, not a few persons may be found, who have realized its fundamental principles in all the forms of thought, have weighed and considered them in all their important bearings, and have experienced the full effect on the character, which belief in that creed ought to produce in a mind thoroughly imbued with it. But when it has come to be an hereditary creed, and to be received passively, not actively – when the mind is no longer compelled, in the same degree as at first, to exercise its vital powers on the questions which its belief presents to it – there is a progressive tendency to forget all of the belief except the formularies, or to give it a dull and torpid assent, as if accepting it on trust dispensed with the necessity of realizing it in consciousness, or testing it by personal experience; until it almost ceases to connect itself at all with the inner life of the human being. Then are seen the cases, so frequent in this age of the world as almost to form the majority, in which the creed remains as it were outside the mind, encrusting and petrifying it against all other influences addressed to the higher parts of our nature; manifesting its power by not suffering any fresh and living conviction to get in, but itself doing nothing for the mind or heart, except standing sentinel over them to keep them vacant.

To what an extent doctrines intrinsically fitted to make the deepest impression upon the mind may remain in it as dead beliefs, without being ever realized in the imagination, the feelings, or the understanding, is exemplified by the manner in which the majority of believers hold the doctrines of Christianity. By Christianity I here mean what is accounted such by all churches and sects – the maxims and precepts contained in the New Testament. These are considered sacred, and accepted as laws, by all professing Christians. Yet it is scarcely too much to say that not one Christian in a thousand guides or tests his individual conduct by reference to those laws. The standard to which he does refer it, is the custom of his nation, his class, or his religious profession. He has thus, on the one hand, a collection of ethical maxims, which he believes to have been vouchsafed to him by infallible wisdom as rules for his government; and on the other, a set of everyday judgements and practices, which go a certain length with some of those maxims, not so great a length with others, stand in direct opposition to some, and are, on the whole, a compromise between the Christian creed and the interests and suggestions of worldly life. To the first of these standards he gives his homage; to the other his real allegiance. All Christians believe that the blessed are the poor and humble, and those who are ill-used by the world; that it is easier for a camel to pass through the eye of a needle than for a rich man to enter the kingdom of heaven; that they should judge not, lest they be judged; that they should swear not at all; that they should love their neighbour as themselves; that if one take their cloak, they should give him their coat also; that they should take no thought for the morrow; that if they would be perfect, they should sell all that they have and give it to the poor. They are not insincere when they say that they believe these things. They do believe them, as people believe what they have always heard lauded and never discussed. But in the sense of that living belief which regulates conduct, they believe these doctrines just up to the point to which it is usual to act upon them. The doctrines in their integrity are serviceable to pelt adversaries with; and it is understood that they are to be put forward (when possible) as the reasons for whatever people do that they think laudable. But any one who reminded them that the maxims require an infinity of things which they never even think of doing, would gain nothing but to be classed among those very unpopular characters who affect to be better than other people. The doctrines have no hold on ordinary believers – are not a power in their minds. They have an habitual respect for the sound of them, but no feeling which spreads from the words to the things signified, and forces the mind to take *them* in, and make them conform to the formula. Whenever conduct is concerned, they look round for Mr A and B to direct them how far to go in obeying Christ.

Now we may be well assured that the case was not thus, but far otherwise, with the early Christians. Had it been thus, Christianity never would have expanded from an obscure sect of the despised Hebrews into the religion of the Roman empire. When their enemies said, 'See how these Christians love one another' (a remark not likely to be made by anybody now), they assuredly had a much livelier feeling of the meaning of their creed than they have ever had since. And to this cause, probably it is chiefly owing that Christianity now makes so little progress in extending its domain, and after eighteen centuries, is still nearly confined to Europeans and the descendants of Europeans. Even with the strictly religious, who are much in earnest about their doctrines, and attach a greater amount of meaning to many of them than people in general, it commonly happens that the part which is thus comparatively active in their minds is that which was made by Calvin, or Knox, or some such person much nearer in character to themselves. The sayings of Christ co-exist passively in their minds, producing hardly any effect beyond what is caused by mere listening to words so amiable and bland. There are many reasons, doubtless, why doctrines which are the badge of a sect retain more of their vitality than those common to all recognized sects, and why more pains are taken by teachers to keep their meaning alive; but one reason certainly is, that the peculiar doctrines are more questioned, and have to be oftener defended against open gainsayers. Both teachers and learners go to sleep at their post, as soon as there is no enemy in the field.

The same thing holds true, generally speaking, of all traditional doctrines – those of prudence and knowledge of life, as well as of morals or religion. All languages and literatures are full of general observations on life, both as to what it is, and how to conduct oneself in it; observations which everybody knows, which everybody repeats, or hears with acquiescence, which are received as truisms, yet of which most people first truly learn the meaning, when experience, generally of a painful kind, has made it a reality to them. How often, when smarting under some unforeseen misfortune or disappointment, does a person call to mind some proverb or common saying, familiar to him all his life, the meaning of which, if he had ever before felt it as he does now, would have saved him from the calamity. There are indeed reasons for this, other than the absence of discussion; there are many truths of which the full meaning *cannot* be realized, until personal experience has brought it home. But much more of the meaning even of these would have been understood, and what was understood would have been far more deeply impressed on the mind, if the man had been accustomed to hear it argued *pro* and *con* by people who did understand it. The fatal tendency of mankind to leave off thinking about a thing when it is no longer doubtful, is the cause of half their errors. A contemporary author has well spoken of 'the deep slumber of a decided opinion'.

But what! (it may be asked) Is the absence of unanimity an indispensable condition of true knowledge? Is it necessary that some part of mankind should persist in error, to enable any to realize the truth? Does a belief cease to be real and vital as soon as it is generally received – and is a proposition never thoroughly understood and felt unless some doubt of it remains? As soon as mankind have unanimously accepted a truth, does the truth perish within them? The highest aim and best result of improved intelligence, it has hitherto been thought, is to unite mankind more and more in the acknowledgement of all important truths: and does the intelligence only last as long as it has not achieved its object? Do the fruits of conquest perish by the very completeness of the victory?

I affirm no such thing. As mankind improve, the number of doctrines which are no longer disputed or doubted will be constantly on the increase: and the well-being of mankind may almost be measured by the number and gravity of the truths which have reached the point of being uncontested. The cessation, on one question after another, of serious controversy, is one of the necessary incidents of the consolidation of opinion; a consolidation as salutary in the case of true opinions, as it is dangerous and noxious when the opinions are erroneous. But though this gradual narrowing of the bounds of diversity of opinion is necessary in both senses of the term, being at once inevitable and indispensable, we are not therefore obliged to conclude that all its consequences must be beneficial. The loss of so important an aid to the intelligent and living apprehension of a truth, as is afforded by the necessity of explaining it to, or defending it against, opponents, though not sufficient to outweigh, is no trifling drawback from, the benefit of its universal recognition. Where this advantage can no longer be had, I confess I should like to see the teachers of mankind endeavouring to provide a substitute for it; some contrivance for making the difficulties of the question as present to the learner's consciousness, as if they were pressed upon him by a dissentient champion, eager for his conversion.

But instead of seeking contrivances for this purpose, they have lost those they formerly had. The Socratic dialectics, so magnificently exemplified in the dialogues of Plato, were a contrivance of this description. They were essentially a negative discussion of the great questions of philosophy and life, directed with consummate skill to the purpose of convincing any one who had merely adopted the commonplaces of received opinion, that he did not understand the subject – that he as yet attached no definite meaning to the doctrines he professed; in order that, becoming aware of his ignorance, he might be put in the way to attain a stable belief, resting on a clear apprehension both of the meaning of doctrines and of their evidence. The school disputations of the middle ages had a somewhat similar object. They were intended to make sure that the pupil understood his own opinion, and (by necessary correlation) the opinion opposed to it, and could enforce the grounds of the one and confute those of the other. These last-mentioned contests had indeed the incurable defect, that the premisses appealed to were taken from authority, not from reason; and, as a discipline to the mind, they were in every respect inferior to the powerful dialectics which formed the intellects of the 'Socratici viri': but the modern mind owes far more to both than it is generally willing to admit, and the present modes of education contain nothing which in the smallest degree supplies the place either of the one or of the other. A person who derives all his instruction from teachers or books, even if he escape the besetting temptation of contenting himself with cram, is under no compulsion to hear both sides; accordingly it is far from a frequent accomplishment, even among thinkers, to know both sides; and the weakest part of what everybody says in defence of his opinion, is what he intends as a reply to antagonists. It is the fashion of the present time to disparage negative logic – that which points out weaknesses in theory or errors in practice, without establishing positive truths. Such negative criticism would indeed be poor enough as an ultimate result; but as a means to attaining any positive knowledge or conviction worthy of the name, it cannot be valued too highly; and until people are again systematically trained to it, there will be few great thinkers, and a low general average of intellect, in any but the mathematical and physical departments of speculation. On any other subject no one's opinions deserve the name of knowledge, except so far as he has either had forced upon him by others, or gone through of himself, the same mental process which would have been required of him in carrying on an active controversy with opponents. That, therefore, which when absent, it is so indispensable, but so difficult, to create, how worse than absurd it is to forgo, when spontaneously offering itself! If there are any persons who contest a received opinion, or who will do so if law or opinion will let them, let us thank them for it, open our minds to listen to them, and rejoice that there is some one to do for us what we otherwise ought, if we have any regard for either the certainty or the vitality of our convictions, to do with much greater labour for ourselves.

It still remains to speak of one of the principal causes which make diversity of opinion advantageous, and will continue to do so until mankind shall have entered a stage of intellectual advancement which at present seems at an incalculable distance. We have hitherto considered only two possibilities: that the received opinion may be false, and some other opinion, consequently, true; or that, the received opinion being true, a conflict with the opposite error is essential to a clear apprehension and deep feeling of its truth. But there is a commoner case than either of these; when the conflicting doctrines, instead of being one true and the other false, share the truth between them; and the nonconforming opinion is needed to supply the remainder of the truth, of which the received doctrine embodies only a part. Popular opinions, on subjects not palpable to sense, are often true, but seldom or never the whole truth. They are a part of the truth; sometimes a greater, sometimes a smaller part, but exaggerated, distorted, and disjoined from the truths by which they ought to be accompanied and limited. Heretical opinions, on the other hand, are generally some of these suppressed and neglected truths, bursting the bonds which kept them down, and either seeking reconciliation with the truth contained in the common opinion, or fronting it as enemies, and setting themselves up, with similar exclusiveness, as the whole truth. The latter case is hitherto the most frequent, as, in the human mind, one-sidedness has always been the rule, and many-sidedness the exception. Hence, even in revolutions of opinion, one part of the truth usually sets while another rises. Even progress, which ought to superadd, for the most part only substitutes, one partial and incomplete truth for another; improvement consisting chiefly in this, that the new fragment of truth is more wanted, more adapted to the needs of the time, than that which it displaces. Such being the partial character of prevailing opinions, even when resting on a true foundation, every opinion which embodies somewhat of the portion of truth which the common opinion omits, ought to be considered precious, with whatever amount of error and confusion that truth may be blended. No sober judge of human affairs will feel bound to be indignant because those who force on our notice truths which we should otherwise have overlooked, overlook some of those which we see. Rather, he will think that so long as popular truth is one-sided, it is more desirable than otherwise that unpopular truth should have one-sided asserters too; such being usually the most energetic, and the most likely to compel reluctant attention to the fragment of wisdom which they proclaim as if it were the whole.

Thus, in the eighteenth century, when nearly all the instructed, and all those of the uninstructed who were led by them, were lost in admiration of what is called civilization, and of the marvels of modern science, literature, and philosophy, and while greatly overrating the amount of unlikeness between men of modern and those of ancient times, indulged the belief that the whole of the difference was in their own favour; with what a salutary shock did the paradoxes of Rousseau explode like bombshells in the midst, dislocating the compact mass of one-sided opinion, and forcing its elements to recombine in a better form and with additional ingredients. Not that the current opinions were on the whole farther from the truth than Rousseau's were; on the contrary, they were nearer to it; they contained more of positive truth, and very much less of error. Nevertheless there lay in Rousseau's doctrine, and has floated down the stream of opinion along with it, a considerable amount of exactly those truths which the popular opinion wanted; and these are the deposit which was left behind when the flood subsided. The superior worth of simplicity of life, the enervating and demoralizing effect of the trammels and hypocrisies of artificial society, are ideas which have never been entirely absent from cultivated minds since Rousseau wrote; and they will in time produce their due effect, though at present needing to be asserted as much as ever, and to be asserted by deeds, for words, on this subject, have nearly exhausted their power.

In politics, again, it is almost a commonplace, that a party of order or stability, and a party of progress or reform, are both necessary elements of a healthy state of political life; until the one or the other shall have so enlarged its mental grasp as to be a party equally of order and of progess, knowing and distinguishing what is fit to be preserved from what ought to be swept away. Each of these modes of thinking derives its utility from the deficiencies of the other; but it is in a great measure the opposition of the other that keeps each within the limits of reason and sanity. Unless opinions favourable to democracy and to aristocracy, to property and to equality, to co-operation and to competition, to luxury and to abstinence, to sociality and individuality, to liberty and discipline, and all the other standing antagonisms of practical life, are expressed with equal freedom, and enforced and defended with equal talent and energy, there is no chance of both elements obtaining their due; one scale is sure to go up, and the other down. Truth, in the great practical concerns of life, is so much a question of the reconciling and combining of opposites, that very few have minds sufficiently capacious and impartial to make the adjustment with an approach to correctness, and it has to be made by the rough process of a struggle between combatants fighting under hostile banners. On any of the great open questions just enumerated, if either of the two opinions has a better claim than the other, not merely to be tolerated, but to be encouraged and countenanced, it is the one which happens at the particular time and place to be in a minority. That is the opinion which, for the time being, represents the neglected interests, the side of human well-being which is in danger of obtaining less than its share. I am aware that there is not, in this country, any intolerance of differences of opinion on most of these topics. They are adduced to show, by admitted and multiplied examples, the universality of the fact, that only through diversity of opinion is there, in the existing state of human intellect, a chance of fair play to all sides of the truth. When there are persons to be found, who form an exception to the apparent unanimity of the world on any subject, even if the world is in the right, it is always probable that dissentients have something worth hearing to say for themselves, and that truth would lose something by their silence.

It may be objected, 'But *some* received principles, especially on the highest and most vital subjects, are more than half-truths. The Christian morality, for instance, is the whole truth on that subject, and if any one teaches a morality which varies from it, he is wholly in error.' As this is of all cases the most important in practice, none can be fitter to test the general maxim. But before pronouncing what Christian morality is or is not, it would be desirable to decide what is meant by Christian morality. If it means the morality of the New Testament, I wonder that any one who derives his knowledge of this from the book itself, can suppose that it was announced, or intended, as a complete doctrine of morals. The Gospel always refers to a pre-existing morality, and confines its precepts to the particulars in which that morality was to be corrected, or superseded by a wider and higher; expressing itself, moreover, in terms most general, often impossible to be interpreted literally, and possessing rather the impressiveness of poetry or eloquence than the precision of legislation. To extract from it a body of ethical doctrine, has never been possible without eking it out from the Old Testament, that is, from a system elaborate indeed, but in many respects barbarous, and intended only for a barbarous people. St Paul, a declared enemy to this Judaical mode of interpreting the doctrine and filling up the scheme of his Master, equally assumes a pre-existing morality, namely that of the Greeks and Romans; and his advice to Christians is in a great measure a system of accommodation to that; even to the extent of giving an apparent sanction to slavery. What is called Christian, but should rather be termed theological, morality, was not the work of Christ or the Apostles, but is of much later origin, having been gradually built up by the Catholic Church of the first five centuries, and though not implicitly adopted by moderns and Protestants, has been much less modified by them than might have been expected. For the most part, indeed, they have contented themselves with cutting off the additions which had been made to it in the middle ages, each sect supplying the place by fresh additions, adapted to its own character and tendencies. That mankind owe a great debt to this morality, and to its early teachers, I should be the last person to deny; but I do not scruple to say of it, that it is, in many important points, incomplete and one-sided, and that unless ideas and feelings, not sanctioned by it, had contributed to the formation of European life and character, human affairs would have been in a worse condition than they now are. Christian morality (so called) has all the characters of a reaction; it is, in great part, a protest against Paganism. Its ideal is negative rather than positive; passive rather than active; Innocence rather than Nobleness; Abstinence from Evil, rather than energetic Pursuit of Good: in its precepts (as has been well said) 'thou shalt not' predominates unduly over 'thou shalt'. In its horror of sensuality, it made an idol of asceticism, which has been gradually compromised away into one of legality. Its holds out the hope of heaven and the threat of hell, as the appointed and appropriate motives to a virtuous life: in this falling far below the best of the ancients, and doing what lies in it to give to human morality an essentially selfish character, by disconnecting each man's feelings of duty from the interests of his fellow-creatures, except so far as a self-interested inducement is offered to him for consulting them. It is essentially a doctrine of passive obedience; it inculcates submission to all authorities found established; who indeed are not to be actively obeyed when they command what religion forbids, but who are not to be resisted, far less rebelled against, for any amount of wrong to ourselves. And while, in the morality of the best Pagan nations, duty to the State holds even a disproportionate place, infringing on the just liberty of the individual; in purely Christian ethics, that grand department of duty is scarcely noticed or acknowledged. It is in the Koran, not the New Testament, that we read the maxim – 'A ruler who appoints any man to an office, when there is in his dominions another man better qualified for it, sins against God and against the State.' What little recognition the idea of obligation to the public obtains in modern morality, is derived from Greek and Roman sources, not from Christian; as, even in the morality of private life, whatever exists of magnanimity, high-mindedness, personal dignity, even the sense of honour, is derived from the purely human, not the religious part of our education, and never could have grown out of a standard of ethics in which the only worth, professedly recognized, is that of obedience.

I am as far as any one from pretending that these defects are necessarily inherent in the Christian ethics, in every manner in which it can be conceived, or that the many requisites of a complete moral doctrine which it does not contain, do not admit of being reconciled with it. Far less would I insinuate this of the doctrines and precepts of Christ himself. I believe that the sayings of Christ are all, that I can see any evidence of their having been intended to be; that they are irreconcilable with nothing which a comprehensive morality requires; that everything which is excellent in ethics may be brought within them, with no greater violence to their language than has been done to it by all who have attempted to deduce from them any practical system of conduct whatever. But it is quite consistent with this, to believe that they contain, and were meant to contain, only a part of the truth; that many essential elements of the highest morality are among the things which are not provided for, nor intended to be provided for, in the recorded deliverances of the Founder of Christianity, and which have been entirely thrown aside in the system of ethics erected on the basis of those deliverances by the Christian Church. And this being so, I think it a great error to persist in attempting to find in the Christian doctrine that complete rule for our guidance, which its author intended it to sanction and enforce, but only partially to provide. I believe, too, that this narrow theory is becoming a grave practical evil, detracting greatly from the value of the moral training and instruction, which so many well-meaning persons are now at length exerting themselves to promote. I much fear that by attempting to form the mind and feelings on an exclusively religious type, and discarding those secular standards (as for want of a better name they may be called) which heretofore co-existed with and supplemented the Christian ethics, receiving some of its spirit, and infusing into it some of theirs, there will result, and is even now resulting, a low, abject, servile type of character, which, submit itself as it may to what it deems the Supreme Will, is incapable of rising to or sympathizing in the conception of Supreme Goodness. I believe that other ethics than any which can be evolved from exclusively Christian sources, must exist side by side with Christian ethics to produce the moral regeneration of mankind; and that the Christian system is no exception to the rule, that in an imperfect state of the human mind, the interests of truth require a diversity of opinions. It is not necessary that in ceasing to ignore the moral truths not contained in Christianity, men should ignore any of those which it does contain. Such prejudice, or oversight, when it occurs, is altogether an evil; but it is one from which we cannot hope to be always exempt, and must be regarded as the price paid for an inestimable good. The exclusive pretension made by a part of the truth to be the whole, must and ought to be protested against; and if a reactionary impulse should make the protestors unjust in their turn, this one-sidedness, like the other, may be lamented, but must be tolerated. If Christians would teach infidels to be just to Christianity, they should themselves be just to infidelity. It can do truth no service to blink the fact, known to all who have the most ordinary acquaintance with literary history, that a large portion of the noblest and most valuable moral teaching has been the work, not only of men who did not know, but of men who knew and rejected, the Christian faith.

I do not pretend that the most unlimited use of the freedom of enunciating all possible opinions would put an end to the evils of religious or philosophical sectarianism. Every truth which men of narrow capacity are in earnest about, is sure to be asserted, inculcated, and in many ways even acted on, as if no other truth existed in the world, or at all events none that could limit or qualify the first. I acknowledge that the tendency of all opinions to become sectarian is not cured by the freest discussion, but is often heightened and exacerbated thereby; the truth which ought to have been, but was not, seen, being rejected all the more violently because proclaimed by persons regarded as opponents. But it is not on the impassioned partisan, it is on the calmer and more disinterested bystander, that this collision of opinions works its salutary effect. Not the violent conflict between parts of the truth, but the quiet suppression of half of it, is the formidable evil; there is always hope when people are forced to listen to both sides; it is when they attend only to one that errors harden into prejudices, and truth itself ceases to have the effect of truth, by being exaggerated into falsehood. And since there are few mental attributes more rare than that judicial faculty which can sit in intelligent judgement between two sides of a question, of which only one is represented by an advocate before it, truth has no chance but in proportion as every side of it, every opinion which embodies any fraction of the truth, not only finds advocates, but is so advocated as to be listened to.

We have now recognized the necessity to the mental well-being of mankind (on which all their other well-being depends) of freedom of opinion, and freedom of the expression of opinion, on four distinct grounds; which we will now briefly recapitulate.

First, if any opinion is compelled to silence, that opinion may, for aught we can certainly know, be true. To deny this is to assume our own infallibility.

Secondly, though the silenced opinion be an error, it may, and very commonly does, contain a portion of truth; and since the general or prevailing opinion on any subject is rarely or never the whole truth, it is only by the collision of adverse opinions that the remainder of the truth has any chance of being supplied.

Thirdly, even if the received opinion be not only true, but the whole truth; unless it is suffered to be, and actually is, vigorously and earnestly contested, it will, by most of those who receive it, be held in the manner of a prejudice, with little comprehension or feeling of its rational grounds. And not only this, but, fourthly, the meaning of the doctrine itself will be in danger of being lost, or enfeebled, and deprived of its vital effect on the character and conduct: the dogma becoming a mere formal profession, inefficacious for good, but cumbering the ground, and preventing the growth of any real and heartfelt conviction, from reason or personal experience.

Before quitting the subject of freedom of opinion, it is fit to take some notice of those who say, that the free expression of all opinions should be permitted, on condition that the manner be temperate, and do not pass the bounds of fair discussion. Much might be said on the impossibility of fixing where these supposed bounds are to be placed; for if the test be offence to those whose opinion is attacked, I think experience testifies that this offence is given whenever the attack is telling and powerful, and that every opponent who pushes them hard, and whom they find it difficult to answer, appears to them, if he shows any strong feeling on the subject, an intemperate opponent. But this, though an important consideration in a practical point of view, merges in a more fundamental objection. Undoubtedly the manner of asserting an opinion, even though it be a true one, may be very objectionable, and may justly incur severe censure. But the principal offences of the kind are such as it is mostly impossible, unless by accidental self-betrayal, to bring home to conviction. The gravest of them is, to argue sophistically, to suppress facts or arguments, to misstate the elements of the case, or misrepresent the opposite opinion. But all this, even to the most aggravated degree, is so continually done in perfect good faith, by persons who are not considered, and in many other respects may not deserve to be considered, ignorant or incompetent, that it is rarely possible on adequate grounds conscientiously to stamp the misrepresentation as morally culpable; and still less could law presume to interfere with this kind of controversial misconduct. With regard to what is commonly meant by intemperate discussion, namely invective, sarcasm, personality, and the like, the denunciation of these weapons would deserve more sympathy if it were ever proposed to interdict them equally to both sides; but it is only desired to restrain the employment of them against the prevailing opinion: against the unprevailing they may not only be used without general disapproval, but will be likely to obtain for him who uses them the praise of honest zeal and righteous indignation. Yet whatever mischief arises from their use, is greatest when they are employed against the comparatively defenceless; and whatever unfair advantage can be derived by any opinion from this mode of asserting it, accrues almost exclusively to received opinions. The worst offence of this kind which can be committed by a polemic, is to stigmatize those who hold the contrary opinion as bad and immoral men. To calumny of this sort, those who hold any unpopular opinion are peculiarly exposed, because they are in general few and uninfluential, and nobody but themselves feels much interested in seeing justice done them; but this weapon is, from the nature of the case, denied to those who attack a prevailing opinion: they can neither use it with safety to themselves, nor, if they could, would it do anything but recoil on their own cause. In general, opinions contrary to those commonly received can only obtain a hearing by studied moderation of language, and the most cautious avoidance of unnecessary offence, from which they hardly ever deviate even in a slight degree without losing ground: while unmeasured vituperation employed on the side of the prevailing opinion, really does deter people from professing contrary opinions, and from listening to those who profess them. For the interest, therefore, of truth and justice, it is far more important to restrain this employment of vituperative language than the other; and, for example, if it were necessary to choose, there would be much more need to discourage offensive attacks on infidelity, than on religion. It is, however, obvious that law and authority have no business with restraining either, while opinion ought, in every instance, to determine its verdict by the circumstances of the individual case; condemning every one, on whichever side of the argument he places himself, in whose mode of advocacy either want of candour, or malignity, bigotry, or intolerance of feeling manifest themselves; but not inferring these vices from the side which a person takes, though it be the contrary side of the question to our own: and giving merited honour to every one, whatever opinion he may hold, who has calmness to see and honesty to state what his opponents and their opinions really are, exaggerating nothing to their discredit, keeping nothing back which tells, or can be supposed to tell, in their favour. This is the real morality of public discussion: and if often violated, I am happy to think that there are many controversialists who to a great extent observe it, and a still greater number who conscientiously strive towards it.

71

3 OF INDIVIDUALITY, AS ONE OF THE ELEMENTS OF WELL-BEING

Such being the reasons which make it imperative that human beings should be free to form opinions, and to express their opinions without reserve; and such the baneful consequences to the intellectual, and through that to the moral nature of man, unless this liberty is either conceded, or asserted in spite of prohibition; let us next examine whether the same reasons do not require that men should be free to act upon their opinions – to carry these out in their lives, without hindrance, either physical or moral, from their fellow men, so long as it is at their own risk and peril. This last proviso is of course indispensable. No one pretends that actions should be as free as opinions. On the contrary, even opinions lose their immunity, when the circumstances in which they are expressed are such as to constitute their expression a positive instigation to some mischievous act. An opinion that corn-dealers are starvers of the poor, or that private property is robbery, ought to be unmolested when simply circulated through the press, but may justly incur punishment when delivered orally to an excited mob assembled before the house of a corn-dealer, or when handed about among the same mob in the form of a placard. Acts, of whatever kind, which, without justifiable cause, do harm to others, may be, and in the more important cases absolutely require to be, controlled by the unfavourable sentiments, and, when needful, by the active interference of mankind. The liberty of the individual must be thus far limited; he must not make himself a nuisance to other people. But if he refrains from molesting others in what concerns them, and merely acts according to his own inclination and judgement in things which concern himself, the same reasons which show that opinion should be free, prove also that he should be allowed, without molestation, to carry his opinions into practice at his own cost. That mankind are not infallible; that their truths, for the most part, are only half-truths; that unity of opinion, unless resulting from the fullest and freest comparison of opposite opinions, is not desirable, and diversity not an evil, but a good, until mankind are much more capable than at present of recognizing all sides of the truth, are principles applicable to men's modes of action, not less than to their opinions. As it is useful that while mankind are imperfect there should be different opinions, so is it that there should be different experiments of living; that free scope should be given to varieties of character, short of injury to others; and that the worth of different modes of life should be proved practically, when any one thinks fit to try them. It is desirable, in short, that in things which do not primarily concern others, individuality should assert itself. Where, not the person's own character, but the traditions or customs of other people are the rule of conduct, there is wanting one of the principal ingredients of human happiness, and quite the chief ingredient of individual and social progress.

In maintaining this principle, the greatest difficulty to be encountered does not lie in the appreciation of means towards an acknowledged end, but in the indifference of persons in general to the end itself. If it were felt that the free development of individuality is one of the leading essentials of well-being; that it is not only a co-ordinate element with all that is designated by the terms civilization, instruction, education, culture, but is itself a necessary part and condition of all those things; there would be no danger that liberty should be undervalued, and the adjustment of the boundaries between it and social control would present no extraordinary difficulty. But the evil is, that individual spontaneity is hardly recognized by the common modes of thinking, as having any intrinsic worth, or deserving any regard on its own account. The majority, being satisfied with the ways of mankind as they now are (for it is they who make them what they are), cannot comprehend why those ways should not be good enough for everybody; and what is more, spontaneity forms no part of the ideal of the majority of moral and social reformers, but is rather looked on with jealousy, as a troublesome and perhaps rebellious obstruction to the general acceptance of what these reformers, in their own judgement, think would be best for mankind. Few persons, out of Germany, even comprehend the meaning of the doctrine which Wilhelm von Humboldt, so eminent both as a savant and as a politician, made the text of a treatise – that 'the end of man, or that which is prescribed by the eternal or immutable dictates of reason, and not suggested by vague and transient desires, is the highest and most harmonious development of his powers to a complete and consistent whole'; that, therefore, the object 'towards which every human being must ceaselessly direct his efforts, and on which especially those who design to influence their fellow men must ever keep their eyes, is the individuality of power and development'; that for this there are two requisites, 'freedom, and variety of situations'; and that from the union of these arise 'individual vigour and manifold diversity', which combine themselves in 'originality'.[1]

Little, however, as people are accustomed to a doctrine like that of Von Humboldt, and surprising as it may be to them to find so high a value attached to individuality, the question, one must nevertheless think, can only be one of degree. No one's idea of excellence in conduct is that people should do absolutely nothing but copy one another. No one would assert that people ought not to put into their mode of life, and into the conduct of their concerns, any impress whatever of their own judgement, or of their own individual character. On the other hand, it would be absurd to pretend that people ought to live as if nothing whatever had been known in the world before they came into it; as if experience had as yet done nothing towards showing that one mode of existence, or of conduct, is preferable to another. Nobody denies that people should be so taught and trained in youth, as to know and benefit by the ascertained results of human experience. But it is the privilege and proper condition of a human being, arrived at the maturity of his faculties, to use and interpret experience in his own way. It is for him to find out what part of recorded experience is properly applicable to his own circumstances and character. The traditions and customs of other people are, to a certain extent, evidence of what their experience has taught *them*; presumptive evidence, and as such, have a claim to his deference: but, in the first place, their experience may be too narrow; or they may not have interpreted it rightly. Secondly, their interpretation of experience may be correct, but unsuitable to him. Customs are made for customary circumstances, and customary characters; and his circumstances or his character may be uncustomary. Thirdly, though the customs be both good as customs, and suitable to him, yet to conform to custom, merely *as* custom, does not educate or develop in him any of the qualities which are the distinctive endowment of a human being. The human faculties of perception, judgement, discriminative feeling, mental activity, and even moral preference, are exercised only in making a choice. He who does anything because it is the custom, makes no choice. He gains no practice either in discerning or in desiring what is best. The mental and moral, like the muscular powers, are improved only by being

1 *The Sphere and Duties of Government*, from the German of Baron Wilhelm von Humboldt, 11–13.

used. The faculties are called into no exercise by doing a thing merely because others do it, no more than by believing a thing only because others believe it. If the grounds of an opinion are not conclusive to the person's own reason, his reason cannot be strengthened, but is likely to be weakened, by his adopting it: and if the inducements to an act are not such as are consentaneous to his own feelings and character (where affection, or the rights of others, are not concerned) it is so much done towards rendering his feelings and character inert and torpid, instead of active and energetic.

He who lets the world, or his own portion of it, choose his plan of life for him, has no need of any other faculty than the ape-like one of imitation. He who chooses his plan for himself, employs all his faculties. He must use observation to see, reasoning and judgement to foresee, activity to gather materials for decision, discrimination to decide, and when he has decided, firmness and self-control to hold to his deliberate decision. And these qualities he requires and exercises exactly in proportion as the part of his conduct which he determines according to his own judgement and feelings is a large one. It is possible that he might be guided in some good path, and kept out of harm's way, without any of these things. But what will be his comparative worth as a human being? It really is of importance, not only what men do, but also what manner of men they are that do it. Among the works of man, which human life is rightly employed in perfecting and beautifying, the first in importance surely is man himself. Supposing it were possible to get houses built, corn grown, battles fought, causes tried, and even churches erected and prayers said, by machinery – by automatons in human form – it would be a considerable loss to exchange for these automatons even the men and women who at present inhabit the more civilized parts of the world, and who assuredly are but starved specimens of what nature can and will produce. Human nature is not a machine to be built after a model, and set to do exactly the work prescribed for it, but a tree, which requires to grow and develop itself on all sides, according to the tendency of the inward forces which make it a living thing.

It will probably be conceded that it is desirable people should exercise their understandings, and that an intelligent following of custom, or even occasionally an intelligent deviation from custom, is better than a blind and simply mechanical adhesion to it. To a certain extent it is admitted, that our understanding should be our own: but there is not the same willingness to admit that our desires and impulses should be our own likewise; or that to possess impulses of our own, and of any strength, is anything but a peril and a snare. Yet desires and impulses are as much a part of a perfect human being, as beliefs and restraints: and strong impulses are only perilous when not properly balanced; when one set of aims and inclinations is developed into strength, while others, which ought to co-exist with them, remain weak and inactive. It is not because men's desires are strong that they act ill; it is because their consciences are weak. There is no natural connexion between strong impulses and a weak conscience. The natural connexion is the other way. To say that one person's desires and feelings are stronger and more various than those of another, is merely to say that he has more of the raw material of human nature, and is therefore capable, perhaps of more evil, but certainly of more good. Strong impulses are but another name for energy. Energy may be turned to bad uses; but more good may always be made of an energetic nature, than of an indolent and impassive one. Those who have most natural feeling, are always those whose cultivated feelings may be made the strongest. The same strong susceptibilities which make the personal impulses vivid and powerful, are also the source from whence are generated the most passionate love of virtue, and the sternest self-control. It is through the cultivation of these, that society both does its duty and protects its interests: not by rejecting the stuff of which heroes are made, because it knows not how to make them. A person whose desires and impulses are his own – are the expression of his own nature, as it has been developed and modified by his own culture – is said to have a character. One whose desires and impulses are not his own, has no character, no more than a steam-engine has a character. If, in addition to being his own, his impulses are strong, and are under the government of a strong will, he has an energetic character. Whoever thinks that individuality of desires and impulses should not be encouraged to unfold itself, must maintain that society has no need of strong natures – is not the better for containing many persons who have much character – and that a high general average of energy is not desirable.

In some early states of society, these forces might be, and were, too much ahead of the power which society then possessed of disciplining and controlling them. There has been a time when the element of spontaneity and individuality was in excess, and the social principle had a hard struggle with it. The difficulty then was, to induce men of strong bodies or minds to pay obedience to any rules which required them to control their impulses. To overcome this difficulty, law and discipline, like the Popes struggling against the Emperors, asserted a power over the whole man, claiming to control all his life in order to control his character – which society had not found any other sufficient means of binding. But society has now fairly got the better of individuality; and the danger which threatens human nature is not the excess, but the deficiency, of personal impulses and preferences. Things are vastly changed, since the passions of those who were strong by station or by personal endowment were in a state of habitual rebellion against laws and ordinances, and required to be rigorously chained up to enable the persons within their reach to enjoy any particle of security. In our times, from the highest class of society down to the lowest, every one lives as under the eye of a hostile and dreaded censorship. Not only in what concerns others, but in what concerns only them-selves, the individual or the family do not ask themselves – what do I prefer? or, what would suit my character and disposition? or, what would allow the best and highest in me to have fair play, and enable it to grow and thrive? They ask themselves, what is suitable to my position? what is usually done by persons of my station and pecuniary circumstances? or (worse still) what is usually done by persons of a station and circumstances superior to mine? I do not mean that they choose what is customary, in preference to what suits their own inclination. It does not occur to them to have any inclination, except for what is customary. Thus the mind itself is bowed to the yoke: even in what people do for pleasure, conformity is the first thing thought of; they like in crowds; they exercise choice only among things commonly done: peculiarity of taste, eccentricity of conduct, are shunned equally with crimes: until by dint of not following their own nature, they have no nature to follow: their human capacities are withered and starved: they become incapable of any strong wishes or native pleasures, and are generally without either opinions or feelings of home growth, or properly their own. Now is this, or is it not, the desirable condition of human nature?

It is so, on the Calvinistic theory. According to that, the one great offence of man is self-will. All the good of which humanity is capable, is comprised in obedience. You have no choice; thus you must do, and not otherwise: 'whatever is not a duty, is a sin'. Human nature being radically corrupt, there is no redemption for any one until human nature is killed within him. To one holding this theory of life, crushing out any of the human faculties, capacities, and susceptibilities, is no evil: man needs no capacity, but that of surrendering himself to the will of God: and if he uses any of his faculties for any other purpose but to do that supposed will more effectually, he is better without them. This is the theory of Calvinism; and it is held, in a mitigated form, by many who do not consider themselves Calvinists; the mitigation consisting in giving a less ascetic interpretation to the alleged will of God; asserting it to be his will that mankind should gratify some of their inclinations; of course not in the manner they themselves prefer, but in the way of obedience, that is, in a way prescribed to them by authority; and, therefore, by the necessary conditions of the case, the same for all.

In some such insidious form there is at present a strong tendency to this narrow theory of life, and to the pinched and hidebound type of human character which it patronizes. Many persons, no doubt, sincerely think that human beings thus cramped and dwarfed, are as their Maker designed them to be; just as many have thought that trees are a much finer thing when clipped into pollards, or cut into figures of animals, than as nature made them. But if it be any part of religion to believe that man was made by a good Being, it is more consistent with that faith to believe, that this Being gave all human faculties that they might be cultivated and unfolded, not rooted out and consumed, and that he takes delight in every nearer approach made by his creatures to the ideal conception embodied in them, every increase in any of their capabilities or comprehension, of action, or of enjoyment. There is a different type of human excellence from the Calvinistic; a conception of humanity as having its nature bestowed on it for other purposes than merely to be abnegated. 'Pagan self-assertion' is one of the elements of human worth, as well as 'Christian self-denial'.[2] There is a Greek ideal of self-development, which the Platonic and Christian ideal of self-government blends with, but does not supersede. It may be better to be a John Knox than an Alcibiades, but it is better to be a Pericles than either; nor would a Pericles, if we had one in these days, be without anything good which belonged to John Knox.

It is not by wearing down into uniformity all that is individual in themselves, but by cultivating it and calling it forth, within the limits imposed by the rights and interests of others, that human

2 Sterling's *Essays*.

beings become a noble and beautiful object of contemplation; and as the works partake the character of those who do them, by the same process human life also becomes rich, diversified, and animating, furnishing more abundant aliment to high thoughts and elevating feelings, and strengthening the tie which binds every individual to the race, by making the race infinitely better worth belonging to. In proportion to the development of his individuality, each person becomes more valuable to himself, and is therefore capable of being more valuable to others. There is a greater fullness of life about his own existence, and when there is more life in the units there is more in the mass which is composed of them. As much compression as is necessary to prevent the stronger specimens of human nature from encroaching on the rights of others, cannot be dispensed with; but for this there is ample compensation even in the point of view of human development. The means of development which the individual loses by being prevented from gratifying his inclinations to the injury of others, are chiefly obtained at the expense of the development of other people. And even to himself there is a full equivalent in the better development of the social part of his nature, rendered possible by the restraint put upon the selfish part. To be held to rigid rules of justice for the sake of others, develops the feelings and capacities which have the good of others for their object. But to be restrained in things not affecting their good, by their mere displeasure, develops nothing valuable, except such force of character as may unfold itself in resisting the restraint. If acquiesced in, it dulls and blunts the whole nature. To give any fair play to the nature of each, it is essential that different persons should be allowed to lead different lives. In proportion as this latitude has been exercised in any age, has that age been noteworthy to posterity. Even despotism does not produce its worst effects, so long as individuality exists under it; and whatever crushes individuality is despotism, by whatever name it may be called, and whether it professes to be enforcing the will of God or the injunctions of men.

Having said that Individuality is the same thing with development, and that it is only the cultivation of individuality which produces, or can produce, well-developed human beings, I might here close the argument: for what more or better can be said of any condition of human affairs, than that it brings human beings themselves nearer to the best thing they can be? or what worse can be said of any obstruction to good, than that it prevents this?

Doubtless, however, these considerations will not suffice to convince those who most need convincing; and it is necessary further to show, that these developed human beings are of some use to the underdeveloped – to point out to those who do not desire liberty, and would not avail themselves of it, that they may be in some intelligible manner rewarded for allowing other people to make use of it without hindrance.

In the first place, then, I would suggest that they might possibly learn something from them. It will not be denied by anybody, that originality is a valuable element in human affairs. There is always need of persons not only to discover new truths, and point out when what were once truths are true no longer, but also to commence new practices, and set the example of more enlightened conduct, and better taste and sense in human life. This cannot well be gainsaid by anybody who does not believe that the world has already attained perfection in all its ways and practices. It is true that this benefit is not capable of being rendered by everybody alike: there are but few persons, in comparison with the whole of mankind, whose experiments, if adopted by others, would be likely to be any improvement on established practice. But these few are the salt of the earth; without them, human life would become a stagnant pool. Not only is it they who introduce good things which did not before exist; it is they who keep the life in those which already existed. It there were nothing new to be done, would human intellect cease to be necessary? Would it be a reason why those who do the old things should forget why they are done, and do them like cattle, not like human beings? There is only too great a tendency in the best beliefs and practices to degenerate into the mechanical; and unless there were a succession of persons whose ever-recurring originality prevents the grounds of those beliefs and practices from becoming merely traditional, such dead matter would not resist the smallest shock from anything really alive, and there would be no reason why civilization should not die out, as in the Byzantine Empire. Persons of genius, it is true, are, and are always likely to be, a small minority; but in order to have them, it is necessary to preserve the soil in which they grow. Genius can only breathe freely in an *atmosphere* of freedom. Persons of genius are, *ex vi termini, more* individual than any other people – less capable, consequently, of fitting themselves, without hurtful compression, into any of the small number of moulds which society provides in order to save its members the trouble of forming their own character. If from timidity they consent to be forced into one of these moulds, and to let all that part of themselves which cannot expand under the pressure remain unexpanded, society will be little the better for their genius. If they are of a strong character, and break their fetters, they become a mark for the society which has not succeeded in reducing them to commonplace, to point at with solemn warning as 'wild', 'erratic', and the like; much as if one should complain of the Niagara river for not flowing smoothly between its banks like a Dutch canal.

I insist thus emphatically on the importance of genius, and the necessity of allowing it to unfold itself freely both in thought and in practice, being well aware that no one will deny the position in theory, but knowing also that almost every one, in reality, is totally indifferent to it. People think genius a fine thing if it enables a man to write an exciting poem, or paint a picture. But in its true sense, that of originality in thought and action, though no one says that it is not a thing to be admired, nearly all, at heart, think that they can do very well without it. Unhappily this is too natural to be wondered at. Originality is the one thing which unoriginal minds cannot feel the use of. They cannot see what it is to do for them: how should they? If they could see what it would do for them, it would not be originality. The first service which originality has to render them, is that of opening their eyes: which being once fully done, they would have a chance of being themselves original. Meanwhile, recollecting that nothing was ever yet done which some one was not the first to do, and that all good things which exist are the fruits of originality, let them be modest enough to believe that there is something still left for it to accomplish, and assure themselves that they are more in need of originality, the less they are conscious of the want.

In sober truth, whatever homage may be professed, or even paid, to real or supposed mental superiority, the general tendency of things throughout the world is to render mediocrity the ascendant power among mankind. In ancient history, in the middle ages, and in a diminishing degree through the long transition from feudality to the present time, the individual was a power in himself; and if he had either great talents or a high social position, he was a considerable power. At present individuals are lost in the crowd. In politics it is almost a triviality to say that public opinion now rules the world. The only power deserving the name is that of masses, and of governments while they make themselves the organ of the tendencies and instincts of masses. This is as true in the moral and social relations of private life as in public transactions. Those whose opinions go by the name of public opinion, are not always the same sort of public: in America they are the whole white population; in England, chiefly the middle class. But they are always a mass, that is to say, collective mediocrity. And what is a still greater novelty, the mass do not now take their opinions from dignitaries in Church or State, from ostensible leaders, or from books. Their thinking is done for them by men much like themselves, addressing them or speaking in their name, on the spur of the moment, through the newspapers. I am not complaining of all this. I do not assert that anything better is compatible, as a general rule, with the present low state of the human mind. But that does not hinder the government of mediocrity from being mediocre government. No government by a democracy or a numerous aristocracy, either in its political acts or in the opinions, qualities, and tone of mind which it fosters, ever did or could rise above mediocrity, except in so far as the sovereign Many have let themselves be guided (which in their best times they always have done) by the counsels and influence of a more highly gifted and instructed One or Few. The initiation of all wise or noble things, comes and must come from individuals; generally at first from some one individual. The honour and glory of the average man is that he is capable of following that initiative; that he can respond internally to wise and noble things, and be led by them with his eyes open. I am not countenancing the sort of 'hero-worship' which applauds the strong man of genius for forcibly seizing on the government of the world and making it do his bidding in spite of itself. All he can claim is, freedom to point out the way. The power of compelling others into it, is not only inconsistent with the freedom and development of all the rest, but corrupting to the strong man himself. It does seem, however, that when the opinions of masses of merely average men are everywhere become or becoming the dominant power, the counterpoise and corrective to that tendency would be, the more and more pro-nounced individuality of those who stand on the higher eminences of thought. It is in these circumstances most especially, that exceptional individuals, instead of being deterred, should be encouraged in acting differently from the mass. In other times there was no advantage in their doing so, unless they acted not only differently, but better. In this age, the mere example of non-conformity, the mere refusal to bend the knee to custom, is itself a service. Precisely because the tyranny of opinion is such as to make eccentricity a reproach, it is desirable, in order to break through that tyranny, that people should be eccentric. Eccentricity has always abounded when and where strength of character has abounded; and the amount of eccentricity in a society has generally been proportional to the amount of genius, mental vigour, and moral courage which it contained. That so few now dare to be eccentric, marks the chief danger of the time.

I have said that it is important to give the freest scope possible to uncustomary things, in order that it may in time appear which of these are fit to be converted into customs. But independence of action, and disregard of custom, are not solely deserving of encouragement for the chance they afford that better modes of action, and customs more worthy of general adoption, may be struck out; nor is it only persons of decided mental superiority who have a just claim to carry on their lives in their own way. There is no reason that all human existence should be constructed on some one or some small number of patterns. If a person possesses any tolerable amount of common sense and experience, his own mode of laying out his existence is the best, not because it is the best in itself, but because it is his own mode. Human beings are not like sheep; and even sheep are not undistinguishably alike. A man cannot get a coat or a pair of boots to fit him, unless they are either made to his measure, or he has a whole warehouseful to choose from: and is it easier to fit him with a life than with a coat, or are human beings more like one another in their whole physical and spiritual conformation than in the shape of their feet? If it were only that people have diversities of taste, that is reason enough for not attempting to shape them all after one model. But different persons also require different conditions for their spiritual development; and can no more exist healthily in the same moral, than all the variety of plants can in the same physical, atmosphere and climate. The same things which are helps to one person towards the cultivation of his higher nature, are hindrances to another. The same mode of life is a healthy excitement to one, keeping all his faculties of action and enjoyment in their best order, while to another it is a distracting burthen, which suspends or crushes all internal life. Such are the differences among human beings in their sources of pleasure, their susceptibilities of pain, and the operation on them of different physical and moral agencies, that unless there is a corresponding diversity in their modes of life, they neither obtain their fair share of happiness, nor grow up to the mental, moral, and aesthetic stature of which their nature is capable. Why then should tolerance, as far as the public sentiment is concerned, extend only to tastes and modes of life which extort acquiescence by the multitude of their adherents? Nowhere (except in some monastic institutions) is diversity of taste entirely unrecognized; a person may, without blame, either like or dislike rowing, or smoking, or music, or athletic exercises, or chess, or cards, or study, because both those who like each of these things, and those who dislike them, are too numerous to be put down. But the man, and still more the woman, who can be accused either of doing 'what nobody does', or of not doing 'what everybody does', is the subject of as much depreciatory remark as if he or she had committed some grave moral delinquency. Persons require to possess a title, or some other badge of rank, or of the consideration of people of rank, to be able to indulge somewhat in the luxury of doing as they like without detriment to their estimation. To indulge somewhat, I repeat: for whoever allow themselves much of that indulgence, incur the risk of something worse than disparaging speeches – they are in peril of a commission *de lunatico*, and of having their property taken from them and given to their relations.[3]

There is one characteristic of the present direction of public opinion, peculiarly calculated to make it intolerant of any marked

3 There is something both contemptible and frightful in the sort of evidence on which, of late years, any person can be judicially declared unfit for the management of his affairs; and after his death, his disposal of his property can be set aside, if there is enough of it to pay the expenses of litigation – which are charged on the property itself. All the minute details of his daily life are pried into, and whatever is found which, seen through the medium of the perceiving and describing faculties of the lowest of the low, bears an appearance unlike absolute commonplace, is laid before the jury as evidence of insanity, and often with success; the jurors being little, if at all, less vulgar and ignorant than the witnesses; while the judges, with that extraordinary want of knowledge of human nature and life which continually astonishes us in English lawyers, often help to mislead them. These trials speak volumes as to the state of feeling and opinion among the vulgar with regard to human liberty. So far from setting any value on individuality – so far from respecting the right of each individual to act, in things indifferent, as seems good to his own judgement and inclinations, judges and juries cannot even conceive that a person in a state of sanity can desire such freedom. In former days, when it was proposed to burn atheists, charitable people used to suggest putting them in a mad-house instead: it would be nothing surprising nowadays were we to see this done, and the doers applauding themselves, because, instead of persecuting for religion, they had adopted so humane and Christian a mode of treating these unfortunates, not without a silent satisfaction at their having thereby obtained their deserts.

demonstration of individuality. The general average of mankind are not only moderate in intellect, but also moderate in inclinations: they have no tastes or wishes strong enough to incline them to do anything unusual, and they consequently do not understand those who have, and class all such with the wild and intemperate whom they are accustomed to look down upon. Now, in addition to this fact which is general, we have only to suppose that a strong movement has set in towards the improvement of morals, and it is evident what we have to expect. In these days such a movement has set in; much has actually been effected in the way of increased regularity of conduct, and discouragement of excesses; and there is a philanthropic spirit abroad, for the exercise of which there is no more inviting field than the moral and prudential improvement of our fellow creatures. These tendencies of the times cause the public to be more disposed than at most former periods to prescribe general rules of conduct, and endeavour to make every one conform to the approved standard. And that standard, express or tacit, is to desire nothing strongly. Its ideal of character is to be without any marked character; to maim by compression, like a Chinese lady's foot, every part of human nature which stands out prominently, and tends to make the person markedly dissimilar in outline to commonplace humanity.

As is usually the case with ideals which exclude one-half of what is desirable, the present standard of approbation produces only an inferior imitation of the other half. Instead of great energies guided by vigorous reason, and strong feelings strongly controlled by a conscientious will, its result is weak feelings and weak energies, which therefore can be kept in outward conformity to rule without any strength either of will or of reason. Already energetic characters on any large scale are becoming merely traditional. There is now scarcely any outlet for energy in this country except business. The energy expended in this may still be regarded as considerable. What little is left from that employment, is expended on some hobby; which may be a useful, even a philanthropic hobby, but is always some one thing, and generally a thing of small dimensions. The greatness of England is now all collective: individually small, we only appear capable of anything great by our habit of combining; and with this our moral and religious philanthropists are perfectly contented. But it was men of another stamp than this that made England what it has been; and men of another stamp will be needed to prevent its decline.

The despotism of custom is everywhere the standing hindrance to human advancement, being in unceasing antagonism to that disposition to aim at something better than customary, which is called, according to circumstances, the spirit of liberty, or that of progress or improvement. The spirit of improvement is not always a spirit of liberty, for it may aim at forcing improvements on an unwilling people; and the spirit of liberty, in so far as it resists such attempts, may ally itself locally and temporarily with the opponents of improvement; but the only unfailing and permanent source of improvement is liberty, since by it there are as many possible independent centres of improvement as there are individuals. The progressive principle, however, in either shape, whether as the love of liberty or of improvement, is antagonistic to the sway of Custom, involving at least emancipation from that yoke; and the contest between the two constitutes the chief interest of the history of mankind. The greater part of the world has, properly speaking, no history, because the despotism of Custom is complete. This is the case over the whole East. Custom is there, in all things, the final appeal; justice and right mean conformity to custom; the argument of custom no one, unless some tyrant intoxicated with power, thinks of resisting. And we see the result. Those nations must once have had originality; they did not start out of the ground populous, lettered, and versed in many of the arts of life; they made themselves all this, and were then the greatest and most powerful nations of the world. What are they now? The subjects or dependants of tribes whose forefathers wandered in the forests when theirs had magnificent palaces and gorgeous temples, but over whom custom exercised only a divided rule with liberty and progress. A people, it appears, may be progressive for a certain length of time, and then stop: when does it stop? When it ceases to possess individuality. If a similar change should befall the nations of Europe, it will not be in exactly the same shape: the despotism of custom with which these nations are threatened is not precisely stationariness. It proscribes singularity, but it does not preclude change, provided all change together. We have discarded the fixed costumes of our forefathers; every one must still dress like other people, but the fashion may change once or twice a year. We thus take care that when there is change it shall be for change's sake, and not from any idea of beauty or convenience; for the same idea of beauty or convenience would not strike all the world at the same moment, and be simultaneously thrown aside by all at another moment. But we are progressive as well as changeable: we continually make new inventions in mechanical things, and keep them until they are again superseded by better; we are eager for improvement in politics, in education, even in morals, though in this last our idea of improvement chiefly consists in persuading or forcing other people to be as good as ourselves. It is not progress that we object to; on the contrary, we flatter ourselves that we are the most progressive people who ever lived. It is individuality that we war against: we should think we had done wonders if we had made ourselves all alike; forgetting that the unlikeness of one person to another is generally the first thing which draws the attention of either to the imperfection of his own type, and the superiority of another, or the possibility, by combining the advantages of both, of producing something better than either. We have a warning example in China – a nation of much talent, and, in some respects, even wisdom, owing to the rare good fortune of having been provided at an early period with a particularly good set of customs, the work, in some measure, of men to whom even the most enlightened European must accord, under certain limitations, the title of sages and philosophers. They are remarkable, too, in the excellence of their apparatus for impressing, as far as possible, the best wisdom they possess upon every mind in the community, and securing that those who have appropriated most of it shall occupy the posts of honour and power. Surely the people who did this have discovered the secret of human progressiveness, and must have kept themselves steadily at the head of the movement of the world. On the contrary, they have become stationary – have remained so for thousands of years; and if they are ever to be farther improved, it must be by foreigners. They have succeeded beyond all hope in what English philanthropists are so industriously working at – in making a people all alike, all governing their thoughts and conduct by the same maxims and rules; and these are the fruits. The modern *régime* of public opinion is, in an unorganized form, what the Chinese educational and political systems are in an organized; and unless individuality shall be able successfully to assert itself against this yoke, Europe, notwithstanding its noble antecedents and its professed Christianity, will tend to become another China.

What is it that has hitherto preserved Europe from this lot? What has made the European family of nations an improving, instead of a stationary portion of mankind? Not any superior excellence in them, which, when it exists, exists as the effect, not as the cause;

but their remarkable diversity of character and culture. Individuals, classes, nations, have been extremely unlike one another: they have struck out a great variety of paths, each leading to something valuable; and although at every period those who travelled in different paths have been intolerant of one another, and each would have thought it an excellent thing if all the rest could have been compelled to travel his road, their attempts to thwart each other's development have rarely had any permanent success, and each has in time endured to receive the good which the others have offered. Europe is, in my judgement, wholly indebted to this plurality of paths for its progressive and many-sided development. But it already begins to possess this benefit in a considerably less degree. It is decidedly advancing towards the Chinese ideal of making all people alike. M. de Tocqueville, in his last important work, remarks how much more the Frenchmen of the present day resemble one another, than did those even of the last generation. The same remark might be made of Englishmen in a far greater degree. In a passage already quoted from Wilhelm von Humboldt, he points out two things as necessary conditions of human development, because necessary to render people unlike one another: namely, freedom, and variety of situations. The second of these two conditions is in this country every day diminishing. The circumstances which surround different classes and individuals, and shape their characters, are daily becoming more assimilated. Formerly, different ranks, different neighbourhoods, different trades and professions, lived in what might be called different worlds; at present, to a great degree in the same. Comparatively speaking, they now read the same things, listen to the same things, see the same things, go to the same places, have their hopes and fears directed to the same objects, have the same rights and liberties, and the same means of asserting them. Great as are the differences of position which remain, they are nothing to those which have ceased. And the assimilation is still proceeding. All the political changes of the age promote it, since they all tend to raise the low and to lower the high. Every extension of education promotes it, because education brings people under common influences, and gives them access to the general stock of facts and sentiments. Improvements in the means of communication promote it, by bringing the inhabitants of distant places into personal contact, and keeping up a rapid flow of changes of residence between one place and another. The increase of commerce and manufactures promotes it, by diffusing more widely the advantages of easy circumstances, and opening all objects of ambition, even the highest, to general competition, whereby the desire of rising becomes no longer the character of a particular class, but of all classes. A more powerful agency than even all these, in bringing about a general similarity among mankind, is the complete establishment, in this and other free countries, of the ascendancy of public opinion in the State. As the various social eminences which enabled persons entrenched on them to disregard the opinion of the multitude, gradually become levelled; as the very idea of resisting the will of the public, when it is positively known that they have a will, disappears more and more from the minds of practical politicians; there ceases to be any social support for nonconformity – any substantive power in society, which, itself opposed to the ascendancy of numbers, is interested in taking under its protection opinions and tendencies at variance with those of the public.

The combination of all these causes forms so great a mass of influences hostile to Individuality, that it is not easy to see how it can stand its ground. It will do so with increasing difficulty, unless the intelligent part of the public can be made to feel its value – to see that it is good there should be differences, even though not for the better, even though, as it may appear to them, some should be for the worse. If the claims of Individuality are ever to be asserted, the time is now, while much is still wanting to complete the enforced assimilation. It is only in the earlier stages that any stand can be successfully made against the encroachment. The demand that all other people shall resemble ourselves, grows by what it feeds on. If resistance waits till life is reduced *nearly* to one uniform type, all deviations from that type will come to be considered impious, immoral, even monstrous and contrary to nature. Mankind speedily become unable to conceive diversity, when they have been for some time unaccustomed to see it.

4   OF THE LIMITS TO THE AUTHORITY OF SOCIETY OVER THE INDIVIDUAL

What, then, is the rightful limit to the sovereignty of the individual over himself? Where does the authority of society begin? How much of human life should be assigned to individuality, and how much to society?

Each will receive its proper share, if each has that which more particularly concerns it. To individuality should belong the part of life in which it is chiefly the individual that is interested; to society, the part which chiefly interests society.

Though society is not founded on a contract, and though no good purpose is answered by inventing a contract in order to deduce social obligations from it, every one who receives the protection of society owes a return for the benefit, and the fact of living in society renders it indispensable that each should be bound to observe a certain line of conduct towards the rest. This conduct consists, first, in not injuring the interests of one another; or rather certain interests, which, either by express legal provision or by tacit understanding, ought to be considered as rights; and secondly, in each person's bearing his share (to be fixed on some equitable principle) of the labours and sacrifices incurred for defending the society or its members from injury and molestation. These conditions society is justified in enforcing at all costs to those who endeavour to withhold fulfilment. Nor is this all that society may do. The acts of an individual may be hurtful to others, or wanting in due consideration for their welfare, without going the length of violating any of their constituted rights. The offender may then be justly punished by opinion, though not by law. As soon as any part of a person's conduct affects prejudicially the interests of others, society has jurisdiction over it, and the question whether the general welfare will or will not be promoted by interfering with it, becomes open to discussion. But there is no room for entertaining any such question when a person's conduct affects the interests of no persons besides himself, or needs not affect them unless they like (all the persons concerned being of full age, and the ordinary amount of understanding). In all such cases there should be perfect freedom, legal and social, to do the action and stand the consequences.

It would be a great misunderstanding of this doctrine to suppose that it is one of selfish indifference, which pretends that human beings have no business with each other's conduct in life, and that they should not concern themselves about the well-doing or well-being of one another, unless their own interest is involved. Instead of any diminution, there is need of a great increase of disinterested exertion to promote the good of others. But disinterested benevolence can find other instruments to persuade people to their good, than whips and scourges, either of the literal or the metaphorical sort. I am the last person to undervalue the self-regarding virtues; they are only second in importance, if even second, to the social. It is equally the business of education to cultivate both. But even education works by conviction and persuasion as well as by compulsion, and it is by the former only that, when the period of education is past, the self-regarding virtues should be inculcated. Human beings owe to each other help to distinguish the better from the worse, and encouragement to choose the former and avoid the latter. They should be for ever stimulating each other to increased exercise of their higher faculties, and increased direction of their feelings and aims towards wise instead of foolish, elevating instead of degrading, objects and contemplations. But neither one person, nor any number of persons, is warranted in saying to another human creature of ripe years, that he shall not do with his life for his own benefit what he chooses to do with it. He is the person most interested in his own well-being: the interest which any other person, except in cases of strong personal attachment, can have in it, is trifling, compared with that which he himself has; the interest which society has in him individually (except as to his conduct to others) is fractional, and altogether indirect: while, with respect to his own feelings and circumstances, the most ordinary man or woman has means of knowledge immeasurably surpassing those that can be possessed by any one else. The interference of society to overrule his judgement and purposes in what only regards himself, must be grounded on general presumptions; which may be altogether wrong, and even if right, are as likely as not to be misapplied to individual cases, by persons no better acquainted with the circumstances of such cases than those are who look at them merely from without. In this department, therefore, of human affairs, Individuality has its proper field of action. In the conduct of human beings towards one another, it is necessary that general rules should for the most part be observed, in order that people may know what they have to expect; but in each person's own concerns, his individual spontaneity is entitled to free exercise.

Considerations to aid his judgement, exhortations to strengthen his will, may be offered to him, even obtruded on him, by others; but he himself is the final judge. All errors which he is likely to commit against advice and warning, are far outweighed by the evil of allowing others to constrain him to what they deem his good.

I do not mean that the feelings with which a person is regarded by others, ought not to be in any way affected by his self-regarding qualities or deficiencies. This is neither possible nor desirable. If he is eminent in any of the qualities which conduce to his own good, he is, so far, a proper object of admiration. He is so much the nearer to the ideal perfection of human nature. If he is grossly deficient in those qualities, a sentiment the opposite of admiration will follow. There is a degree of folly, and a degree of what may be called (though the phrase is not unobjectionable) lowness or depravation of taste, which, though it cannot justify doing harm to the person who manifests it, renders him necessarily and properly a subject of distaste, or, in extreme cases, even of contempt: a person could not have the opposite qualities in due strength without entertaining these feelings. Though doing no wrong to any one, a person may so act as to compel us to judge him, and feel to him, as a fool, or as a being of an inferior order: and since this judgement and feeling are a fact which he would prefer to avoid, it is doing him a service to warn him of it beforehand, as of any other disagreeable consequence to which he exposes himself. It would be well, indeed, if this good office were much more freely rendered than the common notions of politeness at present permit, and if one person could honestly point out to another that he thinks him in fault, without being considered unmannerly or presuming. We have a right, also, in various ways, to act upon our unfavourable opinion of any one, not to the oppression of his individuality, but in the exercise of ours. We are not bound, for example, to seek his society; we have a right to avoid it (though not to parade the avoidance), for we have a right to choose the society most acceptable to us. We have a right, and it may be our duty, to caution others against him, if we think his example or conversation likely to have a pernicious effect on those with whom he associates. We may give others a preference over him in optional good offices, except those which tend to his improvement. In these various modes a person may suffer very severe penalties at the hands of others, for faults which directly concern only himself; but he suffers these penalties only in so far as they are the natural, and, as it were, the spontaneous consequences of the faults themselves, not because they are purposely inflicted on him for the sake of punishment. A person who shows rashness, obstinacy, self-conceit – who cannot live within moderate means – who cannot restrain himself from hurtful indulgencies – who pursues animal pleasures at the expense of those of feeling and intellect – must expect to be lowered in the opinion of others, and to have a less share of their favourable sentiments; but of this he has no right to complain, unless he has merited their favour by special excellence in his social relations, and has thus established a title to their good offices, which is not affected by his demerits towards himself.

What I contend for is, that the inconveniences which are strictly inseparable from the unfavourable judgement of the others, are the only ones to which a person should ever be subjected for that portion of his conduct and character which concerns his own good, but which does not affect the interests of others in their relations with him. Acts injurious to others require a totally different treatment. Encroachment on their rights; infliction on them of any loss or damage not justified by his own rights; falsehood or duplicity in dealing with them; unfair or ungenerous use of advantages over them; even selfish abstinence from defending them against injury – these are fit objects of moral reprobation, and, in grave cases, of moral retribution and punishment. And not only these acts, but the dispositions which lead to them, are properly immoral, and fit subjects of disapprobation which may rise to abhorrence. Cruelty of disposition; malice and ill nature; that most anti-social and odious of all passions, envy; dissimulation and insincerity; irascibility on insufficient cause, and resentment disproportioned to the provocation; the love of domineering over others; the desire to engross more than one's share of advantages (the πλεονεξια of the Greeks); the pride which derives gratification from the abasement of others; the egotism which thinks self and its concerns more important than everything else, and decides all doubtful questions in its own favour; – these are moral vices, and constitute a bad and odious moral character: unlike the self-regarding faults previously mentioned, which are not properly immoralities, and to whatever pitch they may be carried, do not constitute wickedness. They may be proofs of any amount of folly, or want of personal dignity and self-respect; but they are only a subject of moral reprobation when they involve a breach of duty to others, for whose sake the individual is bound to have care for

93

himself. What are called duties to ourselves are not socially obligatory, unless circumstances render them at the same time duties to others. The term duty to oneself, when it means anything more than prudence, means self-respect or self-development; and for none of these is any one accountable to his fellow creatures, because for none of them is it for the good of mankind that he be held accountable to them.

The distinction between the loss of consideration which a person may rightly incur by defect of prudence or of personal dignity, and the reprobation which is due to him for an offence against the rights of others, is not a merely nominal distinction. It makes a vast difference both in our feelings and in our conduct towards him, whether he displeases us in things in which we think we have a right to control him, or in things in which we know that we have not. If he displeases us, we may express our distaste, and we may stand aloof from a person as well as from a thing that displeases us; but we shall not therefore feel called on to make his life uncomfortable. We shall reflect that he already bears, or will bear, the whole penalty of his error; if he spoils his life by mismanagement, we shall not, for that reason, desire to spoil it still further; instead of wishing to punish him, we shall rather endeavour to alleviate his punishment, by showing him how he may avoid or cure the evils his conduct tends to bring upon him. He may be to us an object of pity, perhaps of dislike, but not of anger or resentment; we shall not treat him like an enemy of society: the worst we shall think ourselves justified in doing is leaving him to himself, if we do not interfere benevolently by showing interest or concern for him. It is far otherwise if he has infringed the rules necessary for the protection of his fellow creatures, individually or collectively. The evil consequences of his acts do not then fall on himself, but on others; and society, as the protector of all its members, must retaliate on him; must inflict pain on him for the express purpose of punishment, and must take care that it be sufficiently severe. In the one case, he is an offender at our bar, and we are called on not only to sit in judgement on him, but, in one shape or another, to execute our own sentence; in the other case, it is not our part to inflict any suffering on him, except what may incidentally follow from our using the same liberty in the regulation of our own affairs, which we allow to him in his.

The distinction here pointed out between the part of a person's life which concerns only himself, and that which concerns others, many persons will refuse to admit. How (it may be asked) can any part of the conduct of a member of society be a matter of indifference to the other members? No person is an entirely isolated being; it is impossible for a person to do anything seriously or permanently hurtful to himself, without mischief reaching at least to his near connexions, and often far beyond them. If he injures his property, he does harm to those who directly or indirectly derived support from it, and usually diminishes, by a greater or less amount, the general resources of the community. If he deteriorates his bodily or mental faculties, he not only brings evil upon all who depended on him for any portion of their happiness, but disqualifies himself for rendering the services which he owes to his fellow creatures generally; perhaps becomes a burthen on their affection or benevolence; and if such conduct were very frequent, hardly any offence that is committed would detract more from the general sum of good. Finally, if by his vices or follies a person does no direct harm to others, he is nevertheless (it may be said) injurious by his example; and ought to be compelled to control himself, for the sake of those whom the sight or knowledge of his conduct might corrupt or mislead.

And even (it will be added) if the consequences of misconduct could be confined to the vicious or thoughtless individual, ought society to abandon to their own guidance those who are manifestly unfit for it? If protection against themselves is confessedly due to children and persons under age, is not society equally bound to afford it to persons of mature years who are equally incapable of self-government? If gambling, or drunkenness, or incontinence, or idleness, or uncleanliness, are as injurious to happiness, and as great a hindrance to improvement, as many or most of the acts prohibited by law, why (it may be asked) should not law, so far as is consistent with practicability and social convenience, endeavour to repress these also? And as a supplement to the unavoidable imperfections of law, ought not opinion at least to organize a powerful police against these vices, and visit rigidly with social penalties those who are known to practise them? There is no question here (it may be said) about restricting individuality, or impeding the trial of new and original experiments in living. The only things it is sought to prevent are things which have been tried and condemned from the beginning of the world until now; things which experience has shown not to be useful or suitable to any person's individuality. There must be some length of time and amount of experience, after which a moral or prudential truth may be regarded as established: and it is merely desired to prevent generation after generation from falling over the same precipice which has been fatal to their predecessors.

I fully admit that the mischief which a person does to himself may seriously affect, both through their sympathies and their interests, those nearly connected with him, and in a minor degree, society at large. When, by conduct of this sort, a person is led to violate a distinct and assignable obligation to any other person or persons, the case is taken out of the self-regarding class, and becomes amenable to moral disapprobation in the proper sense of the term. If, for example, a man, through intemperance or extravagance, becomes unable to pay his debts, or, having undertaken the moral responsibility of a family, becomes from the same cause incapable of supporting or educating them, he is deservedly reprobated, and might be justly punished; but it is for the breach of duty to his family or creditors, not for the extravagance. If the resources which ought to have been devoted to them, had been diverted from them for the most prudent investment, the moral culpability would have been the same. George Barnwell murdered his uncle to get money for his mistress, but if he had done it to set himself up in business, he would equally have been hanged. Again, in the frequent case of a man who causes grief to his family by addiction to bad habits, he deserves reproach for his unkindness or ingratitude; but so he may for cultivating habits not in themselves vicious, if they are painful to those with whom he passes his life, or who from personal ties are dependent on him for their comfort. Whoever fails in the consideration generally due to the interests and feelings of others, not being compelled by some more imperative duty, or justified by allowable self-preference, is a subject of moral disapprobation for that failure, but not for the cause of it, nor for the errors, merely personal to himself, which may have remotely led to it. In like manner, when a person disables himself, by conduct purely self-regarding, from the performance of some definite duty incumbent on him to the public, he is guilty of a social offence. No person ought to be punished simply for being drunk; but a soldier or a policeman should be punished for being drunk on duty. Whenever, in short, there is a definite damage, or a definite risk of damage, either to an individual or to the public, the case is taken out of the province of liberty, and placed in that of morality or law.

But with regard to the merely contingent, or, as it may be called, constructive injury which a person causes to society, by conduct which neither violates any specific duty to the public, nor occasions perceptible hurt to any assignable individual except himself; the inconvenience is one which society can afford to bear, for the sake of the greater good of human freedom. If grown persons are to be punished for not taking proper care of themselves, I would rather it were for their own sake, than under pretence of preventing them from impairing their capacity of rendering to society benefits which society does not pretend it has a right to exact. But I cannot consent to argue the point as if society had no means of bringing its weaker members up to its ordinary standard of rational conduct, except waiting till they do something irrational, and then punishing them, legally or morally, for it. Society has had absolute power over them during all the early portion of their existence: it has had the whole period of childhood and nonage in which to try whether it could make them capable of rational conduct in life. The existing generation is master both of the training and the entire circumstances of the generation to come; it cannot indeed make them perfectly wise and good, because it is itself so lamentably deficient in goodness and wisdom; and its best efforts are not always, in individual cases, its most successful ones; but it is perfectly well able to make the rising generation, as a whole, as good as, and a little better than, itself. If society lets any considerable number of its members grow up mere children, incapable of being acted on by rational consideration of distant motives, society has itself to blame for the consequences. Armed not only with all the powers of education, but with the ascendancy which the authority of a received opinion always exercises over the minds who are least fitted to judge for themselves; and aided by the *natural* penalties which cannot be prevented from falling on those who incur the distaste or the contempt of those who know them: let not society pretend that it needs, besides all this, the power to issue commands and enforce obedience in the personal concerns of individuals, in which, on all principles of justice and policy, the decision ought to rest with those who are to abide the consequences. Nor is there anything which tends more to discredit and frustrate the better means of influencing conduct, than a resort to the worse. If there be among those whom it is attempted to coerce into prudence or temperance, any of the material of which vigorous and independent characters are made, they will infallibly rebel against the yoke. No such person will ever feel that others have a right to control him in his concerns, such as they have to prevent him from injuring them in theirs; and it easily comes to be considered a mark of spirit and courage to fly in the face of such usurped authority, and do with ostentation the exact opposite of what it enjoins; as in the fashion of grossness which succeeded, in the time of Charles II, to the fanatical moral intolerance of the Puritans. With respect to what is said of the necessity of protecting society from the bad example set to others by the vicious or the self-indulgent; it is true that bad example may have a pernicious effect, especially the example of doing wrong to others with impunity to the wrong-doer. But we are now speaking of conduct which, while it does no wrong to others, is supposed to do great harm to the agent himself: and I do not see how those who believe this, can think otherwise than that the example, on the whole, must be more salutary than hurtful, since, if it displays the misconduct, it displays also the painful or degrading consequences which, if the conduct is justly censured, must be supposed to be in all or most cases attendant on it.

But the strongest of all the arguments against the interference of the public with purely personal conduct, is that when it does interfere, the odds are that it interferes wrongly, and in the wrong place. On questions of social morality, of duty to others, the opinion of the public, that is, of an overruling majority, though often wrong, is likely to be still oftener right; because on such questions they are only required to judge of their own interests; of the manner in which some mode of conduct, if allowed to be practised, would affect themselves. But the opinion of a similar majority, imposed as a law on the minority, on questions of self-regarding conduct, is quite as likely to be wrong as right; for in these cases public opinion means, at the best, some people's opinion of what is good or bad for other people; while very often it does not even mean that; the public, with the most perfect indifference, passing over the pleasure or convenience of those whose conduct they censure, and considering only their own preference. There are many who consider as an injury to themselves any conduct which they have a distaste for, and resent it as an outrage to their feelings; as a religious bigot, when charged with disregarding the religious feelings of others, has been known to retort that they disregard his feelings, by persisting in their abominable worship or creed. But there is no parity between the feeling of a person for his own opinion, and the feeling of another who is offended at his holding it; no more than between the desire of a thief to take a purse, and the desire of the right owner to keep it. And a person's taste is as much his own peculiar concern as his opinion or his purse. It is easy for any one to imagine an ideal public, which leaves the freedom and choice of individuals in all uncertain matters undisturbed, and only requires them to abstain from modes of conduct which universal experience has condemned. But where has there been seen a public which set any such limit to its censorship? or when does the public trouble itself about universal experience? In its interferences with personal conduct it is seldom thinking of anything but the enormity of acting or feeling differently from itself, and this standard of judgement, thinly disguised, is held up to mankind as the dictate of religion and philosophy, by nine-tenths of all moralists and speculative writers. These teach that things are right because they are right; because we feel them to be so. They tell us to search in our own minds and hearts for laws of conduct binding on ourselves and on all others. What can the poor public do but apply these instructions, and make their own personal feelings of good and evil, if they are tolerably unanimous in them, obligatory on all the world?

The evil here pointed out is not one which exists only in theory; and it may perhaps be expected that I should specify the instances in which the public of this age and country improperly invests its own preferences with the character of moral laws. I am not writing an essay on the aberrations of existing moral feeling. That is too weighty a subject to be discussed parenthetically, and by way of illustration. Yet examples are necessary, to show that the principle I maintain is of serious and practical moment, and that I am not endeavouring to erect a barrier against imaginary evils. And it is not difficult to show, by abundant instances, that to extend the bounds of what may be called moral police, until it encroaches on the most unquestionably legitimate liberty of the individual, is one of the most universal of all human propensities.

As a first instance, consider the antipathies which men cherish on no better grounds than that persons whose religious opinions are different from theirs, do not practise their religious observances, especially their religious abstinences. To cite a rather trivial example, nothing in the creed or practice of Christians does more to envenom the hatred of Mohammedans against them, than the fact of their eating pork. There are few acts which Christians and Europeans regard with more unaffected disgust, than Mussulmans regard this particular mode of satisfying hunger. It is, in the first place, an offence against their religion; but this circumstance by no means explains either the degree or the kind of their repugnance; for wine also is forbidden by their religion, and to partake of it is by all Mussulmans accounted wrong, but not disgusting. Their aversion to the flesh of the 'unclean beast' is, on the contrary, of that peculiar character, resembling an instinctive antipathy, which the idea of uncleanness, when once it thoroughly sinks into the feelings, seems always to excite even in those whose personal habits are anything but scrupulously cleanly, and of which the sentiment of religious impurity, so intense in the Hindoos, is a remarkable example. Suppose now that in a people, of whom the majority were Mussulmans, that majority should insist upon not permitting pork to be eaten within the limits of the country. This would be nothing new in Mohammedan countries.[1] Would it be a legitimate exercise of the moral authority of public opinion? and if not, why not? The practice is really revolting to such a public. They also sincerely think that it is forbidden and abhorred by the Deity. Neither could the prohibition be censured as religious persecution. It might be religious in its origin, but it would not be persecution for religion, since nobody's religion makes it a duty to eat pork. The only tenable ground of condemnation would be, that with the personal tastes and self-regarding concerns of individuals the public has no business to interfere.

To come somewhat nearer home: the majority of Spaniards consider it a gross impiety, offensive in the highest degree to the Supreme Being, to worship him in any other manner than the Roman Catholic; and no other public worship is lawful on Spanish soil. The people of all Southern Europe look upon a married clergy as not only irreligious, but unchaste, indecent, gross, disgusting. What do Protestants think of these perfectly sincere feelings, and of

---

1 The case of the Bombay Parsees is a curious instance in point. When this industrious and enterprising tribe, the descendants of the Persian fire-worshippers, flying from their native country before the Caliphs, arrived in Western India, they were admitted to toleration by the Hindoo sovereigns, on condition of not eating beef. When those regions afterwards fell under the dominion of Mohammedan conquerors, the Parsees obtained from them a continuance of indulgence, on condition of refraining from pork. What was at first obedience to authority became a second nature, and the Parsees to this day abstain both from beef and pork. Though not required by their religion, the double abstinence has had time to grow into a custom of their tribe; and custom, in the East, is a religion.

the attempt to enforce them against non-Catholics? Yet, if mankind are justified in interfering with each other's liberty in things which do not concern the interests of others, on what principle is it possible consistently to exclude these cases? or who can blame people for desiring to suppress what they regard as a scandal in the sight of God and man? No stronger case can be shown for prohibiting anything which is regarded as a personal immorality, than is made out for suppressing these practices in the eyes of those who regard them as impieties; and unless we are willing to adopt the logic of persecutors, and to say that we may persecute others because we are right, and that they must not persecute us because they are wrong, we must beware of admitting a principle of which we should resent as a gross injustice the application to ourselves.

The preceding instances may be objected to, although unreasonably, as drawn from contingencies impossible among us: opinion, in this country, not being likely to enforce abstinence from meats, or to interfere with people for worshipping, and for either marrying or not marrying, according to their creed or inclination. The next example, however, shall be taken from an interference with liberty which we have by no means passed all danger of. Wherever the Puritans have been sufficiently powerful, as in New England, and in Great Britain at the time of the Commonwealth, they have endeavoured, with considerable success, to put down all public, and nearly all private, amusements: especially music, dancing, public games, or other assemblages for purposes of diversion, and the theatre. There are still in this country large bodies of persons by whose notions of morality and religion these recreations are condemned; and those persons belonging chiefly to the middle class, who are the ascendant power in the present social and political condition of the kingdom, it is by no means impossible that persons of these sentiments may at some time or other command a majority in Parliament. How will the remaining portion of the community like to have the amusements that shall be permitted to them regulated by the religious and moral sentiments of the stricter Calvinists and Methodists? Would they not, with considerable peremptoriness, desire these intrusively pious members of society to mind their own business? This is precisely what should be said to every government and every public, who have the pretension that no person shall enjoy any pleasure which they think wrong. But if the principle of the pretension be admitted, no one can reasonably object to its being acted on in the sense of the majority, or other preponderating power in the country; and all persons must be ready to conform to the idea of a Christian commonwealth, as understood by the early settlers in New England, if a religious profession similar to theirs should ever succeed in regaining its lost ground, as religions supposed to be declining have so often been known to do.

To imagine another contingency, perhaps more likely to be realized than the one last mentioned. There is confessedly a strong tendency in the modern world towards a democratic constitution of society, accompanied or not by popular political institutions. It is affirmed that in the country where this tendency is most completely realized – where both society and the government are most democratic, the United States – the feeling of the majority, to whom any appearance of a more showy or costly style of living than they can hope to rival is disagreeable, operates as a tolerably effectual sumptuary law, and that in many parts of the Union it is really difficult for a person possessing a very large income, to find any mode of spending it, which will not incur popular disapprobation. Though such statements as these are doubtless much exaggerated as a representation of existing facts, the state of things they describe is not only a conceivable and possible, but a probable result of democratic feeling, combined with the notion that the public has a right to a veto on the manner in which individuals shall spend their incomes. We have only further to suppose a considerable diffusion of Socialist opinions, and it may become infamous in the eyes of the majority to possess more property than some very small amount, or any income not earned by manual labour. Opinions similar in principle to these, already prevail widely among the artisan class, and weigh oppressively on those who are amenable to the opinion chiefly of that class, namely, its own members. It is known that the bad workmen who form the majority of the operatives in many branches of industry, are decidedly of opinion that bad workmen ought to receive the same wages as good, and that no one ought to be allowed, through piecework or otherwise, to earn by superior skill or industry more than others can without it. And they employ a moral police, which occasionally becomes a physical one, to deter skilful workmen from receiving, and employers from giving, a larger remuneration for a more useful service. If the public have any jurisdiction over private concerns, I cannot see that these people are in fault, or that any individual's particular public can be blamed for asserting the same authority over his individual conduct, which the general public asserts over people in general.

But, without dwelling upon supposititious cases, there are, in our own day, gross usurpations upon the liberty of private life actually practised, and still greater ones threatened with some expectation of success, and opinions propounded which assert an unlimited right in the public not only to prohibit by law everything which it thinks wrong, but in order to get at what it thinks wrong, to prohibit any number of things which it admits to be innocent.

Under the name of preventing intemperance, the people of one English colony, and of nearly half the United States, have been interdicted by law from making any use whatever of fermented drinks, except for medical purposes: for prohibition of their sale is in fact, as it is intended to be, prohibition of their use. And though the impracticability of executing the law has caused its repeal in several of the States which had adopted it, including the one from which it derives its name, an attempt has notwithstanding been commenced, and is prosecuted with considerable zeal by many of the professed philanthropists, to agitate for a similar law in this country. The association, or 'Alliance' as it terms itself, which has been formed for this purpose, has acquired some notoriety through the publicity given to a correspondence between its Secretary and one of the very few English public men who hold that a politician's opinions ought to be founded on principles. Lord Stanley's share in this correspondence is calculated to strengthen the hopes already built on him, by those who know how rare such qualities as are manifested in some of his public appearances, unhappily are among those who figure in political life. The organ of the Alliance, who would 'deeply deplore the recognition of any principle which could be wrested to justify bigotry and persecution', undertakes to point out the 'broad and impassable barrier' which divides such principles from those of the association. 'All matters relating to thought, opinion, conscience, appear to me,' he says, 'to be without the sphere of legislation; all pertaining to social act, habit, relation, subject only to a discretionary power vested in the State itself, and not in the individual, to be within it.' No mention is made of a third class, different from either of these, viz. acts and habits which are not social, but individual; although it is to this class, surely, that the act of drinking fermented liquors belongs. Selling fermented liquors, however, is trading, and trading is a social act. But the infringement complained of is not on the liberty of the seller, but on that of the buyer and consumer; since the State might just as well forbid him to drink wine, as purposely make it impossible for him to obtain it. The Secretary, however, says, 'I claim, as a citizen, a right to legislate whenever my social rights are invaded by the social act of another.' And now for the definition of these 'social rights'. 'If anything invades my social rights, certainly the traffic in strong drink does. It destroys my primary right of security, by constantly creating and stimulating social disorder. It invades my right of equality, by deriving a profit from the creation of a misery I am taxed to support. It impedes my right to free moral and intellectual development, by surrounding my path with dangers, and by weakening and demoralizing society, from which I have a right to claim mutual aid and intercourse.' A theory of 'social rights', the like of which probably never before found its way into distinct language: being nothing short of this – that it is the absolute social right of every individual, that every other individual shall act in every respect exactly as he ought; that whosoever fails thereof in the smallest particular, violates my social right, and entitles me to demand from the legislature the removal of the grievance. So monstrous a principle is far more dangerous than any single interference with liberty; there is no violation of liberty which it would not justify; it acknowledges no right to any freedom whatever, except perhaps to that of holding opinions in secret, without ever disclosing them: for, the moment an opinion which I consider noxious passes any one's lips, it invades all the 'social rights' attributed to me by the Alliance. The doctrine ascribes to all mankind a vested interest in each other's moral, intellectual, and even physical perfection, to be defined by each claimant according to his own standard.

Another important example of illegitimate interference with the rightful liberty of the individual, not simply threatened, but long since carried into triumphant effect, is Sabbatarian legislation. Without doubt, abstinence on one day in the week, so far as the exigencies of life permit, from the usual daily occupation, though in no respect religiously binding on any except Jews, is a highly beneficial custom. And inasmuch as this custom cannot be observed without a general consent to that effect among the industrious classes, therefore, in so far as some persons by working may impose the same necessity on others, it may be allowable and right that the law should guarantee to each the observance by others of the custom, by suspending the greater operations of industry on a particular day. But this justification, grounded on the direct interest which others have in each individual's observance of the practice, does not apply to the self-chosen occupations in which a person may think fit to employ his leisure; nor does it hold good, in the smallest degree, for legal restrictions on amusements. It is true that the amusement of some is the day's work of others; but the pleasure, not to say the useful recreation, of many, is worth the labour of a few, provided the occupation is freely chosen, and can be freely resigned. The operatives are perfectly right in thinking that if all worked on Sunday, seven days' work would have to be given for six days' wages: but so long as the great mass of employments are suspended, the small number who for the enjoyment of others must still work, obtain a proportional increase of earnings; and they are not obliged to follow those occupations, if they prefer leisure to emolument. If a further remedy is sought, it might be found in the establishment by custom of a holiday on some other day of the week for those particular classes of persons. The only ground, therefore, on which restrictions on Sunday amusements can be defended, must be that they are religiously wrong; a motive of legislation which never can be too earnestly protested against. 'Deorum injuriae Diis curae.' It remains to be proved that society or any of its officers holds a commission from on high to avenge any supposed offence to Omnipotence, which is not also a wrong to our fellow creatures. The notion that it is one man's duty that another should be religious, was the foundation of all the religious persecutions ever perpetrated, and if admitted, would fully justify them. Though the feeling which breaks out in the repeated attempts to stop railway travelling on Sunday, in the resistance to the opening of Museums, and the like, has not the cruelty of the old persecutors, the state of mind indicated by it is fundamentally the same. It is a determination not to tolerate others in doing what is permitted by their religion, because it is not permitted by the persecutor's religion. It is a belief that God not only abominates the act of the misbeliever, but will not hold us guiltless if we leave him unmolested.

I cannot refrain from adding to these examples of the little account commonly made of human liberty, the language of downright persecution which breaks out from the press of this country, whenever it feels called on to notice the remarkable phenomenon of Mormonism. Much might be said on the unexpected and instructive fact, that an alleged new revelation, and a religion founded on it, the product of palpable imposture, not even supported by the *prestige* of extraordinary qualities in its founder, is believed by hundreds of thousands, and has been made the foundation of a society, in the age of newspapers, railways, and the electric telegraph. What here concerns us is, that this religion, like other and better religions, has its martyrs; that its prophet and founder was, for his teaching, put to death by a mob; that others of its adherents lost their lives by the same lawless violence; that they were forcibly expelled, in a body from the country in which they first grew up; while, now that they have been chased into a solitary recess in the midst of a desert, many in this country openly declare that it would be right (only that it is not convenient) to send an expedition against them, and compel them by force to conform to the opinions of other people. The article of the Mormonite doctrine which is the chief provocative to the antipathy which thus breaks through the ordinary restraints of religious tolerance, is its sanction of polygamy; which, though permitted to Mohammedans, and Hindoos, and Chinese, seems to excite unquenchable animosity when practised by persons who speak English, and profess to be a kind of Christians. No one has a deeper disapprobation than I have of this Mormon institution; both for other reasons, and because, far from being in any way countenanced by the principle of liberty, it is a direct infraction of that principle, being a mere riveting of the chains of one-half of the community, and an emancipation of the other from reciprocity of obligation towards them. Still, it must be remembered that this relation is as much voluntary on the part of the women concerned in it, and who may be deemed the sufferers by it, as is the case with any other form of the marriage institution; and however surprising this fact may appear, it has its explanation in the common ideas and customs of the world, which teaching women to think marriage the one thing needful, make it intelligible that many a woman should prefer being one of several wives, to not being a wife at all. Other countries are not asked to recognize such unions, or release any portion of their inhabitants from their own laws on the score of Mormonite opinions. But when the dissentients have conceded to the hostile sentiments of others, far more than could justly be demanded; when they have left the countries to which their doctrines were unacceptable, and established themselves in a remote corner of the earth, which they have been the first to render habitable to human beings; it is difficult to see on what principles but those of tyranny they can be prevented from living there under what laws they please, provided they commit no aggression on other nations, and allow perfect freedom of departure to those who are dissatisfied with their ways. A recent writer, in some respects of considerable merit, proposes (to use his own words) not a crusade, but a *civilizade*, against this polygamous community, to put an end to what seems to him a retrograde step in civilization. It also appears so to me, but I am not aware that any community has a right to force another to be civilized. So long as the sufferers by the bad law do not invoke assistance from other communities, I cannot admit that persons entirely unconnected with them ought to step in and require that a condition of things with which all who are directly interested appear to be satisfied, should be put an end to because it is a scandal to persons some thousands of miles distant, who have no part or concern in it. Let them send missionaries, if they please, to preach against it; and let them, by any fair means (of which silencing the teachers is not one), oppose the progress of similar doctrines among their own people. If civilization has got the better of barbarism when barbarism had the world to itself, it is too much to profess to be afraid lest barbarism, after having been fairly got under, should revive and conquer civilization. A civilization that can thus succumb to its vanquished enemy, must first have become so degenerate, that neither its appointed priests and teachers, nor anybody else, has the capacity, or will take the trouble, to stand up for it. If this be so, the sooner such a civilization receives notice to quit, the better. It can only go on from bad to worse, until destroyed and regenerated (like the Western Empire) by energetic barbarians.

5 APPLICATIONS

The principles asserted in these pages must be more generally admitted as the basis for dicussion of details, before a consistent application of them to all the various departments of government and morals can be attempted with any prospect of advantage. The few observations I propose to make on questions of detail, are designed to illustrate the principles, rather than to follow them out to their consequences. I offer, not so much applications, as specimens of application; which may serve to bring into greater clearness the meaning and limits of the two maxims which together form the entire doctrine of this Essay, and to assist the judgement in holding the balance between them, in the cases where it appears doubtful which of them is applicable to the case.

The maxims are, first, that the individual is not accountable to society for his actions, in so far as these concern the interests of no person but himself. Advice, instruction, persuasion, and avoidance by other people if thought necessary by them for their own good, are the only measures by which society can justifiably express its dislike or disapprobation of his conduct. Secondly, that for such actions as are prejudicial to the interests of others, the individual is accountable, and may be subjected either to social or to legal punishment, if society is of opinion that the one or the other is requisite for its protection.

In the first place, it must by no means be supposed, because damage, or probability of damage, to the interests of others, can alone justify the interference of society, that therefore it always does justify such interference. In many cases, an individual, in pursuing a legitimate object, necessarily and therefore legitimately causes pain or loss to others, or intercepts a good which they had a reasonable hope of obtaining. Such oppositions of interest between individuals often arise from bad social institutions, but are unavoidable while those institutions last; and some would be unavoidable under any institutions. Whoever succeeds in an overcrowded profession, or in a competitive examination; whoever is preferred to another in any contest for an object which both desire, reaps benefit from the loss of others, from their wasted exertion and their disappointment. But it is, by common admission, better for the general interest of mankind, that persons should pursue their objects undeterred by this sort of consequence. In other words, society admits no right, either legal or moral, in the disappointed competitors, to immunity from this kind of suffering; and feels called on to interfere, only when means of success have been employed which it is contrary to the general interest to permit – namely, fraud or treachery, and force.

Again, trade is a social act. Whoever undertakes to sell any description of goods to the public, does what affects the interest of other persons, and of society in general; and thus his conduct, in principle, comes within the jurisdiction of society: accordingly, it was once held to be the duty of governments, in all cases which were considered of importance, to fix prices, and regulate the processes of manufacture. But it is now recognized, though not till after a long struggle, that both the cheapness and the good quality of commodities are most effectually provided for by leaving the producers and sellers perfectly free, under the sole check of equal freedom to the buyers for supplying themselves elsewhere. This is the so-called doctrine of Free Trade, which rests on grounds different from, though equally solid with, the principle of individual liberty asserted in this Essay. Restrictions on trade, or on production for purposes of trade, are indeed restraints; and all restraint, *quâ* restraint, is an evil: but the restraints in question affect only that part of conduct which society is competent to restrain, and are wrong solely because they do not really produce the results which it is desired to produce by them. As the principle of individual liberty is not involved in the doctrine of Free Trade, so neither is it in most of the questions which arise respecting the limits of that doctrine; as for example, what amount of public control is admissible for the prevention of fraud by adulteration; how far sanitary precautions, or arrangements to protect work-people employed in dangerous occupations, should be enforced on employers. Such questions involve considerations of liberty, only in so far as leaving people to themselves is always better, *caeteris paribus*, than controlling them: but that they may be legitimately controlled for these ends, is in principle undeniable. On the other hand, there are questions relating to interference with trade, which are essentially questions of liberty; such as the Maine Law, already touched upon; the prohibition of the importation of opium into China; the restriction of the sale of poisons; all cases, in short, where the object of the interference is to make it impossible or difficult to obtain a particular commodity. These interferences are objectionable, not as infringements on the liberty of the producer or seller, but on that of the buyer.

One of these examples, that of the sale of poisons, opens a new question; the proper limits of what may be called the functions of police; how far liberty may legitimately be invaded for the prevention of crime, or of accident. It is one of the undisputed functions of government to take precautions against crime before it has been committed, as well as to detect and punish it afterwards. The preventive function of government, however, is far more liable to be abused, to the prejudice of liberty, than the punitory function; for there is hardly any part of the legitimate freedom of action of a human being which would not admit of being represented, and fairly too, as increasing the facilities for some form or other of delinquency. Nevertheless, if a public authority, or even a private person, sees any one evidently preparing to commit a crime, they are not bound to look on inactive until the crime is committed, but may interfere to prevent it. If poisons were never bought or used for any purpose except the commission of murder, it would be right to prohibit their manufacture and sale. They may, however, be wanted not only for innocent but for useful purposes, and restrictions cannot be imposed in the one case without operating in the other. Again, it is a proper office of public authority to guard against accidents. If either a public officer or any one else saw a person attempting to cross a bridge which had been ascertained to be unsafe, and there were no time to warn him of his danger, they might seize him and turn him back, without any real infringement of his liberty; for liberty consists in doing what one desires, and he does not desire to fall into the river. Nevertheless, when there is not a certainty, but only a danger of mischief, no one but the person himself can judge of the sufficiency of the motive which may prompt him to incur the risk: in this case, therefore (unless he is a child, or delirious, or in some state of excitement or absorption incompatible with the full use of the reflecting faculty), he ought, I conceive, to be only warned of the danger; not forcibly prevented from exposing himself to it. Similar considerations, applied to such a question as the sale of poisons, may enable us to decide which among the possible modes of regulation are or are not contrary to principle. Such a precaution, for example, as that of labelling the drug with some word expressive of its dangerous character, may be enforced without violation of liberty: the buyer cannot wish not to know that the thing he possesses has poisonous qualities. But to require in all cases the certificate of a medical practitioner, would make it sometimes impossible, always

110

expensive, to obtain the article for legitimate uses. The only mode apparent to me, in which difficulties may be thrown in the way of crime committed through this means, without any infringement, worth taking into account, upon the liberty of those who desire the poisonous substance for other purposes, consists in providing what, in the apt language of Bentham, is called 'preappointed evidence'. This provision is familiar to every one in the case of contracts. It is usual and right that the law, when a contract is entered into, should require as the condition of its enforcing performance, that certain formalities should be observed, such as signatures, attestation of witnesses, and the like, in order that in case of subsequent dispute, there may be evidence to prove that the contract was really entered into, and that there was nothing in the circumstances to render it legally invalid: the effect being, to throw great obstacles in the way of fictitious contracts, or contracts made in circumstances which, if known, would destroy their validity. Precautions of a similar nature might be enforced in the sale of articles adapted to be instruments of crime. The seller, for example, might be required to enter in a register the exact time of the transaction, the name and address of the buyer, the precise quality and quantity sold; to ask the purpose for which it was wanted, and record the answer he received. When there was no medical prescription, the presence of some third person might be required, to bring home the fact to the purchaser, in case there should afterwards be reason to believe that the article had been applied to criminal purposes. Such regulations would in general be no material impediment to obtaining the article, but a very considerable one to making an improper use of it without detection.

The right inherent in society, to ward off crimes against itself by antecedent precautions, suggests the obvious limitations to the maxim, that purely self-regarding misconduct cannot properly be meddled with in the way of prevention or punishment. Drunkenness, for example, in ordinary cases, is not a fit subject for legislative interference; but I should deem it perfectly legitimate that a person, who had once been convicted of any act of violence to others under the influence of drink, should be placed under a special legal restriction, personal to himself; that if he were afterwards found drunk, he should be liable to a penalty, and that if when in that state he committed another offence, the punishment to which he would be liable for that other offence should be increased in severity. The making himself drunk, in a person whom drunkenness excites to do harm to others, is a crime against others. So, again, idleness, except in a person receiving support from the public, or except when it constitutes a breach of contract, cannot without tyranny be made a subject of legal punishment; but if, either from idleness or from any other avoidable cause, a man fails to perform his legal duties to others, as for instance to support his children, it is no tyranny to force him to fulfil that obligation, by compulsory labour, if no other means are available.

Again, there are many acts which, being directly injurious only to the agents themselves, ought not to be legally interdicted, but which, if done publicly, are a violation of good manners, and coming thus within the category of offences against others, may rightfully be prohibited. Of this kind are offences against decency; on which it is unnecessary to dwell, the rather as they are only connected indirectly with our subject, the objection to publicity being equally strong in the case of many actions not in themselves condemnable, nor supposed to be so.

There is another question to which an answer must be found, consistent with the principles which have been laid down. In cases of personal conduct supposed to be blameable, but which respect for liberty precludes society from preventing or punishing, because the evil directly resulting falls wholly on the agent; what the agent is free to do, ought other persons to be equally free to counsel or instigate? This question is not free from difficulty. The case of a person who solicits another to do an act, is not strictly a case of self-regarding conduct. To give advice or offer inducements to any one, is a social act, and may, therefore, like actions in general which affect others, be supposed amenable to social control. But a little reflection corrects the first impression, by showing that if the case is not strictly within the definition of individual liberty, yet the reasons on which the principle of individual liberty is grounded, are applicable to it. If people must be allowed, in whatever concerns only themselves, to act as seems best to themselves at their own peril, they must equally be free to consult with one another about what is fit to be so done; to exchange opinions, and give and receive suggestions. Whatever it is permitted to do, it must be permitted to advise to do. The question is doubtful, only when the instigator derives a personal benefit from his advice; when he makes it his occupation, for subsistence or pecuniary gain, to promote what society and the State consider to be an evil. Then, indeed, a new element of complication is introduced; namely, the existence of classes of persons with an interest opposed to what is considered as the public weal, and whose mode of living is grounded on the counteraction of it. Ought this to be interfered with, or not? Fornication, for example, must be tolerated, and so must gambling; but should a person be free to be a pimp, or to keep a gambling-house? The case is one of those which lie on the exact boundary line between two principles, and it is not at once apparent to which of the two it properly belongs. There are arguments on both sides. On the side of toleration it may be said, that the fact of following anything as an occupation, and living or profiting by the practice of it, cannot make that criminal which would otherwise be admissible; that the act should either be consistently permitted or consistently prohibited; that if the principles which we have hitherto defended are true, society has no business, *as* society, to decide anything to be wrong which concerns only the individual; that it cannot go beyond dissuasion, and that one person should be as free to persuade, as another to dissuade. In opposition to this it may be contended, that although the public, or the State, are not warranted in authoritatively deciding, for purposes of repression or punishment, that such or such conduct affecting only the interests of the individual is good or bad, they are fully justified in assuming, if they regard it as bad, that its being so or not is at least a disputable question: that, this being supposed, they cannot be acting wrongly in endeavouring to exclude the influence of solicitations which are not disinterested, of instigators who cannot possibly be impartial – who have a direct personal interest on one side, and that side the one which the State believes to be wrong, and who confessedly promote it for personal objects only. There can surely, it may be urged, be nothing lost, no sacrifice of good, by so ordering matters that persons shall make their election, either wisely or foolishly, on their own prompting, as free as possible from the arts of persons who stimulate their inclinations for interested purposes of their own. Thus (it may be said) though the statutes respecting unlawful games are utterly indefensible – though all persons should be free to gamble in their own or each other's houses, or in any place of meeting established by their own subscriptions, and open only to the members and their visitors – yet public gambling-houses should not be permitted. It is true that the prohibition is never effectual, and that, whatever amount of tyrannical power may be given to the police, gambling-houses can always be maintained under other pretences; but they may be compelled to conduct their operations with a certain degree of secrecy and mystery, so that nobody knows anything about them but those who seek them; and more than this, society ought not to aim at. There is considerable force in these arguments. I will not venture to decide whether they are sufficient to justify the moral anomaly of punishing the accessory, when the principal is (and must be) allowed to go free; of fining or imprisoning the procurer, but not the fornicator, the gambling-house keeper, but not the gambler. Still less ought the common operations of buying and selling to be interfered with on analogous grounds. Almost every article which is bought and sold may be used in excess, and the sellers have a pecuniary interest in encouraging that excess; but no argument can be founded on this, in favour, for instance, of the Maine Law; because the class of dealers in strong drinks, though interested in their abuse, are indispensably required for the sake of their legitimate use. The interest, however, of these dealers in promoting intemperance is a real evil, and justifies the State in imposing restrictions and requiring guarantees which, but for that justification, would be infringements of legitimate liberty.

A further question is, whether the State, while it permits, should nevertheless indirectly discourage conduct which it deems contrary to the best interests of the agent; whether, for example, it should take measures to render the means of drunkenness more costly, or add to the difficulty of procuring them by limiting the number of the places of sale. On this as on most other practical questions, many distinctions require to be made. To tax stimulants for the sole purpose of making them more difficult to be obtained, is a measure differing only in degree from their entire prohibition; and would be justifiable only if that were justifiable. Every increase of cost is a prohibition, to those whose means do not come up to the augmented price; and to those who do, it is a penalty laid on them for gratifying a particular taste. Their choice of pleasures, and their mode of expending their income, after satisfying their legal and moral obligations to the State and to individuals, are their own concern, and must rest with their own judgement. These consider-ations may seem at first sight to condemn the selection of stimulants as special subjects of taxation for purposes of revenue. But it must be remembered that taxation for fiscal purposes is absolutely inevitable; that in most countries it is necessary that a considerable part of that taxation should be indirect; that the State, therefore, cannot help imposing penalties, which to some persons may be prohibitory, on the use of some articles of consumption. It is hence the duty of the State to consider, in the imposition of taxes, what commodities the consumers can best spare; and *a fortiori*, to select in preference those of which it deems the use, beyond a very moderate quantity, to be positively injurious. Taxation, therefore, of stimulants, up to the point which produces the largest amount of revenue (supposing that the State needs all the revenue which it yields) is not only admissible, but to be approved of.

The question of making the sale of these commodities a more or less exclusive privilege, must be answered differently, according to the purposes to which the restriction is intended to be subservient. All places of public resort require the restraint of a police, and places of this kind peculiarly, because offences against society are especially apt to originate there. It is, therefore, fit to confine the power of selling these commodities (at least for consumption on the spot) to persons of known or vouched-for respectability of conduct; to make such regulations respecting hours of opening and closing as may be requisite for public surveillance, and to withdraw the licence if breaches of the peace repeatedly take place through the connivance or incapacity of the keeper of the house, or if it becomes a rendezvous for concocting and preparing offences against the law. Any further restriction I do not conceive to be, in principle, justifiable. The limitation in number, for instance, of beer and spirit houses, for the express purpose of rendering them more difficult of access, and diminishing the occasions of temptation, not only exposes all to an inconvenience because there are some by whom the facility would be abused, but is suited only to a state of society in which the labouring classes are avowedly treated as children or savages, and placed under an education of restraint, to fit them for future admission to the privileges of freedom. This is not the principle on which the labouring classes are professedly governed in any free country; and no person who sets due value on freedom will give his adhesion to their being so governed, unless after all efforts have been exhausted to educate them for freedom and govern them as freemen, and it has been definitively proved that they can only be governed as children. The bare statement of the alternative shows the absurdity of supposing that such efforts have been made in any case which needs be considered here. It is only because the institutions of this country are a mass of inconsistencies, that things find admittance into our practice which belong to the system of despotic, or what is called paternal, government, while the general freedom of our institutions precludes the exercise of the

115

amount of control necessary to render the restraint of any real efficacy as a moral education.

It was pointed out in an early part of this Essay, that the liberty of the individual, in things wherein the individual is alone concerned, implies a corresponding liberty in any number of individuals to regulate by mutual agreement such things as regard them jointly, and regard no persons but themselves. This question presents no difficulty, so long as the will of all the persons implicated remains unaltered; but since that will may change, it is often necessary, even in things in which they alone are concerned, that they should enter into engagements with one another; and when they do, it is fit, as a general rule, that those engagements should be kept. Yet, in the laws, probably, of every country, this general rule has some exceptions. Not only persons are not held to engagements which violate the rights of third parties, but it is sometimes considered a sufficient reason for releasing them from an engagement, that it is injurious to themselves. In this and most other civilized countries, for example, an engagement by which a person should sell himself, or allow himself to be sold, as a slave, would be null and void; neither enforced by law nor by opinion. The ground for thus limiting his power of voluntarily disposing of his own lot in life, is apparent, and is very clearly seen in this extreme case. The reason for not interfering, unless for the sake of others, with a person's voluntary acts, is consideration for his liberty. His voluntary choice is evidence that what he so chooses is desirable, or at the least endurable, to him, and his good is on the whole best provided for by allowing him to take his own means of pursuing it. But by selling himself for a slave, he abdicates his liberty; he forgoes any future use of it beyond that single act. He therefore defeats, in his own case, the very purpose which is the justification of allowing him to dispose of himself. He is no longer free; but is thenceforth in a position which has no longer the presumption in its favour, that would be afforded by his voluntarily remaining in it. The principle of freedom cannot require that he should be free not to be free. It is not freedom, to be allowed to alienate his freedom. These reasons, the force of which is so conspicuous in this peculiar case, are evidently of far wider application; yet a limit is everywhere set to them by the necessities of life, which continually require, not indeed that we should resign our freedom, but that we should consent to this and the other limitation of it. The principle, however, which demands uncontrolled freedom of action in all that concerns only the agents themselves, requires that those who have become bound to one another, in things which concern no third party, should be able to release one another from the engagement: and even without such voluntary release, there are perhaps no contracts or engagements, except those that relate to money or money's worth, of which one can venture to say that there ought to be no liberty whatever of retractation. Baron Wilhelm von Humboldt, in the excellent essay from which I have already quoted, states it as his conviction, that engagements which involve personal relations or services, should never be legally binding beyond a limited duration of time; and that the most important of these engagements, marriage, having the peculiarity that its objects are frustrated unless the feelings of both the parties are in harmony with it, should require nothing more than the declared will of either party to dissolve it. This subject is too important, and too complicated, to be discussed in a parenthesis, and I touch on it only so far as is necessary for purposes of illustration. If the conciseness and generality of Baron Humboldt's dissertation had not obliged him in this instance to content himself with enunciating his conclusion without discussing the premises, he would doubtless have recognized that the question cannot be decided on grounds so simple as those to which he confines himself. When a person, either by express promise or by conduct, has encouraged another to rely upon his continuing to act in a certain way – to build expectations and calculations, and stake any part of his plan of life upon that supposition – a new series of moral obligations arises on his part towards that person, which may possibly be overruled, but cannot be ignored. And again, if the relation between two contracting parties has been followed by consequences to others; if it has placed third parties in any peculiar position, or, as in the case of marriage, has even called third parties into existence, obligations arise on the part of both the contracting parties towards those third persons, the fulfilment of which, or at all events the mode of fulfilment, must be greatly affected by the continuance or disruption of the relation between the original parties to the contract. It does not follow, nor can I admit, that these obligations extend to requiring the fulfilment of the contract at all costs to the happiness of the reluctant party; but they are a necessary element in the question; and even if, as Von Humboldt maintains, they ought to make no difference in the *legal* freedom of the parties to release themselves from the engagement (and I also hold that they ought not to make *much* difference), they necessarily make a great difference in the *moral* freedom. A person is bound to take all these circumstances into account, before resolving on a step which may affect such important interests of others; and if he does not allow proper weight to those interests, he is morally responsible for the wrong. I have made these obvious remarks for the better illustration of the general principle of liberty, and not because they are at all needed on the particular question, which, on the contrary, is usually discussed as if the interest of children was everything, and that of grown persons nothing.

I have already observed that, owing to the absence of any recognized general principles, liberty is often granted where it should be withheld, as well as withheld where it should be granted; and one of the cases in which, in the modern European world, the sentiment of liberty is the strongest, is a case where, in my view, it is altogether misplaced. A person should be free to do as he likes in his own concerns; but he ought not to be free to do as he likes in acting for another, under the pretext that the affairs of the other are his own affairs. The State, while it respects the liberty of each in what specially regards himself, is bound to maintain a vigilant control over his exercise of any power which it allows him to possess over others. This obligation is almost entirely disregarded in the case of the family relations, a case, in its direct influence on human happiness, more important than all others taken together. The almost despotic power of husbands over wives needs not be enlarged upon here, because nothing more is needed for the complete removal of the evil, than that wives should have the same rights, and should receive the protection of law in the same manner, as all other persons; and because, on this subject, the defenders of established injustice do not avail themselves of the plea of liberty, but stand forth openly as the champions of power. It is in the case of children, that misapplied notions of liberty are a real obstacle to the fulfilment by the State of its duties. One would almost think that a man's children were supposed to be literally, and not metaphorically, a part of himself, so jealous is opinion of the smallest interference of law with his absolute and exclusive control over them; more jealous than of almost any interference with his own freedom of action: so much less do the generality of mankind value liberty than power. Consider, for example, the case of education. Is it not almost a self-evident axiom, that the State should require and compel the education, up to a certain standard, of every human being who is born its citizen? Yet who is there that is not afraid to recognize and assert this truth?

Hardly any one indeed will deny that it is one of the most sacred duties of the parents (or, as law and usage now stand, the father), after summoning a human being into the world, to give to that being an education fitting him to perform his part well in life towards others and towards himself. But while this is unanimously declared to be the father's duty, scarcely anybody, in this country, will bear to hear of obliging him to perform it. Instead of his being required to make any exertion or sacrifice for securing education to the child, it is left to his choice to accept it or not when it is provided gratis! It still remains unrecognized, that to bring a child into existence without a fair prospect of being able, not only to provide food for its body, but instruction and training for its mind, is a moral crime, both against the unfortunate offspring and against society; and that if the parent does not fulfil this obligation, the State ought to see it fulfilled, at the charge, as far as possible, of the parent.

Were the duty of enforcing universal education once admitted, there would be an end to the difficulties about what the State should teach, and how it should teach, which now convert the subject into a mere battle-field for sects and parties, causing the time and labour which should have been spent in educating, to be wasted in quarrelling about education. If the government would make up its mind to *require* for every child a good education, it might save itself the trouble of *providing* one. It might leave to parents to obtain the education where and how they pleased, and content itself with helping to pay the school fees of the poorer classes of children, and defraying the entire school expenses of those who have no one else to pay for them. The objections which are urged with reason against State education, do not apply to the enforcement of education by the State, but to the State's taking upon itself to direct that education: which is a totally different thing. That the whole or any large part of the education of the people should be in State hands, I go as far as any one in deprecating. All that has been said of the importance of individuality of character, and diversity in opinions and modes of conduct, involves, as of the same unspeakable importance, diversity of education. A general State education is a mere contrivance for moulding people to be exactly like one another: and as the mould in which it casts them is that which pleases the predominant power in the government, whether this be a monarch, a priesthood, an aristocracy, or the majority of the existing generation in proportion as it is efficient and successful, it establishes a despotism over the mind, leading by natural tendency to one over the body. An education established and controlled by the State should only exist, if it exist at all, as one among many competing experiments, carried on for the purpose of example and stimulus, to keep the others up to a certain standard of excellence. Unless, indeed, when society in general is in so backward a state that it could not or would not provide for itself any proper institutions of education, unless the government undertook the task: then, indeed, the government may, as the less of two great evils, take upon itself the business of schools and universities, as it may that of joint-stock companies, when private enterprise, in a shape fitted for undertaking great works of industry, does not exist in the country. But in general, if the country contains a sufficient number of persons qualified to provide education under government auspices, the same persons would be able and willing to give an equally good education on the voluntary principle, under the assurance of remuneration afforded by a law rendering education compulsory, combined with State aid to those unable to defray the expense.

The instrument for enforcing the law could be no other than public examinations, extending to all children, and beginning at an early age. An age might be fixed at which every child must be examined, to ascertain if he (or she) is able to read. If a child proves unable, the father, unless he has some sufficient ground of excuse, might be subjected to a moderate fine, to be worked out, if necessary, by his labour, and the child might be put to school at his expense. Once in every year the examination should be renewed, with a gradually extending range of subjects, so as to make the universal acquisition, and what is more, retention, of a certain minimum of general knowledge, virtually compulsory. Beyond that minimum, there should be voluntary examinations on all subjects, at which all who come up to a certain standard of proficiency might claim a certificate. To prevent the State from exercising, through these arrangements, an improper influence over opinion, the knowledge required for passing an examination (beyond the merely instrumental parts of knowledge, such as languages and their use) should, even in the higher classes of examinations, be confined to facts and positive science exclusively. The examinations on religion, politics, or other disputed topics, should not turn on the truth or falsehood of opinions, but on the matter of fact that such and such an opinion is held, on such grounds, by such authors, or schools, or churches. Under this system, the rising generation would be no worse off in regard to all disputed truths, than they are at present; they would be brought up either churchmen or dissenters as they now are, the State merely taking care that they should be instructed churchmen, or instructed dissenters. There would be nothing to hinder them from being taught religion, if their parents chose, at the same schools where they were taught other things. All attempts by the State to bias the conclusions of its citizens on disputed subjects, are evil; but it may very properly offer to ascertain and certify that a person possesses the knowledge, requisite to make his conclusions, on any given subject, worth attending to. A student of philosophy would be the better for being able to stand an examination both in Locke and in Kant, whichever of the two he takes up with, or even if with neither: and there is no reasonable objection to examining an atheist in the evidences of Christianity, provided he is not required to profess a belief in them. The examinations, however, in the higher branches of knowledge should, I conceive, be entirely voluntary. It would be giving too dangerous a power to governments, were they allowed to exclude any one from professions, even from the profession of teacher, for alleged deficiency of qualifications: and I think, with Wilhelm von Humboldt, that degrees, or other public certificates of scientific or professional acquirements, should be given to all who present themselves for examination, and stand the test; but that such certificates should confer no advantage over competitors, other than the weight which may be attached to their testimony by public opinion.

It is not in the matter of education only, that misplaced notions of liberty prevent moral obligations on the part of parents from being recognized, and legal obligations from being imposed, where there are the strongest grounds for the former always, and in many cases for the latter also. The fact itself, of causing the existence of a human being, is one of the most responsible actions in the range of human life. To undertake this responsibility – to bestow a life which may be either a curse or a blessing – unless the being on whom it is to be bestowed will have at least the ordinary chances of a desirable existence, is a crime against that being. And in a country either overpeopled, or threatened with being so, to produce children, beyond a very small number, with the effect of reducing the reward of labour by their competition, is a serious offence against all who live by the remuneration of their labour. The laws which, in many countries on the Continent, forbid marriage unless the parties can show that they have the means of supporting a family, do not exceed the legitimate powers of the State: and whether such laws be expedient or not (a question mainly dependent on local circumstances and feelings), they are not objectionable as violations of liberty. Such laws are interferences of the State to prohibit a mischievous act – an act injurious to others, which ought to be a subject of reprobation, and social stigma, even when it is not deemed expedient to superadd legal punishment. Yet the current ideas of liberty, which bend so easily to real infringements of the freedom of the individual in things which concern only himself, would repel the attempt to put any restraint upon his inclinations when the consequence of their indulgence is a life or lives of wretchedness and depravity to the offspring, with manifold evils to those sufficiently within reach to be in any way affected by their actions. When we compare the strange respect of mankind for liberty, with their strange want of respect for it, we might imagine that a man had an indispensable right to do harm to others, and no right at all to please himself without giving pain to any one.

I have reserved for the last place a large class of questions respecting the limits of government interference, which, though closely connected with the subject of this Essay, do not, in strictness, belong to it. These are cases in which the reasons against interference do not turn upon the principle of liberty: the question is not about restraining the actions of individuals, but about helping them: it is asked whether the government should do, or cause to be done, something for their benefit, instead of leaving it to be done by themselves, individually, or in voluntary combination.

The objections to government interference, when it is not such as to involve infringement of liberty, may be of three kinds.

The first is, when the thing to be done is likely to be better done by individuals than by the government. Speaking generally, there is no one so fit to conduct any business, or to determine how or by whom it shall be conducted, as those who are personally interested in it. This principle condemns the interferences, once so common, of the legislature, or the officers of government, with the ordinary processes of industry. But this part of the subject has been sufficiently enlarged upon by political economists, and is not particularly related to the principles of this Essay.

The second objection is more nearly allied to our subject. In many cases, though individuals may not do the particular thing so well, on the average, as the officers of government, it is nevertheless desirable that it should be done by them, rather than by the government, as a means to their own mental education – a mode of strengthening their active faculties, exercising their judgement, and giving them a familiar knowledge of the subjects with which they are thus left to deal. This is a principal, though not the sole, recommendation of jury trial (in cases not political); of free and popular local and municipal institutions; of the conduct of industrial and philanthropic enterprises by voluntary associations. These are not questions of liberty, and are connected with that subject only by remote tendencies; but they are questions of development. It belongs to a different occasion from the present to dwell on these things as parts of national education; as being, in truth, the peculiar training of a citizen, the practical part of the political education of a free people, taking them out of the narrow circle of personal and family selfishness, and accustoming them to the comprehension of joint interests, the management of joint concerns – habituating them to act from public or semi-public motives, and guide their conduct by aims which unite instead of isolating them from one another. Without these habits and powers, a free constitution can neither be worked nor preserved; as is exemplified by the too-often transitory nature of political freedom in countries where it does not rest upon a sufficient basis of local liberties. The management of purely local business by the localities, and of the great enterprises of industry by the union of those who voluntarily supply the pecuniary means, is further recommended by all the advantages which have been set forth in this Essay as belonging to individuality of develop-ment, and diversity of modes of action. Government operations tend to be everywhere alike. With individuals and voluntary associations, on the contrary, there are varied experiments, and endless diversity of experience. What the State can usefully do, is to make itself a central depository, and active circulator and diffuser, of the experience resulting from many trials. Its business is to enable each experimentalist to benefit by the experiments of others; instead of tolerating no experiments but its own.

The third, and most cogent reason for restricting the interference of government, is the great evil of adding unnecessarily to its power. Every function superadded to those already exercised by the government, causes its influence over hopes and fears to be more widely diffused, and converts, more and more, the active and ambitious part of the public into hangers-on of the government, or of some party which aims at becoming the government. If the roads, the railways, the banks, the insurance offices, the great joint-

stock companies, the universities, and the public charities, were all
of them branches of the government; if, in addition, the municipal
corporations and local boards, with all that now devolves on them,
became departments of the central administration; if the employés
of all these different enterprises were appointed and paid by the
government, and looked to the government for every rise in life;
not all the freedom of the press and popular constitution of the
legislature would make this or any other country free otherwise
than in name. And the evil would be greater, the more efficiently
and scientifically the administrative machinery was constructed –
the more skilful the arrangements for obtaining the best qualified
hands and heads with which to work it. In England it has of late
been proposed that all the members of the civil service of government
should be selected by competitive examination, to obtain for those
employments the most intelligent and instructed persons procur-
able; and much has been said and written for and against this
proposal. One of the arguments most insisted on by its opponents,
is that the occupation of a permanent official servant of the State
does not hold out sufficient prospects of emolument and importance
to attract the highest talents, which will always be able to find a more
inviting career in the professions, or in the service of companies and
other public bodies. One would not have been surprised if this
argument had been used by the friends of the proposition, as an
answer to its principal difficulty. Coming from the opponents it is
strange enough. What is urged as an objection is the safety-valve of
the proposed system. If indeed all the high talent of the country *could*
be drawn into the service of the government, a proposal tending to
bring about that result might well inspire uneasiness. If every part of
the business of society which required organized concert, or large
and comprehensive views, were in the hands of the government, and
if government offices were universally filled by the ablest men, all
the enlarged culture and practised intelligence in the country, except
the purely speculative, would be concentrated in a numerous
bureaucracy, to whom alone the rest of the community would look
for all things: the multitude for direction and dictation in all they had
to do; the able and aspiring for personal advancement. To be
admitted into the ranks of this bureaucracy, and when admitted, to
rise therein, would be the sole objects of ambition. Under this
régime, not only is the outside public ill-qualified, for want of
practical experience, to criticize or check the mode of operation of
the bureaucracy, but even if the accidents of despotic or the natural

working of popular institutions occasionally raise to the summit a ruler or rulers of reforming inclinations, no reform can be effected which is contrary to the interest of the bureaucracy. Such is the melancholy condition of the Russian empire, as shown in the accounts of those who have had sufficient opportunity of observation. The Czar himself is powerless against the bureaucratic body; he can send any one of them to Siberia, but he cannot govern without them, or against their will. On every decree of his they have a tacit veto, by merely refraining from carrying it into effect. In countries of more advanced civilization and of a more insurrectionary spirit, the public, accustomed to expect everything to be done for them by the State, or at least to do nothing for themselves without asking from the State not only leave to do it, but even how it is to be done, naturally hold the State responsible for all evil which befalls them, and when the evil exceeds their amount of patience, they rise against the government and make what is called a revolution; whereupon somebody else, with or without legitimate authority from the nation, vaults into the seat, issues his orders to the bureaucracy, and everything goes on much as it did before; the bureaucracy being unchanged, and nobody else being capable of taking their place.

A very different spectacle is exhibited among a people accustomed to transact their own business. In France, a large part of the people having been engaged in military service, many of whom have held at least the rank of non-commissioned officers, there are in every popular insurrection several persons competent to take the lead, and improvise some tolerable plan of action. What the French are in military affairs, the Americans are in every kind of civil business; let them be left without a government, every body of Americans is able to improvise one, and to carry on that or any other public business with a sufficient amount of intelligence, order, and decision. This is what every free people ought to be: and a people capable of this is certain to be free; it will never let itself be enslaved by any man or body of men because these are able to seize and pull the reins of the central administration. No bureaucracy can hope to make such a people as this do or undergo anything that they do not like. But where everything is done through the bureaucracy, nothing to which the bureaucracy is really adverse can be done at all. The constitution of such countries is an organization of the experience and practical ability of the nation, into a disciplined body for the purpose of governing the rest; and the more perfect that organization is in itself, the more successful in drawing to itself and educating for itself the persons of greatest capacity from all ranks of the community, the more complete is the bondage of all, the members of the bureaucracy included. For the governors are as much the slaves of their organization and discipline, as the governed are of the governors. A Chinese mandarin is as much the tool and creature of a despotism as the humblest cultivator. An individual Jesuit is to the utmost degree of abasement the slave of his order, though the order itself exists for the collective power and importance of its members.

It is not, also, to be forgotten, that the absorption of all the principal ability of the country into the governing body is fatal, sooner or later, to the mental activity and progressiveness of the body itself. Banded together as they are – working a system which, like all systems, necessarily proceeds in a great measure by fixed rules – the official body are under the constant temptation of sinking into indolent routine, or, if they now and then desert that mill-horse round, of rushing into some half-examined crudity which has struck the fancy of some leading member of the corps: and the sole check to these closely allied, though seemingly opposite, tendencies, the only stimulus which can keep the ability of the body itself up to a high standard, is liability to the watchful criticism of equal ability outside the body. It is indispensable, therefore, that the means should exist, independently of the government, of forming such ability, and furnishing it with the opportunities and experience necessary for a correct judgement of great practical affairs. If we would possess permanently a skilful and efficient body of functionaries – above all, a body able to originate and willing to adopt improvements; if we would not have our bureaucracy degenerate into a pedantocracy, this body must not engross all the occupations which form and cultivate the faculties required for the government of mankind.

To determine the point at which evils, so formidable to human freedom and advancement, begin, or rather at which they begin to predominate over the benefits attending the collective application of the force of society, under its recognized chiefs, for the removal of the obstacles which stand in the way of its well-being; to secure as much of the advantages of centralized power and intelligence, as can be had without turning into governmental channels too great a proportion of the general activity – is one of the most difficult and complicated questions in the art of government. It is, in a great measure, a question of detail, in which many and various considerations must be kept in view, and no absolute rule can be laid down. But I believe that the practical principle in which safety resides, the ideal to be kept in view, the standard by which to test all arrangements intended for overcoming the difficulty, may be conveyed in these words: the greatest dissemination of power consistent with efficiency; but the greatest possible centralization of information, and diffusion of it from the centre. Thus, in municipal administration, there would be, as in the New England States, a very minute division among separate officers, chosen by the localities, of all business which is not better left to the persons directly interested; but besides this, there would be, in each department of local affairs, a central superintendence, forming a branch of the general government. The organ of this superintendence would concentrate, as in a focus, the variety of information and experience derived from the conduct of that branch of public business in all the localities, from everything analogous which is done in foreign countries, and from the general principles of political science. This central organ should have a right to know all that is done, and its special duty should be that of making the knowledge acquired in one place available for others. Emancipated from the petty prejudices and narrow views of a locality by its elevated position and comprehensive sphere of observation, its advice would naturally carry much authority; but its actual power, as a permanent institution, should, I conceive, be limited to compelling the local officers to obey the laws laid down for their guidance. In all things not provided for by general rules, those officers should be left to their own judgement, under responsibility to their constituents. For the violation of rules, they should be responsible to law, and the rules themselves should be laid down by the legislature; the central administrative authority only watching over their execution, and if they were not properly carried into effect, appealing, according to the nature of the case, to the tribunals to enforce the law, or to the constituencies to dismiss the functionaries who had not executed it according to its spirit. Such, in its general conception, is the central superintendence which the Poor Law Board is intended to exercise over the administrators of the Poor Rate throughout the country. Whatever powers the Board exercises beyond this limit, were right and necessary in that peculiar case, for the cure of rooted habits of maladministration in matters deeply affecting not the localities merely, but the whole community; since no locality has a moral right to make itself by mismanagement a nest of pauperism, necessarily overflowing into other localities, and impairing the moral and physical condition of the whole labouring community. The powers of administrative coercion and subordinate legislation possessed by the Poor Law Board (but which, owing to the state of opinion on the subject, are very scantily exercised by them), though perfectly justifiable in a case of first-rate national interest, would be wholly out of place in the superintendence of interests purely local. But a central organ of information and instruction for all the localities, would be equally valuable in all departments of administration. A government cannot have too much of the kind of activity which does not impede, but aids and stimulates, individual exertion and development. The mischief begins when, instead of calling forth the activity and powers of individuals and bodies, it substitutes its own activity for theirs; when, instead of informing, advising, and, upon occasion, denouncing, it makes them work in fetters, or bids them stand aside and does their work instead of them. The worth of a State, in the long run, is the worth of the individuals composing it; and a State which postpones the interests of *their* mental expansion and elevation, to a little more of administrative skill, or of that semblance of it which practice gives, in the details of business; a State which dwarfs its men, in order that they may be more docile instruments in its hands even for beneficial purposes – will find that with small men no great thing can really be accomplished; and that the perfection of machinery to which it has sacrificed everything, will in the end avail it nothing, for want of the vital power which, in order that the machine might work more smoothly, it has preferred to banish.

CRITICAL
COMMENTARY

JOHN STUART MILL
AND THE ENDS OF LIFE[1]

Isaiah Berlin

> the importance, to man and society . . . of giving full
> freedom to human nature to expand itself in innumerable and
> conflicting directions.
>
> J.S. MILL, Autobiography

I must begin by thanking you for the honour that you have done
me, in inviting me to address you on the subject to which the
Robert Waley Cohen Memorial Lectures are dedicated – tolerance.
In a world in which human rights were never trampled on, and
men did not persecute each other for what they believed or what
they were, this Council would have no reason for existence. This,
however, is not our world. We are a good deal remoter from this
desirable condition than some of our more civilized ancestors, and,
in this respect, unfortunately conform only too well to the common
pattern of human experience. The periods and societies in which
civil liberties were respected, and variety of opinion and faith
tolerated, have been very few and far between – oases in the desert
of human uniformity, intolerance, and oppression. Among the
great Victorian preachers, Carlyle and Marx have turned out to be
better prophets than Macaulay and the Whigs, but not necessarily
better friends to mankind; sceptical, to put it at its lowest, of the
principles which this Council exists to promote. Their greatest
champion, the man who formulated these principles most clearly
and thereby founded modern liberalism, was, as everyone knows,
the author of the *Essay on Liberty*, John Stuart Mill. This book –
this great short book, as Sir Richard Livingstone has justly called it
in his own lecture in this series – was published 100 years ago. The
subject was then in the forefront of discussion. The year 1859 saw
the death of the two best-known champions of individual liberty in

Europe, Macaulay and Tocqueville. It marked the centenary of the birth of Friedrich Schiller, who was acclaimed as the poet of the free and creative personality fighting against great odds. The individual was seen by some as the victim of, by others as rising to his apotheosis in, the new and triumphant forces of nationalism and industrialism which exalted the power and the glory of great disciplined human masses that were transforming the world in factories or battlefields or political assemblies. The predicament of the individual versus the state or the nation or the industrial organization or the social or political group was becoming an acute personal and public problem. In the same year there appeared Darwin's *On the Origin of Species*, probably the most influential work of science of its century, which at once did much to destroy the ancient accumulation of dogma and prejudice, and, in its misapplication to psychology, ethics, and politics, was used to justify violent imperialism and naked competition. Almost simultaneously with it there appeared an essay, written by an obscure economist expounding a doctrine which has had a decisive influence on mankind. The author was Karl Marx, the book was the *Critique of Political Economy*, the preface to which contained the clearest statement of the materialist interpretation of history – the heart of all that goes under the name of Marxism today. But the impact made upon political thought by Mill's treatise was more immediate, and perhaps no less permanent. It superseded earlier formulations of the case for individualism and toleration, from Milton and Locke to Montesquieu and Voltaire, and, despite its outdated psychology and lack of logical cogency, it remains the classic statement of the case for individual liberty. We are sometimes told that a man's behaviour is a more genuine expression of his beliefs than his words. In Mill's case there is no conflict. His life embodied his beliefs. His single-minded devotion to the cause of toleration and reason was unique even among the dedicated lives of the nineteenth century. The centenary of his profession of faith should not, therefore, be allowed to pass without a word before this Council.

I

Everyone knows the story of John Stuart Mill's extraordinary education. His father, James Mill, was the last of the great *raisonneurs* of the eighteenth century, and remained completely unaffected by the new romantic currents of the time in which he lived. Like his teacher Bentham and the French philosophical materialists, he saw man as a natural object and considered that a systematic study of the human species – conducted on lines similar to those of zoology or botany or physics – could and should be established on firm empirical foundations. He believed himself to have grasped the principles of the new science of man, and was firmly convinced that any man educated in the light of it, brought up as a rational being by other rational beings, would thereby be preserved from ignorance and weakness, the two great sources of unreason in thought and action, which were alone responsible for the miseries and vices of mankind. He brought up his son, John Stuart, in isolation from other – less rationally educated – children; his own brothers and sisters were virtually his only companions. The boy knew Greek by the age of five, algebra and Latin by the age of nine. He was fed on a carefully distilled intellectual diet, prepared by his father, compounded of natural science and the classical literatures. No religion, no metaphysics, little poetry – nothing that Bentham had stigmatized as the accumulation of human idiocy and error – were permitted to reach him. Music, perhaps because it was supposed that it could not easily misrepresent the real world, was the only art in which he could indulge himself freely. The experiment was, in a sense, an appalling success. John Mill, by the time he reached the age of twelve, possessed the learning of an exceptionally erudite man of thirty. In his own sober, clear, literal-minded, painfully honest account of himself, he says that his emotions were starved while his mind was violently over-developed. His father had no doubt of the value of his experiment. He had succeeded in producing an excellently informed and perfectly rational being. The truth of Bentham's views on education had been thoroughly vindicated.

The results of such treatment will astonish no one in our psychologically less naïve age. In his early manhood John Mill went through his first agonizing crisis. He felt lack of purpose, a paralysis of the will, and terrible despair. With his well trained and, indeed, ineradicable habit of reducing emotional dissatisfaction to a clearly formulated problem, he asked himself a simple question: supposing that the noble Benthamite ideal of universal happiness which he had been taught to believe, and to the best of his ability did believe, were realized, would this, in fact, fulfil all his desires? He admitted to himself, to his horror, that it would not. What, then, was the true end of life? He saw no purpose in existence: everything in his world now seemed dry and bleak. He tried to analyse his condition. Was he perhaps totally devoid of feeling – was he a monster with a large part of normal human nature atrophied? He felt that he had no motives for continuing to live, and wished for death. One day, as he was reading a pathetic story in the memoirs of the now almost forgotten French writer Marmontel, he was suddenly moved to tears. This convinced him that he was capable of emotion, and with this his recovery began. It took the form of a revolt, slow, concealed, reluctant, but profound and irresistible, against the view of life inculcated by his father and the Benthamites. He read the poetry of Wordsworth, he read and met Coleridge; his view of the nature of man, his history and his destiny, was transformed. John Mill was not by temperament rebellious. He loved and deeply admired his father, and was convinced of the validity of his main philosophical tenets. He stood with Bentham against dogmatism, transcendentalism, obscurantism, all that resisted the march of reason, analysis, and empirical science. To these beliefs he held firmly all his life. Nevertheless, his conception of man, and therefore of much else, suffered a great change. He became not so much an open heretic from the original utilitarian movement, as a disciple who quietly left the fold, preserving what he thought true or valuable, but feeling bound by none of the rules and principles of the movement. He continued to profess that happiness was the sole end of human existence, but his conception of what contributed to it changed into something very different from that of his mentors, for what he came to value most was neither rationality nor contentment, but diversity, versatility, fullness of life – the unaccountable leap of individual genius, the spontaneity and uniqueness of a man, a group, a civilization. What he hated and feared was narrowness, uniformity, the crippling effect of persecution, the crushing of individuals by the weight of authority or of custom or of public opinion; he set himself against the worship of order or tidiness, or even peace, if they were bought at the price of obliterating the variety and colour of untamed human beings with unextinguished passions and untrammelled imaginations. This was, perhaps, a natural enough compensation for his own drilled, emotionally shrivelled, warped, childhood and adolescence.

By the time he was seventeen he was mentally fully formed. John Mill's intellectual equipment was probably unique in that or any other age. He was clear-headed, candid, highly articulate, intensely serious, and without any trace of fear, vanity, or humour. During the next ten years he wrote articles and reviews, with all the weight of the official heir presumptive of the whole utilitarian movement upon his shoulders; and although his articles made him a great name, and he grew to be a formidable publicist and a source of pride to his mentors and allies, yet the note of his writings is not theirs. He praised what his father had praised – rationality, empirical method, democracy, equality, and he attacked what the utilitarians attacked – religion, belief in intuitive and undemonstrable truths and their dogmatic consequences, which, in their view and in his, led to the abandonment of reason, hierarchical societies, vested interests, intolerance of free criticism, prejudice, reaction, injustice, depotism, misery. Yet the emphasis had shifted. James Mill and Bentham had wanted literally nothing but pleasure obtained by whatever means were the most effective. If someone had offered them a medicine which could scientifically be shown to put those who took it into a state of permanent contentment, their premises would have bound them to accept this as the panacea for all that they thought evil. Provided that the largest possible number of men receive lasting happiness, or even freedom from pain, it should not matter how this is achieved. Bentham and Mill believed in education and legislation as the roads to happiness. But, if a shorter way had been discovered, in the form of pills to swallow, techniques of subliminal suggestion, or other means of conditioning human beings in which our century has made such strides, then, being men of fanatical consistency, they might well have accepted this as a better, because more effective and perhaps less costly, alternative than the means that they had advocated. John Stuart Mill, as he made plain both by his life and by his writings, would have rejected with both hands any such solution. He would have condemned it as degrading the nature of man. For him man differs from animals primarily neither as the possessor of reason, nor as an inventor of tools and methods, but as a being capable of choice, one who is most himself in choosing and not being chosen for; the rider and not the horse; the seeker of ends, and not merely of means, ends that he pursues, each in his own fashion: with the corollary that the more various these fashions, the richer the lives of men become; the larger the field of interplay between individuals, the greater the opportunities of the new and the unexpected; the more numerous the possibilities for altering his own character in some fresh or unexplored direction, the more paths open before each individual, and the wider will be his freedom of action and thought.

In the last analysis, all appearances to the contrary, this is what Mill seems to me to have cared about most of all. He is officially committed to the exclusive pursuit of happiness. He believes deeply in justice, but his voice is most his own when he describes the glories of individual freedom, or denounces whatever seeks to curtail or extinguish it. Bentham, too, unlike his French predecessors who trusted in moral and scientific experts, had laid it down that each man is the best judge of his own happiness. Nevertheless, this principle would remain valid for Bentham even after every living man had swallowed the happiness-inducing pill and society was thereby lifted or reduced to a condition of unbroken and uniform bliss. For Bentham individualism is a psychological datum; for Mill it is an ideal. Mill likes dissent, independence, solitary thinkers, those who defy the establishment. In an article written at the age of seventeen (demanding toleration for a now almost forgotten atheist named Carlyle), he strikes a note which sounds and resounds in his writings throughout the rest of his life:

> Christians, whose reformers perished in the dungeon or at the stake as heretics, as apostates, as blasphemers – Christians, whose religion breathes charity, liberty and mercy in every line . . . that they, having gained the power of which they were the victims, should employ it in the self same way . . . in vindictive persecution . . . is most monstrous.[2]

He remained the champion of heretics, apostates, and blasphemers, of liberty and mercy, for the rest of his life.

His acts were in harmony with his professions. The public policies with which Mill's name was associated as a journalist, a reformer, and a politician, were seldom connected with the typically utilitarian projects advocated by Bentham and successfully realized by many of his disciples: great industrial, financial, educational schemes, reforms of public health or the organization of labour or leisure. The issues to which Mill was dedicated, whether in his published views or his actions, were concerned with something different: the extension of individual freedom, especially freedom of speech: seldom with anything else. When Mill declared that war was better than oppression, or that a revolution that would kill all men with an income of more than £500 per annum might improve things greatly, or that the Emperor Napoleon III of France was the vilest man alive; when he expressed delight at Palmerston's fall over the Bill that sought to make conspiracy against foreign despots a criminal offence in England; when he denounced the Southern States in the American Civil War, or made himself violently unpopular by speaking in the House of Commons in defence of Fenian assassins (and thereby probably saving their lives), or for the rights of women, or of workers, or of colonial peoples, and thereby made himself the most passionate and best-known champion in England of the insulted and the oppressed, it is difficult to suppose that it was not liberty and justice (at whatever cost) but utility (which counts the cost) that were uppermost in his mind. His articles and his political support saved Durham and his Report, when both were in danger of being defeated by the combination of right and left-wing adversaries, and thereby did much to ensure self-government in the British Commonwealth. He helped to destroy the reputation of Governor Eyre who had perpetrated brutalities in Jamaica. He saved the right of public meeting and of free speech in Hyde Park, against a government that wished to destroy it. He wrote and spoke for proportional representation because this alone, in his view, would allow minorities (not necessarily virtuous or rational ones) to make their voices heard. When, to the surprise of radicals, he opposed the dissolution of the East India Company for which he, like his father before him, had worked so devotedly, he did this because he feared the dead hand of the government more than the paternalist and not inhumane rule of the Company's officials. On the other hand he did not oppose state intervention as such; he welcomed it in education or labour legislation because he thought that without it the weakest would be enslaved and crushed; and because it would increase the range of choices for the great majority of men, even if it restrained some. What is common to all these causes is not any direct connexion they might have with the 'greater happiness' principle but the fact that they turn on the issue of human rights – that is to say, of liberty and toleration.

I do not, of course, mean to suggest that there was no such connexion in Mill's own mind. He often seems to advocate freedom on the ground that without it the truth cannot be discovered – we cannot perform those experiments either in thought or 'in living' which alone reveal to us new, unthought-of ways of maximizing pleasure and minimizing pain – the only ultimate source of value. Freedom, then, is valuable as a means, not as an end. But when we ask what Mill meant either by pleasure or by happiness, the answer is far from clear. Whatever happiness may be, it is, according to Mill, not what Bentham took it to be: for his conception of human nature is pronounced too narrow and altogether inadequate; he has no imaginative grasp of history or society or individual psychology; he does not understand either what holds, or what should hold, society together – common ideals, loyalties, national character; he is not aware of honour, dignity, self-culture, or the love of beauty, order, power, action; he understands only the 'business' aspects of life. Are these goals, which Mill rightly regards as central, so many means to a single universal goal – happiness? Or are they species of it? Mill never clearly tells us. He says that happiness – or utility – is of no use as a criterion of conduct – destroying at one blow the proudest claim, and indeed the central doctrine, of the Benthamite system. 'We think', he says in his essay on Bentham (published only after his father's death), 'utility or happiness much too complex or indefinite at end to be sought except through the medium of various secondary ends, concerning which there may be, and often is, agreement among persons who differ in the ultimate standard.' This is simple and definite enough in Bentham; but Mill rejects his formula because it rests on a false view of human nature. It is 'complex and indefinite' in Mill because he packs into it the many diverse (and, perhaps, not always compatible) ends which men in fact pursue for their own sake, and which Bentham had either ignored or falsely classified under the head of pleasure: love, hatred, desire for justice, for action, for freedom, for power, for beauty, for knowledge, for self-sacrifice. In J.S. Mill's writings happiness comes to mean something very like 'realization of one's wishes', whatever they may be. This stretches its meaning to the point of vacuity. The letter remains; but the spirit – the old, tough-minded Benthamite view for which happiness, if it was not a clear and concrete criterion of action, was nothing at all, as worthless as the 'transcendental' intuitionist moonshine it was meant to replace – the true utilitarian spirit – has fled. Mill does indeed add that 'when two or more of the secondary principles conflict, direct appeal to some first principle becomes necessary'; this principle is utility; but he gives no indication how this notion, drained of its old, materialistic but intelligible content, is to be applied. It is this tendency of Mill's to escape into what Bentham called 'vague generality' that leads one to ask what, in fact, was Mill's real scale of values as shown in his writings and actions. If his life and the causes he advocated are any evidence, then it seems clear that in public life the highest values for him – whether or not he calls them 'secondary ends' – were individual liberty, variety, and justice. If challenged about variety Mill would have defended it on the ground that without a sufficient degree of it many, at present wholly unforeseeable, forms of human happiness (or satisfaction, or fulfilment, or higher levels of life – however the degrees of these were to be determined and compared) would be left unknown, untried, unrealized; among them happier lives than any yet experienced. This is his thesis and he chooses to call it utilitarianism. But if anyone were to argue that a given, actual or attainable, social arrangement yielded enough happiness – that given the virtually impassable limitations of the nature of men and their environment (e.g. the very high improbability of men's becoming immortal or growing as tall as Everest) it were better to concentrate on the best that we have, since change would, in all empirical likelihood, lead to lowering of general happiness, and should therefore be avoided, we may be sure that Mill would have rejected this argument out of hand. He was committed to the answer that we can never tell (until we have tried) where greater truth or happiness (or any other form of experience) may lie. Finality is therefore in principle impossible: all solutions must be tentative and provisional. This is the voice of a disciple of both Saint-Simon and Constant or Humboldt. It runs directly counter to traditional – that is, eighteenth-century – utilitarianism, which rested on the view that there exists an unalterable nature of things, and answers to social, as to other, problems, can, at least in principle, be scientifically discovered once and for all. It is this perhaps, that, despite his fear of ignorant and irrational democracy and consequent craving for government by the enlightened and the expert (and insistence, early and late in his life, on the importance of objects of common, even uncritical, worship) checked his Saint-Simonism, turned him against Comte, and preserved him from the elitist tendency of his Fabian disciples.

There was a spontaneous and uncalculating idealism in his mind and his actions that was wholly alien to the dispassionate and penetrating irony of Bentham, or the vain and stubborn rationalism of James Mill. He tells us that his father's educational methods had turned him into a desiccated calculating machine, not too far removed from the popular image of the inhuman utilitarian philosopher; his very awareness of this makes one wonder whether it can ever have been wholly true. Despite the solemn bald head, the black clothes, the grave expression, the measured phrases, the total lack of humour, Mill's life is an unceasing revolt against his father's outlook and ideals, the greater for being subterranean and unacknowledged.

Mill had scarcely any prophetic gift. Unlike his contemporaries, Marx, Burckhardt, Tocqueville, he had no vision of what the twentieth century would bring, neither of the political and social consequences of industrialization, nor of the discovery of the strength of irrational and unconscious factors in human behaviour, nor of the terrifying techniques to which this knowledge has led and is leading. The transformation of society which has resulted – the rise of dominant secular ideologies and the wars between them, the awakening of Africa and Asia, the peculiar combination of nationalism and socialism in our day – these were outside Mill's horizon. But if he was not sensitive to the contours of the future, he was acutely aware of the destructive factors at work in his own world. He detested and feared standardization. He perceived that in the name of philanthropy, democracy, and equality a society was being created in which human objectives were artificially made narrower and smaller and the majority of men were being converted, to use his admired friend Tocqueville's phrase, into mere 'industrious sheep', in which, in his own words, 'collective mediocrity' was gradually strangling originality and individual gifts. He was against what have been called 'organization men', a class of persons to whom Bentham could have had in principle no rational objection. He knew, feared, and hated timidity, mildness, natural conformity, lack of interest in human issues. This was common ground between him and his friend, his suspicious and disloyal friend, Thomas Carlyle. Above all he was on his guard against those who, for the sake of being left in peace to cultivate their gardens, were ready to sell their fundamental human right to self-government in the public spheres of life; these characteristics of our lives today he would have recognized with horror. He took human solidarity for granted, perhaps altogether too much for granted. He did not fear the isolation of individuals or groups, the factors that make for the alienation and disintegration of individuals and societies. He was preoccupied with the opposite evils of socialization and uniformity.[3] He longed for the widest variety of human life and character. He saw that this could not be obtained without protecting individuals from each other, and, above all, from the terrible weight of social pressure; this led to his insistent and persistent demands for toleration.

Toleration, Professor Butterfield has told us in his own lecture in this series, implies a certain disrespect. I tolerate your absurd beliefs and your foolish acts, though I know them to be absurd and foolish. Mill would, I think, have agreed. He believed that to hold an opinion deeply is to throw our feelings into it. He once declared[4] that when we deeply care, we must dislike those who hold the opposite views. He preferred this to cold temperaments and opinions. He asked us not necessarily to respect the views of others – very far from it – only to try to understand and tolerate them; only tolerate; disapprove, think ill of, if need be mock or despise, but tolerate; for without conviction, without some antipathetic feeling, there was, he thought, no deep conviction; and without deep conviction there were no ends of life, and then the awful abyss on the edge of which he had himself once stood would yawn before us. But without tolerance the conditions for rational criticism, rational condemnation, are destroyed. He therefore pleads for reason and toleration at all costs. To understand is not necessarily to forgive. We may argue, attack, reject, condemn with passion and hatred. But we may not suppress or stifle: for that is to destroy the bad and the good, and is tantamount to collective moral and intellectual suicide. Sceptical respect for the opinions of our opponents seems to him preferable to indifference or cynicism. But even these attitudes are less harmful than intolerance, or an imposed orthodoxy which kills rational discussion. This is Mill's faith. It obtained its classical formulation in the tract on Liberty, which he began writing in 1855 in collaboration with his wife, who, after his father, was the dominant figure in his life. Until his dying day he believed her to be endowed with a genius vastly superior to his own. He published the essay after her death in 1859 without those improvements which he was sure that her unique gifts would have brought to it. It is this event that I venture to invite you to celebrate today.

II

I shall not impose upon your patience by giving you an abstract of Mill's argument. I should like to remind you only of those salient ideas to which Mill attached the greatest importance – beliefs which his opponents attacked in his lifetime, and attack even more vehemently today. These propostitions are still far from self-evident; time has not turned them to platitudes; they are not even now undisputed assumptions of a civilized outlook. Let me attempt to consider them briefly.

Men want to curtail the liberties of other men, either (*a*) because they wish to impose their power on others; or (*b*) because they want conformity – they do not wish to think differently from others, or others to think differently from themselves; or, finally, (*c*) because they believe that to the question of how one should live there can be (as with any genuine question) one true answer and one only; this answer is discoverable by means of reason, or intuition, or direct revelation, or a form of life or 'unity of theory and practice'; its authority is identifiable with one of these avenues to final knowledge; all deviation from it is error which imperils human salvation; this justifies legislation against, or even extirpation of, those who lead away from the truth, whatever their character or intentions. Mill dismisses the first two motives as being irrational, since they stake out no intellectually argued claim, and are therefore incapable of being answered by rational argument. The only motive which he is prepared to take seriously is the last, namely, that if the true ends of life can be discovered, those who oppose these truths are spreading pernicious falsehood, and must be repressed. To this he replies that men are not infallible; that the supposedly pernicious view might turn out to be true after all; that those who killed Socrates and Christ sincerely believed them to be purveyors of wicked falsehoods, and were themselves men as worthy of respect as any to be found today; that Marcus Aurelius, 'the gentlest and most amiable of rulers', known as the most enlightened man of his time and one of the noblest, nevertheless authorized the persecution of Christianity as a moral and social danger, and that no argument ever used by any other persecutor had not been equally open to him. We cannot suppose that persecution never kills the truth. 'It is a piece of idle sentimentality', Mill observes, 'that truth, merely as truth, has any inherent power denied to error, of prevailing against the dungeon and the stake' (p. 48).[5] Persecution is historically only too effective.

> To speak only of religious opinions: the Reformation broke out at least twenty times before Luther, and was put down. Arnold of Brescia was put down. Fra Dolcino was put down.

Savonarola was put down. The Albigeois were put down. The Vaudois were put down. The Lollards were put down. The Hussites were put down . . . In Spain, Italy, Flanders, the Austrian Empire, Protestantism was rooted out; and most likely would have been so in England had Queen Mary lived or Queen Elizabeth died . . . No reasonable person can doubt that Christianity might have been extirpated in the Roman Empire. (p. 47)

And if it be said against this that, just because we have erred in the past, it is mere cowardice to refrain from striking down evil when we see it in the present in case we may be mistaken again; or, to put it in another way, that, even if we are not infallible, yet, if we are to live at all, we must make decisions and act, and must do so on nothing better than probability, according to our lights, with constant risk of error; for all living involves risk, and what alternative have we? Mill answers that 'There is the greatest difference between presuming an opinion to be true, because with every opportunity for contesting it, it has not been refuted, and assuming its truth for the purpose of not permitting its refutation' (p. 39). You can indeed stop 'bad men from perverting society with false or pernicious views' (p. 39), but only if you give men liberty to deny that what you yourself call bad, or pernicious, or perverted, or false, is such; otherwise your conviction is founded on mere dogma and is not rational, and cannot be analysed or altered in the light of any new facts and ideas. Without infallibility how can truth emerge save in discussion? there is no *a priori* road towards it; a new experience, a new argument, can in principle always alter our views, no matter how strongly held. To shut doors is to blind yourself to the truth deliberately, to condemn yourself to incorrigible error.

Mill had a strong and subtle brain and his arguments are never negligible. But it is, in this case, plain that his conclusion only follows from premises which he does not make explicit. He was an empiricist; that is, he believed that no truths are – or could be – rationally established, except on the evidence of observation. New observations could in principle always upset a conclusion founded on earlier ones. He believed this rule to be true of the laws of physics, even of the laws of logic and mathematics; how much more, therefore, in 'ideological' fields where no scientific certainty prevailed – in ethics, politics, religion, history, the entire field of human affairs, where only probability reigns; here, unless full liberty of opinion and argument is permitted, nothing can ever be rationally established. But those who disagree with him, and believe in intuited truths, in principle not corrigible by experience, will disregard this argument. Mill can write them off as obscurantists, dogmatists, irrationalists. Yet something more is needed than mere contemptuous dismissal if their views, more powerful today perhaps than even in Mill's own century, are to be rationally contested. Again, it may well be that without full freedom of discussion the truth cannot emerge. But this may be only a necessary, not a sufficient, condition of its discovery; the truth may, for all our efforts, remain at the bottom of a well, and in the meantime the worse cause may win, and do enormous damage to mankind. Is it so clear that we must permit opinions advocating, say, race hatred to be uttered freely, because Milton has said that 'though all the winds of doctrine are let loose upon the earth . . . whoever knew truth put to the worse in a free and open encounter?' because 'the truth must always prevail in a fair fight with falsehood'? These are brave and optimistic judgements, but how good is the empirical evidence for them today? Are demagogues and liars, scoundrels and blind fanatics, always, in liberal societies, stopped in time, or refuted in the end? How high a price is it right to pay for the great boon of freedom of discussion? A very high one, no doubt; but is it limitless? And if not, who shall say what sacrifice is, or is not, too great? Mill goes on to say that an opinion believed to be false may yet be partially true; for there is no absolute truth, only different roads towards it; the suppression of an apparent falsehood may also suppress what is true in it, to the loss of mankind. This argument, again, will not tell with those who believe that absolute truth is discoverable once and for all, whether by metaphysical or theological argument, or by some direct insight, or by leading a certain kind of life, or, as Mill's own mentors believed, by scientific or empirical methods.

His argument is plausible only on the assumption which, whether he knew it or not, Mill all too obviously made, that human knowledge was in principle never complete, and always fallible; that there was no single, universally visible, truth; that each man, each nation, each civilization might take its own road towards its own goal, not necessarily harmonious with those of others; that men are altered, and the truths in which they believe are altered, by new experiences and their own actions – what he calls 'experiments in living'; that consequently the conviction, common to

Aristotelians and a good many Christian scholastics and atheistical materialists alike, that there exists a basic knowable human nature, one and the same, at all times, in all places, in all men – a static, unchanging substance underneath the altering appearances, with permanent needs, dictated by a single, discoverable goal, or pattern of goals, the same for all mankind – is mistaken; and so, too, is the notion that is bound up with it, of a single true doctrine carrying salvation to all men everywhere, contained in natural law, or the revelation of a sacred book, or the insight of a man of genius, or the natural wisdom of ordinary men, or the calculations made by an elite of utilitarian scientists set up to govern mankind.

Mill – bravely for a professed utilitarian – observes that the human (that is the social) sciences are too confused and uncertain to be properly called sciences at all – there are in them no valid generalizations, no laws, and therefore no predictions or rules of action can properly be deduced from them. He honoured the memory of his father, whose whole philosophy was based on the opposite assumption; he respected Auguste Comte, and subsidized Herbert Spencer, both of whom claimed to have laid the foundations for just such a science of society. Yet his own half-articulate assumption contradicts this. Mill believes that man is spontaneous, that he has freedom of choice, that he moulds his own character, that as a result of the interplay of men with nature and with other men something novel continually arises, and that this novelty is precisely what is most characteristic and most human in men. Because Mill's entire view of human nature turns out to rest not on the notion of the repetition of an identical pattern, but on his perception of human lives as subject to perpetual incompleteness, self-transformation, and novelty, his words are today alive and relevant to our own problems; whereas the works of James Mill, and of Buckle and Comte and Spencer, remain huge half-forgotten hulks in the river of nineteenth-century thought. He does not demand or predict ideal conditions for the final solution of human problems or for obtaining universal agreement on all crucial issues. He assumes that finality is impossible, and implies that it is undesirable too. He does not demonstrate this. Rigour in argument is not among his accomplishments. Yet it is this belief, which undermines the foundations on which Helvétius, Bentham, and James Mill built their doctrines – a system never formally repudiated by him – that gives his case both its plausibility and its humanity.

His remaining arguments are weaker still. He says that unless it is contested, truth is liable to degenerate into dogma or prejudice; men would no longer feel it as a living truth; opposition is needed to keep it alive. 'Both teachers and learners go to sleep at their post, as soon as there is no enemy in the field', overcome as they are by 'the deep slumber of a decided opinion' (p. 61). So deeply did Mill believe this, that he declared that if there were no genuine dissenters, we had an obligation to invent arguments against ourselves, in order to keep ourselves in a state of intellectual fitness. This resembles nothing so much as Hegel's argument for war as keeping human society from stagnation. Yet if the truth about human affairs were in principle demonstrable, as it is, say, in arithmetic, the invention of false propositions in order to be knocked down would scarcely be needed to preserve our understanding of it. What Mill seems really to be asking for is diversity of opinion for its own sake. He speaks of the need for 'fair play to all sides of the truth' (p. 65) – a phrase that a man would scarcely employ if he believed in simple, complete truths as the earlier utilitarians did; and he makes use of bad arguments to conceal this scepticism, perhaps even from himself. 'In an imperfect state of the human mind', he says, 'the interests of the truth require a diversity of opinions' (p. 68). Or again, 'Do we really accept the logic of the persecutors [and say] we may persecute others because we are right, and they may not persecute us because they are wrong?' (p. 101) Catholics, Protestants, Jews, Muslims have all justified persecution by this argument in their day; and on their premises there may be nothing logically amiss with it. It is these premises that Mill rejects, and rejects not, it seems to me, as a result of a chain of reasoning, but because he believes – even if he never, so far as I know, admits this explicitly – that there are no final truths not corrigible by experience, at any rate in what is now called the ideological sphere – that of value judgements and of general outlook and attitude to life. Yet within this framework of ideas and values, despite all the stress on the value of 'experiments in living' and what they may reveal, Mill is ready to stake a very great deal on the truth of his convictions about what he thinks to be the deepest and most permanent interests of men. Although his reasons are drawn from experience and not *a priori* knowledge, the propositions themselves are very like those defended on metaphysical grounds by the traditional upholders of the doctrine of natural rights. Mill believes in liberty, that is, the rigid limitation of the right to coerce, because he is sure that men cannot develop and flourish and become fully human unless they are left free from interference by other men within a certain minimum area of their lives, which he regards as – or wishes to make – inviolable. This is his view of what men are, and therefore of their basic moral and intellectual needs, and he formulates his conclusions in the celebrated maxims according to which 'The individual is not accountable to society for his actions, in so far as these concern the interests of no person but himself' (p. 108), and that

> The only reason for which power can be rightfully exercised over any member of a civilised community against his will is to prevent harm to others. His own good, either physical or moral, is not a sufficient warrant. He cannot rightfully be compelled to do or to forbear . . . because in the opinion of others to do so would be wise or even right. (p. 30)

This is Mill's profession of faith, and the ultimate basis of political liberalism, and therefore the proper target of attack – both on psychological and moral (and social) grounds – by its opponents during Mill's lifetime and after. Carlyle reacted with characteristic fury in a letter to his brother Alexander: 'As if it were a sin to control or coerce into better methods human swine in any way . . . Ach Gott in Himmel!'[6]

Milder and more rational critics have not failed to point out that the limits of private and public domain are difficult to demarcate, that anything a man does could, in principle, frustrate others; that no man is an island; that the social and the individual aspects of human beings often cannot, in practice, be disentangled. Mill was told that when men look upon forms of worship in which other men persist as being not merely 'abominable' in themselves, but as an offence to them or to their God, they may be irrational and bigoted, but they are not necessarily lying; and that when he asks rhetorically why Muslims should not forbid the eating of pork to everyone, since they are genuinely disgusted by it, the answer, on utilitarian premisses, is by no means self-evident. It might be argued that there is no *a priori* reason for supposing that most men would not be happier – if that is the goal – in a wholly socialized world where private life and personal freedom are reduced to vanishing point, than in Mill's individualist order; and that whether this is so or not is a matter for experimental verification. Mill constantly protests against the fact that social and legal rules are too often determined merely by 'the likings and dislikings of society', and correctly points out that these are often irrational or are founded on ignorance. But if damage to others is what concerns him most (as he professes), then the fact that their resistance to this or that belief is instinctive, or intuitive, or founded on no rational ground, does not make it the less painful, and, to that extent, damaging to them. Why should rational men be entitled to the satisfaction of their ends more than the irrational? Why not the irrational, if the greatest happiness of the greatest number (and the greatest number are seldom rational) is the sole justified purpose of action? Only a competent social psychologist can tell what will make a given society happiest. If happiness is the sole criterion, then human sacrifice, or the burning of witches, at times when such practices had strong public feeling behind them, did doubtless, in their day, contribute to the happiness of the majority. If there is no other moral criterion, then the question whether the slaughter of innocent old women (together with the ignorance and prejudice which made this acceptable) or the advance in knowledge and rationality (which ended such abominations but robbed men of comforting illusions) – which of these yielded a higher balance of happiness is only a matter of actuarial calculation. Mill paid no attention to such considerations: nothing could go more violently against all that he felt and believed. At the centre of Mill's thought and feeling lies, not his utilitarianism, nor the concern about enlightenment, nor about dividing the private from the public domain – for he himself at times concedes that the state may invade the private domain, in order to promote education, hygiene, or social security or justice – but his passionate belief that men are made human by their capacity for choice – choice of evil and good equally. Fallibility, the right to err, as a corollary of the capacity for self-improvement; distrust of symmetry and finality as enemies of freedom – these are the principles which Mill never abandons. He is acutely aware of the many-sidedness of the truth and of the irreducible complexity of life, which rules out the very possibility of any simple solution, or the idea of a final answer to any concrete problem. Greatly daring, and without looking back at the stern intellectual puritanism in which he was brought up, he preaches the necessity of understanding and gaining illumination from doctrines that are incompatible with one another – say those of Coleridge and Bentham; he explained in his autobiography the need to understand and learn from both.[7]

III

Kant once remarked that 'out of the crooked timber of humanity no straight thing was ever made'. Mill believed this deeply. This, and his almost Hegelian distrust of simple models and of cut-and-dried formulae to cover complex, contradictory, and changing situations, made him a very hesitant and uncertain adherent of organized parties and programmes. Despite his father's advocacy, despite Mrs Taylor's passionate faith in the ultimate solution of all social evils by some great institutional change (in her case that of socialism), he could not rest in the notion of a clearly discernible final goal, because he saw that men differed and evolved, not merely as a result of natural causes, but also because of what they themselves did to alter their own characters, at times in unintended ways. This alone makes their conduct unpredictable, and renders laws or theories, whether inspired by analogies with mechanics or with biology, nevertheless incapable of embracing the complexity and qualitative properties of even an individual character, let alone of a group of men. Hence the imposition of any such construction upon a living society is bound, in his favourite words of warning, to dwarf, maim, cramp, wither the human faculties.

His greatest break with his father was brought about by this conviction: by his belief (which he never explicitly admitted) that particular predicaments required each its own specific treatment; that the application of correct judgement, in curing a social malady, mattered at least as much as knowledge of the laws of anatomy or pharmacology. He was a British empiricist and not a French rationalist, or a German metaphysician, sensitive to day-to-day play of circumstances, differences of 'climate', as well as to the individual nature of each case, as Helvétius or Saint-Simon or Fichte, concerned as they were with the *grandes lignes* of development, were not. Hence his unceasing anxiety, as great as Tocqueville's and greater than Montesquieu's, to preserve variety, to keep doors open to change, to resist the dangers of social pressure, and above all his hatred of the human pack in full cry against a victim, his desire to protect dissidents and heretics as such. The whole burden of his charge against the 'progressives' (he means utilitarians and perhaps socialists) is that, as a rule, they do no more than try to alter social opinion in order to make it more favourable to this or that scheme or reform, instead of assailing the monstrous principle itself which says that social opinion 'should be a law for individuals' (p. 28).

Mill's overmastering desire for variety and individuality for their own sake emerges in many shapes. He notes that 'Mankind are greater gainers by suffering each other to live as seems good to themselves, than by compelling each to live as seems good to the rest' (p. 33) – a truism which, he declares, 'stands opposed to the general tendency of existing opinion and practice'. At other times he speaks in sharper terms. He remarks that

> it is the habit of our time to desire nothing strongly. Its ideal of character is to be without any marked character; to maim by compression, like a Chinese lady's foot, every part of human nature which stands out prominently, and tends to make the person markedly dissimilar in outline to common-place humanity (p. 85).

And again:

> The greatness of England is now all collective; individually small, we only appear capable of anything great by combining; and with this our moral and religious philanthropists are perfectly content. But it was men of another stamp that made England what it has been; and men of another stamp will be needed to prevent its decline (p. 85).

The tone of this, if not the content, would have shocked Bentham; so indeed would this bitter echo of Tocqueville:

> Comparatively speaking, they now read the same things, listen to the same things, see the same things, go to the same places, have their hopes and fears directed to the same objects, have the same rights and liberties and the same means of asserting them . . . All the political changes of the age promote it, since they all tend to raise the low and lower the high. Every extension of education promotes it, because education brings people under common influences. Improvement in the means of communication promotes it . . . Increase of commerce and manufacture promotes it . . . The ascendancy of public opinion . . . forms so great a mass of influence hostile to individuality (pp. 88–9) [that] in this age the mere example of non-conformity, the mere refusal to bend the knee to custom, is itself a service (pp. 82–3).

We have come to such a pass that mere differences, resistance for its own sake, protest as such, is now enough. Conformity, and the intolerance which is its offensive and defensive arm, are for Mill always detestable, and peculiarly horrifying in an age which thinks itself enlightened; in which, nevertheless, a man can be sent to prison for twenty-one months for atheism; jurymen are rejected and foreigners denied justice because they hold no recognized religious beliefs; no public money is given for Hindu or Muslim schools because an 'imbecile display' (p. 50) is made by an Under-Secretary, who declares that toleration is desirable only among Christians but not for unbelievers. It is no better when workers employ 'moral police' to prevent some members of their trade union being paid higher wages earned by superior skill or industry than the wages paid to those who lack these attributes. Such conduct is even more loathsome when it interferes with private relations between individuals. He declared that 'what any person might freely do with respect to sexual relations' should be deemed to be an unimportant and purely private matter which concerns no one but themselves; that to have held any human being responsible to other people, and to the world, for the fact itself (apart from such of its consequences as the birth of children, which clearly created duties which should be socially enforced) would one day be thought one of the superstitions and barbarisms of the infancy of the human race. The same seemed to him to apply to the enforcement of temperance or Sabbath observance, or any of the matters on which 'intrusively pious members of society should be told to mind their own business' (p. 101). No doubt the gossip to which Mill was exposed during his relationship with Mrs Taylor before his marriage to her – the relationship which Carlyle mocked at as platonic – made him peculiarly sensitive to this form of social persecution. But it is of a piece with his deepest and most permanent convictions.

Mill's suspicion of democracy as the only just, and yet potentially the most oppressive, form of government, springs from the same roots. He wondered uneasily whether centralization of authority and the inevitable dependence of each on all and 'surveillance of each by all' would not end by grinding all down into 'a tame uniformity of thought, dealings and actions', and produce 'automatons in human form' and 'liberticide'. Tocqueville had written pessimistically about the moral and intellectual effects of democracy in America. Mill agreed. He said that even if such power did not destroy, it prevented existence; it compressed, enervated, extinguished, and stupefied a people; and turned them into a flock of 'timid and industrious animals of whom the government is a shepherd'. Yet the only cure for this, as Tocqueville himself maintained (it may be a little half-heartedly), is more democracy,[8] which can alone educate a sufficient number of individuals to independence, resistance, and strength. Men's disposition to impose their own views on others is so strong that, in Mill's view, only want of power restricts it; this power is growing; hence unless further barriers are erected it will increase, leading to a proliferation of 'conformers, time servers, hyprocrites, created by silencing opinion',[9] and finally to a society where timidity has killed independent thought, and men confine themselves to safe subjects. Yet if we make the barriers too high, and do not interfere with opinion at all, will this not end, as Burke or the Hegelians have warned in the dissolution of the social texture, atomization of society – anarchy? To this Mill replies that 'the inconvenience arising from conduct which neither violates specific duty to the public, nor hurts any assignable individual, is one which society can afford to bear for the sake of the greater good of human freedom' (p. 97). This is tantamount to saying that if society, despite the need for social cohesion, has itself failed to educate its citizens to be civilized men, it has no right to punish them for irritating others, or being misfits, or not conforming to some standard which the majority accepts. A smooth and harmonious society could perhaps be created, at any rate for a time, but it would be purchased at too high a price. Plato saw correctly that if a frictionless society is to emerge the poets must be driven out; what horrifies those who revolt against this policy is not so much the expulsion of the fantasy-mongering poets as such, but the underlying desire for an end to variety, movement, individuality of any kind; a craving for a fixed pattern of life and thought, timeless, changeless, and uniform. Without the right of protest, and the capacity for it, there is for Mill no justice, there are no ends worth pursuing.

> If all mankind minus one were of one opinion, and only one person were of a contrary opinion, mankind would be no more justified in silencing that one person than he, if he had the power, would be justified in silencing mankind. (p. 37)

In his lecture in this series, to which I have already referred, Sir Richard Livingstone, whose sympathy with Mill is not in doubt, charges him with attributing too much rationality to human beings: the ideal of untrammelled freedom may be the right of those who have reached the maturity of their faculties, but of how many men today, or at most times, is this true? Surely Mill asks far too much and is far too optimistic? There is certainly an important sense in which Sir Richard is right: Mill was no prophet. Many social developments caused him grief, but he had no inkling of the mounting strength of the irrational forces that have moulded the history of the twentieth century. Burckhardt and Marx, Pareto and Freud, were more sensitive to the deeper currents of their own times, and saw a good deal more deeply into the springs of individual and social behaviour. But I know of no evidence that Mill overestimated the enlightenment of his own age, or that he supposed that the majority of men of his own time were mature or rational or likely soon to become so. What he did see before him was the spectacle of some men, civilized by any standards, who were kept down, or discriminated against, or persecuted by prejudice, stupidity, 'collective mediocrity'; he saw such men deprived of what he regarded as their most essential rights, and he protested. He believed that all human progress, all human greatness and virtue and freedom, depended chiefly on the preservation of such men and the clearing of paths before them. But he did not[10] want them appointed Platonic Guardians. He thought that others like them could be educated, and, when they were educated, would be entitled to make choices, and that these choices must not, within certain limits, be blocked or directed by others. He did not merely advocate education and forget the freedom to which it would entitle the educated (as communists have), or press for total freedom of choice, and forget that without adequate education it would lead to chaos and, as a reaction to it, a new slavery (as anarchists do). He demanded both. But he did not think that this process would be rapid, or easy, or universal; he was on the whole a pessimistic man, and consequently at once defended and distrusted democracy, for which he has been duly attacked, and is still sharply criticized. Sir Richard has observed that Mill was acutely conscious of the circumstances of his age, and saw no further than that. This seems to me a just comment. The disease of Victorian England was claustrophobia – there was a sense of suffocation, and the best and most gifted men of the period, Mill and Carlyle, Nietzsche and Ibsen, men both of the left and of the right – demanded more air and more light. The mass neurosis of our age is agoraphobia; men are terrified of disintegration and of too little direction: they ask, like Hobbes's masterless men in a state of nature, for walls to keep out the raging ocean, for order, security, organization, clear and recognizable authority, and are alarmed by the prospect of too

153

much freedom, which leaves them lost in a vast, friendless vacuum, a desert without paths or landmarks or goals. Our situation is different from that of the nineteenth century, and so are our problems: the area of irrationality is seen to be vaster and more complex than any that Mill had dreamed of. Mill's psychology has become antiquated and grows more so with every discovery that is made. He is justly criticized for paying too much attention to purely spiritual obstacles to the fruitful use of freedom – lack of moral and intellectual light; and too little (although nothing like as little as his detractors have maintained) to poverty, disease, and their causes, and to the common sources and the interaction of both, and for concentrating too narrowly on freedom of thought and expression. All this is true. Yet what solutions have we found, with all our new technological and psychological knowledge and great new powers, save the ancient prescription advocated by the creators of humanism – Erasmus and Spinoza, Locke and Montesquieu, Lessing and Diderot – reason, education, self-knowledge, responsibility – above all, self-knowledge? What other hope is there for men, or has there ever been?

IV

Mill's ideal is not original. It is an attempt to fuse rationalism and romanticism: the aim of Goethe and Wilhelm Humboldt, a rich, spontaneous, many-sided, fearless, free, and yet rational, self-directed character. Mill notes that Europeans owe much to 'plurality of paths'. From sheer differences and disagreements sprang toleration, variety, humanity. In a sudden outburst of anti-egalitarian feeling, he praises the Middle Ages because men were then more individual and more responsible: men died for ideas, and women were equal to men. 'The poor Middle Ages, its Papacy, its chivalry, its feudality, under what hands did they perish? Under that of the attorney, and fraudulent bankrupt, the false coiner.'[11] This is the language not of a philosophical radical, but of Burke, or Carlyle, or Chesterton. In his passion for the colour and the texture of life Mill has forgotten his list of martyrs, he has forgotten the teachings of his father, of Bentham, or Condorcet. He remembers only Coleridge, only the horrors of a levelling, middle-class society – the grey, conformist, congregation that worships the wicked principle that 'it is the absolute social right of every individual that every other individual should act in every respect exactly as he ought' (p. 104)' or, worse still, 'that it is one man's duty that another should be religious', for 'God not only abominates the acts of the misbeliever, but will not hold us guiltless if we leave them unmolested' (p. 105). These are the shibboleths of Victorian England, and if that is its conception of social justice, it were better dead. In a similar, earlier moment of acute indignation with the self-righteous defences of the exploitation of the poor, Mill had expressed his enthusiasm for revolution and slaughter, since justice was more precious than life. He was twenty-five years old when he wrote that. A quarter of a century later, he declared that a civilization which had not the inner strength to resist barbarism had better succumb (p. 107). This may not be the voice of Kant, but it is not that of utilitarianism; rather that of Rousseau or Mazzini.

But Mill seldom continues in this tone. His solution is not revolutionary. If human life is to be made tolerable, information must be centralized and power disseminated. If everyone knows as much as possible, and has not too much power, then we may yet avoid a state which 'dwarfs its men', in which 'there is the absolute rule of the head of the executive over a congregation of isolated individuals, all equals but all slaves'. With small men 'no great thing can really be accomplished' (p. 128). There is a terrible danger in creeds and forms of life which 'compress', 'stunt', 'dwarf' men. The acute consciousness in our day of the dehumanizing effect of mass culture; of the destruction of genuine purposes, both individual and communal, by the treatment of men as irrational creatures to be deluded and manipulated by the media of mass advertising, and mass communication – and so 'alienated' from the basic purposes of human beings by being left exposed to the play of the forces of nature interacting with human ignorance, vice, stupidity, tradition, and above all self-deception and institutional blindness – all this was as deeply and painfully felt by Mill as by Ruskin or William Morris. In this matter he differs from them only in his clearer awareness of the dilemma created by the simultaneous needs for individual self-expression and for human community. It is on this theme that the tract on Liberty was composed. 'It is to be feared', Mill added gloomily, 'that the teachings' of his essay 'will retain their value for a long time.'

It was, I think, Bertrand Russell – Mill's godson – who remarked somewhere that the deepest convictions of philosophers are seldom contained in their formal arguments: fundamental beliefs, comprehensive views of life, are like citadels which must be guarded against the enemy. Philosophers expend their intellectual power in arguments against actual and possible objections to their doctrines, and although the reasons they find, and the logic that they use, may be complex, ingenious, and formidable, they are defensive weapons; the inner fortress itself – the vision of life for the sake of which the war is being waged – will, as a rule, turn out to be relatively simple and unsophisticated. Mill's defence of his position in the tract on Liberty is not, as has often been pointed out, of the highest intellectual quality: most of his arguments can be turned against him; certainly none is conclusive, or such as would convince a determined or unsympathetic opponent. From the days of James Stephen, whose powerful attack on Mill's position appeared in the year of Mill's death, to the conservatives and socialists and authoritarians and totalitarians of our day, the critics of Mill have, on the whole, exceeded the number of his defenders. Nevertheless, the inner citadel – the central thesis – has stood the test. It may need elaboration or qualification, but it is still the clearest, most candid, persuasive, and moving exposition of the point of view of those who desire an open and tolerant society. The reason for this is not merely the honesty of Mill's mind, or the moral and intellectual charm of his prose, but the fact that he is saying something true and important about some of the most fundamental characteristics and aspirations of human beings. Mill is not merely uttering a string of clear propositions (each of which, viewed by itself, is of doubtful plausibility) connected by such logical links as he can supply. He perceived something profound and essential about the destructive effect of man's most successful efforts at self-improvement in modern society; about the unintended consequences of modern democracy, and the fallaciousness and practical dangers of the theories by which some of the worst of these consequences were (and still are) defended. That is why, despite the weakness of the argument, the loose ends, the dated examples, the touch of the finishing governess that Disraeli so maliciously noted, despite the total lack of that boldness of conception which only men of original genius possess, his essay educated his generation, and is controversial still. Mill's central propositions are not truisms, they are not at all self-evident. They are statements of a position which has been resisted and rejected by the modern descendants of his most notable contemporaries, Marx, Carlyle, Dostoevsky, Newman, Comte, and they are still assailed because they are still contemporary. The *Essay on Liberty* deals with specific social issues in terms of examples drawn from genuine and disturbing issues of its day, and its principles and conclusions are alive in part because they spring from acute moral crises in a man's life, and thereafter from a life spent in working for concrete causes and taking genuine – and therefore at times dangerous – decisions. Mill looked at the questions that puzzled him directly, and not through spectacles provided by any orthodoxy. His revolt against his father's education, his bold avowal of the values of Coleridge and the Romantics was the liberating act that dashed these spectacles to the ground. From these half-truths, too, he liberated himself in turn, and became a thinker in his own right. For this reason, while Spencer and Comte, Taine and Buckle – even Carlyle and Ruskin, figures who loomed very large in their generation – are fast receding into (or have been swallowed by) the shadows of the past, Mill himself remains real.

One of the symptoms of this kind of three-dimensional, rounded, authentic quality is that we feel sure that we can tell where he would have stood on the issues of our own day. Can anyone doubt what position he would have taken on the Dreyfus case, or the Boer War, or fascism, or communism? Or, for that matter, on Munich, or Suez, or Budapest, or Apartheid, or colonialism, or the Wolfenden report? Can we be so certain with regard to other eminent Victorian moralists? Carlyle or Ruskin or Dickens? or even Kingsley or Wilberforce or Newman? Surely that alone is some evidence of the permanence of the issues with which Mill dealt and the degree of his insight into them.

V

Mill is usually represented as a just and high-souled Victorian schoolmaster, honourable, sensitive, humane, but 'sober, censorious and sad'; something of a goose, something of a prig, a good and noble man, but bleak, sententious, and desiccated; a waxwork among other waxworks in an age now dead and gone and stiff with such effigies. His autobiography – one of the most moving accounts of a human life – modifies this impression. Mill was certainly an intellectual, and was well aware, and not at all ashamed, of this fact. He knew that his main interest lay in general ideas in a society largely distrustful of them: 'the English', he wrote to his friend d'Eichthal, 'invariably mistrust the most evident truths if he who propounds them is suspected of having general ideas'. He was excited by ideas and wanted them to be as interesting as possible. He admired the French for respecting intellectuals as the English did not. He noted that there was a good deal of talk in England about the march of intellect at home, but he remained sceptical. He wondered whether 'our march of intellect be not rather a march towards doing without intellect, and supplying our deficiency in giants by the united effort of the constantly increasing multitude of dwarfs'. The word 'dwarfs', and the fear of smallness, pervades all his writings.

Because he believed in the importance of ideas, he was prepared to change his own if others could convince him of their inadequacy, or when a new vision was revealed to him, as it was by Coleridge or Saint-Simon, or, as he believed, by the transcendent genius of Mrs Taylor. He liked criticism for its own sake. He detested adulation, even praise of his own work. He attacked dogmatism in others and was genuinely free from it himself. Despite the efforts of his father and his mentors, he retained an unusually open mind, and his 'still and cold appearance' and 'the head that reasons as a great steam engine works'[12] were united (to quote his friend Stirling) with a 'warm, upright and really lofty soul' and a touching and pure-hearted readiness to learn from anyone, at any time. He lacked vanity and cared little for his reputation, and therefore did not cling to consistency for its own sake, nor to his own personal dignity, if a human issue was at stake. He was loyal to movements, to causes, and to parties, but could not be prevailed upon to support them at the price of saying what he did not think to be true. A characteristic instance of this is his attitude to religion. His father brought him up in the strictest and narrowest atheist dogma. He rebelled against it. He embraced no recognized faith, but he did not dismiss religion, as the French encyclopaedists or the Benthamites had done, as a tissue of childish fantasies and emotions, comforting illusions, mystical gibberish and deliberate lies. He held that the existence of God was possible, indeed probable, but unproven, but that if God was good he could not be omnipotent, since he permitted evil to exist. He would not hear of a being at once wholly good and omnipotent whose nature defied the canons of human logic, since he rejected belief in mysteries as mere attempts to evade agonizing issues. If he did not understand (this must have happened often), he did not pretend to understand. Although he was prepared to fight for the rights of others to hold a faith detached from logic, he rejected it himself. He revered Christ as the best man who ever lived, and regarded theism as a noble, though to him unintelligible, set of beliefs. He regarded immortality as possible, but rated its probability very low. He was, in fact, a Victorian agnostic who was uncomfortable with atheism and regarded religion as something that was exclusively the individual's own affair. When he was invited to stand for parliament, to which he was duly elected, he declared that he was prepared to answer any questions that the electors of Westminster might choose to put to him, save those on his religious views. This was not cowardice – his behaviour throughout the election was so candid and imprudently fearless, that someone remarked that on Mill's platform God Almighty Himself could not expect to be elected. His reason was that a man had an indefeasible right to keep his private life to himself and to fight for this right, if need be. When, at a later date, his stepdaughter Helen Taylor and others upbraided him for not aligning himself more firmly with the atheists, and accused him of temporizing and shilly-shallying, he remained unshaken. His doubts were his own property: no one was entitled to extort a confession of faith from him, unless it could be shown that his silence harmed others; since this could not be shown, he saw no reason for publicly committing himself. Like Acton after him, he regarded liberty and religious toleration as the indispensable protection of all true religion, and the distinction made by the Church between spiritual and temporal realms as one of the great achievements of Christianity, inasmuch as it had made possible freedom of opinion. This last he valued beyond all things, and he defended Bradlaugh passionately, although, and because, he did not agree with his opinions.

He was the teacher of a generation, of a nation, but still no more than a teacher, not a creator or an innovator. He is known for no lasting discovery or invention. He made scarcely any significant advance in logic or philosophy or economics or political thought. Yet his range, and his capacity for applying ideas to fields in which they would bear fruit was unexampled. He was not original, yet he transformed the structure of the human knowledge of his age.

Because he had an exceptionally honest, open, and civilized mind, which found natural expression in lucid and admirable prose; because he combined an unswerving pursuit of the truth with the belief that its house had many mansions, so that even 'one-eyed men like Bentham might see what men with normal vision would not';[13] because, despite his inhibited emotions and his over-developed intellect, despite his humourless, cerebral, solemn character, his conception of man was deeper, and his vision of

159

history and life wider and less simple than that of his utilitarian predecessors or liberal followers, he has emerged as a major political thinker in our own day. He broke with the pseudo-scientific model, inherited from the classical world and the age of reason, of a determined human nature, endowed at all times, everywhere, with the same unaltering needs, emotions, motives, responding differently only to differences of situation and stimulus, or evolving according to some unaltering pattern. For this he substituted (not altogether consciously) the image of man as creative, incapable of self-completion, and therefore never wholly predictable: fallible, a complex combination of opposites, some reconcilable, others incapable of being resolved or harmonized; unable to cease from his search for truth, happiness, novelty, freedom, but with no guarantee, theological or logical or scientific, of being able to attain them: a free, imperfect being, capable of determining his own destiny in circumstances favourable to the development of his reason and his gifts. He was tormented by the problem of free will, and found no better solution for it than anyone else, although at times he thought he had solved it. He believed that it is neither rational thought, nor domination over nature, but freedom to choose and to experiment that distinguishes men from the rest of nature; of all his ideas it is this view that has ensured his lasting fame.[14] By freedom he meant a condition in which men were not prevented from choosing both the object and the manner of their worship. For him only a society in which this condition was realized could be called fully human. No man deserves commemoration by this Council more than Mill, for it was created to serve an ideal which he regarded as more precious than life itself.

NOTES

1 This Robert Waley Cohen Memorial Lecture, delivered at The Conference Hall, London, on 2 December 1959, was first published by The Council of Christians and Jews, Kingsway Chambers, 162a Strand, London WC2, in the same year.
2 From a tribute to John Stuart Mill by James Bain, quoted in the full and interesting *Life of John Stuart Mill* by Michael St John Packe, (London, Secker & Warburg, 1954), 54.
3 He did not seem to look on socialism, which under the influence of Mrs Taylor he advocated in the *Political Economy* and later, as a danger to individual liberty in the way in which democracy, for example, might be so. This is not the place to examine the very peculiar relationship of Mill's socialist to his individualist convictions. Despite his socialist

professions, none of the socialist leaders of his time – neither Louis Blanc nor Proudhon nor Lassalle nor Herzen – not to speak of Marx, appears to have regarded him even as a fellow traveller. He was to them the very embodiment of a mild reformist liberal or bourgeois radical. Only the Fabians claimed him as an ancestor.

4 Mill, *CW*, 1:51–3.

5 Mill, *On Liberty*, all page references in the text refer to this volume.

6 A. Carlyle, ed., *New Letters of Thomas Carlyle*, 2 vols (London, John Lane, 1904), 2:196.

7 And in the essays on 'Coleridge' and 'Bentham', *CW*, 10.

8 Which in any case he regarded as inevitable and, perhaps, to a vision wider than his own time-bound one, ultimately more just and more generous.

9 Packe, *The Life of John Stuart Mill*, 203.

10 This is the line which divides him from Saint-Simon and Comte, and from H.G. Wells and the technocrats.

11 Packe, *The Life of John Stuart Mill*, 294–5.

12 ibid., 222.

13 He goes on: 'Almost all rich veins of original and striking speculation have been opened by systematic half-thinkers'. 'Bentham', *CW*, 10:94.

14 It will be seen from the general tenor of this essay that I am not in agreement with those who wish to represent Mill as favouring some kind of hegemony of right-minded intellectuals. I do not see how this can be regarded as Mill's considered conclusion; not merely in view of the considerations that I have urged, but of his own warnings against Comtian despotism, which contemplated precisely such a hierarchy. At the same time, he was, in common with a good many other liberals in the nineteenth century both in England and elsewhere, not merely hostile to the influence of uncriticized traditionalism, or the sheer power of inertia, but apprehensive of the rule of the uneducated democratic majority, consequently he tried to insert into his system some guarantees against the vices of uncontrolled democracy, plainly hoping that, at any rate while ignorance and irrationality were still widespread (he was not over-optimistic about the rate of the growth of education), authority would tend to be exercised by the more rational, just, and well-informed persons in the community. It is, however, one thing to say that Mill was nervous of majorities as such, and another to accuse him of authoritarian tendencies, of favouring the rule of a rational élite, whatever the Fabians may or may not have derived from him. He was not responsible for the views of his disciples, particularly of those whom he himself had not chosen and never knew. Mill was the last man to be guilty of advocating what Bakunin, in the course of an attack on Marx, described as *la pédantocratie*, the government by professors, which he regarded as one of the most oppressive of all forms of despotism.

161

JOHN STUART MILL'S ART OF LIVING

Alan Ryan

The commonly accepted view about John Stuart Mill is that he tried to draw a line between the area of morality and the area of law, and hence that what *On Liberty* condemned was legislation on moral matters. Most people – whether critics or supporters of Mill – think that when the Wolfenden Committee declared that 'there must remain a realm of private morality and immorality, which is, in brief and crude terms, not the law's business', they were reiterating Mill's doctrine; though they did not explicitly refer to him. Similarly, when Lord Devlin attacks the committee and denies that there is a realm of private morality and immorality, it is thought that he it tilting at the shade of Mill as well; certainly Devlin thinks so, and in his recent book he fastens the offending view on Mill in no uncertain way. The received view of Mill's case, therefore, is that he held that a man's behaviour might be wicked or wrong or immoral, but that his was no concern of the law unless the wrong or wicked behaviour also harmed other people.

But Mill's principle is of a wider scope than this. *On Liberty* is not an isolated libertarian plea in a utilitarian ethics with which it is largely inconsistent; it is, rather, a working out of the consequences of a social and philosophical doctrine, the other elements of which may be traced in the *System of Logic*, in Mill's essay on Bentham, and in *Utilitarianism*. And the distinction which runs through all these works is not the one which the usual view of Mill finds there; it is not a distinction between law and morality, but between the sort of conduct subject to law-or-morality on the one hand and that which is subject to neither of these but to prudential or aesthetic appraisal on the other. The importance of this distinction for any sensible discussion of the extent to which society ought to control the private lives of its members is enormous.

162

To see that Mill was not doing what he is always said to have been doing, we need only turn to two letters which he wrote to Pasquale Villari in 1858. In these he explained that the subject matter of *On Liberty* was not legal or political freedom, but social, intellectual, psychological, and religious freedom; these forms of freedom were badly lacking in England, where the law was not oppressive, but where public opinion was. And the whole essay reflects precisely this concern. Government and law are rarely mentioned; the tyranny feared is always the tyranny of opinion; in so far as Mill expects the law to be oppressive it is only because he expects public opinion to mould the law in its own image. There is, too, every good reason why Mill should not have discussed at any length the relations of law and morality. To a utilitarian, their relations are in theory simple, whatever practical difficulties they may pose. To say that an action is immoral is, on Mill's account of it, to say that the action will harm persons other than the agent. People live in society in order to protect themselves against actions aimed at harming them, so, if an action is wrong or immoral, then society must stop it. The only question is, how? At the least, the pressure of public opinion should be brought to bear, so that the weight of social disapproval can act as a deterrent and as a punishment to offenders.

If the case requires it, then opinion must be supplemented by the state organized system of punishment involved in the criminal law. The question of when to supplement public opinion by the apparatus of the law is itself to be settled on utilitarian grounds. We have to ask ourselves whether the inconveniences of legislation, police action, judicial procedure, and the rest will be outweighed by the utility of having the action in question more effectively controlled than it would be by public opinion unaided. Thus, for example, it is wrong to break a promise; but we have to calculate in what cases of breach of promise it is right to employ the law. If the good achieved by legal enforcement outweighs the inevitable drawbacks of the law, then the matter is one for the law; if not, then it must remain within the realm of morals alone.

Law and morality thus cover, for utilitarians, the same area of human conduct; they have a similar subject matter and a similar logic; for they both involve general rules which aim at promoting such interpersonal goods as peace, justice, and honesty. And both law and morality are backed by what is supposed to be an impartial sanction. It is only in the nature of the sanction that they differ –

for moral rules have behind them the sanction of public opinion, while laws have behind them the whole organized coercive apparatus of the state. Of course, the difference of sanction is enormously important; and no one would want to deny it – but it is not a *logically* basic distinction in ethics.

The doctrine which emerges from a comparison of what Mill says in several places is crudely this: there is, he says in the *System of Logic*, or at least there might be created, an art of life, a body of directions for our conduct in three branches. These branches are morality, prudence, and aesthetics; and their subject matter, respectively the right, the expedient, and the beautiful or noble.

In each of these branches of the art of life, the aim is to achieve happiness and avoid pain, but in different ways. Morality is concerned with social relations, with dealings with other people. It is concerned largely with rules directing us to abstain from conduct calculated to harm others; thus, as we said, it is aimed at achieving *interpersonal* goods such as peace, justice, and honesty. For this reason, Mill says in the essay on Bentham that morality is essentially concerned with the business side of life, with preserving minimal forbearances. Prudence, by contrast, is concerned with the good of the agent, with his own happiness and misery, not that of other people. The rules of prudence indicate what to do and what to avoid doing if we are to make ourselves happy. Prudence thus aims at private goods, and whatever rules we formulate to promote the good of the agent, these rules are part of prudence.

One important conclusion which Mill draws from this is that there can be no such things as duties to oneself. If the expression means anything, he says, it must mean either prudence or else self-development. Aesthetics seems to involve another sort of appraisal altogether. Whereas morality and prudence both involve calculating the consequences of our behaviour, the first to others, the second to ourselves, aesthetics seems to involve something more akin to perception than to calculation. It is not concerned with the efficacy of means to some good, whether this good be private or inter-personal; rather it is concerned with the quality of the good sought. There are many problems about this sort of appraisal, but the only thing that needs saying now is that it must be very plain that *morality* is distinct from both prudence and aesthetics. The logical form of morality is that of law, not that of prudence or aesthetics. Its subject matter is different from that of prudence, and while it can be that of aesthetics, the two forms of appraisal are very different.

Aesthetics is critical and revisionary; morality is concerned with clearing a space within which aesthetic and personal ideals can flourish, within which people can pursue their own goods. An example will bring out the way the different considerations are to be handled. Suppose a man repays a debt. This has an other-regarding side to it; we ask the moral question 'Did he do what was right?' and we are told yes, he paid back money, fulfilling an obligation and thus contributing to the maintenance of honesty, trust, and so on. It also has a self-regarding aspect, a prudential aspect, for we can ask 'What did he get out of it?' and we may learn that he succeeded in creating a good climate for a larger loan, or else that he had ruined himself in the repayment. And it also has an aesthetic aspect; whether the man is to be regarded as rash, or unfortunate, or brave, we prefer to see him go to his ruin with his head up rather than bemoaning his fate.

This puts a new complexion on Mill's famous principle, stated in *On Liberty*, that the only part of a man's behaviour for which he should be subject to social coercion is that which concerns others without their free and undeceived consent. For what this principle amounts to is a limitation of morality to this sort of behaviour; it is only to this sort of conduct that appraisal in terms of *wrong, immoral,* or *wicked* is appropriate. And, crucially, it is only in the area of this sort of conduct that deterrence and retribution as they operate in morals – that is, social approval and disapproval, the weapons of public opinion – can ever be justified. Where only the agent is involved – where, that is, the other-regarding question cannot be asked, or where others are involved only with their free and undeceived consent – the matter is not a moral one; therefore it cannot be a matter involving punishment.

That this position is a good deal more radical than that of the Wolfenden Committee needs little argument; if, for instance, it is true that homosexuality harms no one beyond the consenting participants, then no sort of punishment is appropriate. The Wolfenden Committee's view that *legal* penalties are out of place is only a special case of the wider judgement. In a well known passage, Mill distinguishes what we can and what we cannot say about a man who drinks too much; he may be said to behave foolishly, his life may be said to be ugly, but he cannot properly be said to be immoral or wicked, even though his life may be uglier than many forms of wickedness are. And this distinction it is that Mill maintains throughout his discussion of fornication, drug-taking, and the rest. The importance of the distinction to Mill is enormous. If we say that an action is wrong, we are committing ourselves to the view that the action is socially harmful, and we are invoking the aid of public opinion in stopping that action.

Mill wants us to see clearly whether we really want to do these two things, and he wants us to ask carefully whether we have any grounds for doing them; if we see that we do not or that we have not, the way is open for that moral outlook which Mill so wanted to encourage. One major component of it is the willingness to make and encourage others to make experiments in living, individual attempts to find new or deeper, or even merely different, sources of happiness in life. The other major component is a finer discrimination in what we do want to say about people's behaviour. Once we rule out coercion, there is room for sympathy, advice, criticism, and exhortation. Mill, indeed, is clear that a good deal more mutual criticism and advice than custom allows would be a thoroughly good thing; what he is against is coercion, and the sort of coercion he is chiefly against is the coercion of public opinion. This coercion, justified where the matter really is a moral one, is simply tyranny where it is not; and Mill's fear was that because of its mildness and unobtrusiveness, the tyranny of public opinion would prove the most deadly of all despotisms.

There are two great merits in Mill's case, which are of continuing importance. Both are connected with clarifying our moral outlook. The first sort of clarity Mill offers us is classificatory; the utilitarian scheme does include and exclude virtually everything which we all want to include and exclude when talking of morals. For example, in the case of lying, it is part of our concept of a lie that a liar should aim at getting another person to do what that other does not want to – namely, believe a known untruth. You logically cannot lie to a man with his free and undeceived consent; if he is undeceived he cannot have been lied to. Equally, in no sense other than a dubious analogical one can a man lie to himself. And over the whole range of such cases as promise-breaking, stealing, and the like, the application of Mill's test is simple enough. If you have my free and undeceived consent to break a promise to me, then you cannot have broken it, but have been released from it. If you have my free and undeceived consent to steal my watch, you cannot have stolen it at all; I must have given it to you. Of course there are problems about when consent is free and undeceived; and of course there are problems about when my actions involve others. But the existence of hard cases in practice is no obstacle to our drawing the line where Mill wants it drawn; indeed, the fact that we recognize the hard cases as such rather suggests that we do habitually make the distinction which Mill wants made, without any great difficulty.

The second sort of clarity which Mill forces on us is a need to be much surer of our facts, since the variety of objections to a given line of conduct which Mill suggests means that we have to see carefully what facts we are to appeal to in our support. The muddles of Devlin and Wolfenden illustrate this well. The Wolfenden Committee is, on Mill's terms, not entitled to talk of 'private immorality' at all; either it can produce facts which show that homosexuality can be reasonably foreseen to cause harm to non-consenting parties, or else it must take the plunge and admit that homosexuality is not wrong or immoral at all; though the committee is at liberty to say it finds homosexuality distasteful, or foolish. The committee's line would have incensed Mill, because it is precisely the sort of view which could remove legal pressures while leaving untouched the greater evil of social prejudice and social coercion. Equally Lord Devlin is caught in the same cleft stick; it is true that he and Mill are in agreement over the fact that there is no such thing as 'private immorality'; but this is cold comfort for Devlin, since the question he is faced with is 'What factual grounds are there for calling this sort of conduct immoral at all?' Mill's case is that the conduct is private in the required sense, and thus not immoral; Devlin's sometimes seems to be that the conduct is immoral and thus cannot be private. But this will not do, for it leaves unanswered the question of what makes the action immoral in the first place. Devlin never answers this question; at one point he appears to argue that whatever people dislike enough is immoral, but – quite apart from the extreme illiberalism of this attitude, from which even Devlin shrinks – this ignores the vital fact that the dislike which people feel is felt just because they suppose the conduct in question to be immoral. Somehow and somewhere the question of what are the facts which make such and such immoral has to be answered. Indeed, Lord Devlin often enough resorts to arguments about the effects of actions on society in the most straightforward utilitarian way. The trouble is that he never sees that these are utilitarian arguments, and hence never asks himself what his evidence is, what facts he is appealing to.

In this unconcern for the facts in the face of sheer indignation,

Devlin is much too like most self-appointed preachers, and most unlike Mill. In the way it brings us constantly to the question 'what are the facts?', a wider acceptance of Mill's utilitarian outlook would do a lot of good to current moral debates.

A RE-READING OF MILL ON LIBERTY

J.C. Rees

I

My aim in this article is to discuss what Mill was trying to do in his essay *On Liberty*. Or, to put it more precisely, to consider whether the commonly accepted version of 'the very simple principle' asserted in the essay is a fair account of Mill's intentions. Before setting out what I take to be the traditional version and giving my reasons for questioning it, we ought to remind ourselves of the general purpose Mill had in publishing his work.

In his *Autobiography* Mill describes the essay as 'a philosophic text-book of a single truth . . . the importance, to man and society, of a large variety in types of character, and of giving full freedom to human nature to expand itself in innumerable and conflicting directions'.[1] The book deals with one of the recurring questions of politics but was written in circumstances which gave that question a new significance. For behind Mill's question – 'What is the nature and extent of the power which society ought to exercise over the individual?' – was his anxiety lest the tendencies which he claimed to see at work in the civilized world would eventually extinguish spontaneity in all the important branches of human conduct. 'Society has now [the manuscript was completed in 1857] fairly got the better of individuality . . . in our times, from the highest class of society down to the lowest, every one lives as under the eye of a hostile and dreaded censorship.' (p. 77)[2] The essay had, therefore, the practical aim of helping to ward off the dangers which the trends of the age seemed to carry with them and, in particular, to counter 'the general tendency of things throughout the world to render mediocrity the ascendant power among mankind'. (p. 81) The work, Mill tells us, was conceived and written as a short essay in 1854.[3] In a letter to Harriet from Rome in January 1855 he wrote:

> On my way here cogitating thereon I came back to an idea we have talked about, and thought that the best thing to write and publish at present would be a volume on Liberty. So many things might be brought into it and nothing seems more to be needed – it is a growing need too, for opinion tends to encroach more and more on liberty, and almost all the projects of social reformers of these days are really liberticide – Comte's particularly so.[4]

But Mill's fears and anxieties go back long before this period. They were clearly expressed in an essay on 'Civilization' published in 1836 and there are definite signs that they were taking root in even earlier years.[5]

One of the tasks Mill set himself in *On Liberty* was to fix a limit 'to the legitimate interference of collective opinion with individual independence' (p. 26). This seemed to him to be at least as important as 'protection against political despotism', for the 'yoke of opinion in England is perhaps heavier, that of the law is lighter, than in most other countries of Europe' (p. 29). The preservation of individuality and variety of character was possible, he believed, if a principle were observed whereby every person was accorded an area of liberty in thought and action. His father and Bentham had argued the case for representative government, but its practical consequences, whether in the United States as revealed by de Tocqueville or experienced in England since the Reform Act, were in his view by no means wholly favourable to liberty.[6] And even more menacing than the now apparent weaknesses of a system of government whose establishment was the great aim of the orthodox Utilitarians were the informal pressures of society that the coming of democracy tended to strengthen and make still more relentless. Progress and the attainment of the truth were, as Mill saw it, the work of a select few; and to promote and safeguard the conditions for the distinctive activity of this *élite* in face of the growing power of the mediocre mass was a result he hoped his essay would help to achieve. Yet to a number who have shared his aspirations the specific principle he offered has always seemed defective. Mill's attachment to liberty has been admired on all sides and the many eloquent and moving passages he dedicates to its virtues have been widely acclaimed as classic utterances on behalf of one of the most cherished of western ideals, but, it has been generally said, the principle he advances for its protection cannot do what is expected of it. My purpose here is to look again at that principle and to discuss whether it has been properly understood by its critics.

II

'The object of this Essay', says Mill, 'is to assert one very simple principle . . . that the sole end for which mankind are warranted, individually or collectively, in interfering with the liberty of action of any of their number is self-protection . . . to prevent harm to others . . . His own good, either physical or moral, is not a sufficient warrant . . . The only part of the conduct of any one, for which he is amenable to society, is that which concerns others. In the part which merely concerns himself, his independence is, of right, absolute' (pp. 30–1). This passage appears in the first chapter of the essay. In the last chapter, where Mill offers some examples of how his principle might be applied in practical cases, he restates

the two maxims which together form the entire doctrine of this Essay . . . first, that the individual is not accountable to society for his actions, in so far as these concern the interests of no person but himself . . . Secondly, that for such actions as are prejudicial to the interests of others, the individual is accountable, and may be subjected either to social or to legal punishment, if society is of opinion that the one or the other is requisite for its protection (p. 108).

A study of the comments on Mill's essay during the century since its publication shows that the principle just stated has been widely criticized because it appears to rest on the possibility of classifying human actions into two categories – actions which concern only the agent and actions that concern others besides the agent. The distinction between these two categories, it has been repeatedly argued, is impossible to sustain. As one of the critics has put it: 'The greater part of English history since his day has been a practical commentary on the fallacy of this distinction. No action, however intimate, is free from social consequences. No human being can say that what he is, still less what he does, affects no one but himself.'[7] The crucial point in this criticism is clearly the supposition that Mill's principle depends for its validity on there being some actions, including some important ones, which are free from social consequences, i.e. that they affect no one but the agent himself.[8] I shall argue that this assumption on the part of the critics is false and that it derives from a failure to observe the form of words which Mill often employs in the text and to take at its full value Mill's firm assertion that actions of the so-called 'self-regarding' variety may frequently affect, even harmfully, persons other than the agent. Before elaborating this claim I want to pass briefly in review the evidence for my contention that the traditional account of Mill's principle makes just this assumption about his classification of human actions.

I begin with a commonly made criticism, drawn from among the first reviews of *On Liberty*. There is no conduct whose impact is confined to the agent, said the *London Review* in 1859, because 'no moral quality is limited in its action to the sphere of its possessor's own history and doings . . . society has an interest, over and above that of mere self-defence, in the conduct of everyone of its members'.[9] Fourteen years later, Fitzjames Stephen, whose *Liberty, Equality, Fraternity* has set the pattern for much of the criticism directed against Mill up to the present time, asserted with characteristic vigour that

> the attempt to distinguish between self-regarding acts and acts which regard others, is like an attempt to distinguish between acts which happen in time and acts which happen in space. Every act happens at some time and in some place, and in like manner every act that we do either does or may affect both ourselves and others . . . the distinction is altogether fallacious and unfounded.[10]

Further, in defence of the attitude of a temperance reformer whom Mill had attacked in *On Liberty*, Stephen remarks:

> It is surely a simple matter of fact that every human creature is deeply interested not only in the conduct, but in the thoughts, feelings, and opinions of millions of persons who stand in no other assignable relation to him than that of being his fellow-creatures. . . . A man would no more be a man if he was alone in the world than a hand would be a hand without the rest of the body.[11]

The view of human relations expressed in this last passage was, of course, shared by the Oxford Idealists and we should expect from them too a decided lack of sympathy with Mill's principle. Thus

Ritchie considers the conception of the individual implied in Mill's doctrine to be abstract and negative, for the individual finds his true self 'not in distinction and separation from others, but in community with them'. 'We may very well doubt', he continues,

> whether any acts, nay, even thoughts, of the individual can, in the strictest sense, be merely self-regarding, and so matters of indifference to other individuals. . . . The more we learn of human society, the more we discover that there are no absolute divisions, but that every atom influences and is influenced by every other. It may be very inexpedient to meddle with particular acts, or it may be practically impossible to do so; but we can lay down no hard and fast line, separating self-regarding acts from acts which affect others.[12]

And Bosanquet: 'every act of mine affects both myself and others. . . . It may safely be said that no demarcation between self-regarding and other-regarding action can possibly hold good.'[13]

Closer to our own day, MacIver in his *Modern State* remarks of Mill's principle:

> This statement has a form which suggests that the full significance of the interdependence of social beings is hardly realized by Mill . . . he thinks of man as in certain categories social, but in others wholly 'individual'. But if we realize that the nature of man is a unity, that in every *aspect* he is a social being at the same time that he is also autonomous and self-legislating, so that his sociality and his individuality cannot belong to two different spheres . . . we can no longer be content with an abstract doctrine of liberty.[14]

In similar vein Sir Ernest Barker says that Mill's assumption of the existence of two different spheres of conduct is open to the criticism that Mill separates the inseparable. 'The conduct of any man', maintains Sir Ernest, 'is a single whole: there can be nothing in it that concerns himself only, and does not concern other men: whatever he is, and whatever he does, affects others and therefore concerns them.'[15] Finally, to conclude with a quotation from one of the best studies of Mill's philosophy that has appeared in recent decades, here is the view of Professor R.P. Anschutz. He is commenting on Mill's principle of self-protection ('the argument for insulation' as Anschutz calls it) and says: 'It is a completely untenable as well as a completely impracticable doctrine. It is quite impossible to distinguish between that part of a person's behaviour which affects himself and that part which also affects others; and there is nothing to be gained by attempting to make the distinction.'[16]

This, then, is the case which has been built up against Mill over the last hundred years. The essential point in the criticism is, as I have said, that Mill wrongly assumes some human actions to be free of social consequences. But if we look carefully at the two passages quoted above (p. 171) where Mill is explicitly stating his principle, it will be noticed that, although in the first case he writes of conduct which 'merely concerns' the agent and of conduct which 'concerns others', he introduces the word 'interests' in the second passage. He says that the individual is to be held accountable only for those actions which 'are prejudicial to the *interests* of others'.[17] Elsewhere in the essay both types of phrase appear, with a number of variations within each type. Thus we find on the one hand: 'what only regards himself', 'conduct which affects only himself', 'which concerns only himself', 'things wherein the individual alone is concerned'; and on the other: 'concern the interests of others', 'affects the interests of no one but himself', 'affect the interests of others', 'damage to the interests of others'. Traditional commentary has assumed that all these expressions were intended to convey the same meaning and that Mill's distinction was simply between actions which affect no one but the agent and actions which affect others. My case in this chapter is that we ought not to gloss over these different modes of expression, that there is an important difference between just 'affecting others' and 'affecting the interests of others', and that there are passages in the essay which lend support to the view that Mill was thinking of 'interests' and not merely 'effects'. As a first step I wish to support my claim that there is a significant difference between saying, on the one hand, that an action affects another person and, on the other, that it affects his interests.

It seems to me quite clear that a person may be affected by another's behaviour without his interests being affected. For example, when we speak of a man's equilibrium not being affected in trying circumstances we are not thinking of his interests. Indeed a man's interests may well be seriously injured without his equilibrium being affected to any marked degree. And even if it were, there would be two things affected, not one. Similarly, if we heard of someone's outlook on life being fundamentally affected by an event such as a religious experience we should not have to conclude that his interests had likewise been affected. True, a religious convert has an interest in religion that he did not have before, but we are not speaking of interests in that sense. My interests in literature can undergo a radical change without anything like business, professional, or property interests being affected to the slightest extent. To bring out the distinction I am trying to make between interests and effects, but with no pretence at offering a definitive account of the nature of interests, one might say that interests – and I do not wish to imply that they are necessarily legal – depend for their existence on social recognition and are closely connected with prevailing standards about the sort of behaviour a man can legitimately expect from others. A claim that something should be recognized as an interest is one we should require to be supported by reasons and one capable of being made the subject of discussion. On the other hand, I could be very seriously affected by the action of another person merely because I had an extraordinarily sensitive nature and no claim to have others respect these tender spots would be recognized as amounting to an interest. How one is affected by a theatrical performance depends partly on one's tastes, but the interests of a businessman would be affected by a tax on business property no matter what his tastes or susceptibilities; just as the interests of a university are affected by a scheme to establish a research institute in the same area (in a common subject of course) whether the university authorities welcome the idea or not. Moreover, 'effects' is a concept applicable to plants and animals as well as human beings, but no one talks about the interests of plants. Crops are affected by fertilizers or drought in much the same way as a certain drug would have an effect on, say, chronic lassitude. And dogs are affected by thunder in the kind of way that I might be affected by the news that my favourite football team had been beaten in the cup final. There are no interests necessarily at stake here, though drought could affect my interests as well as the crops, and gamblers stand to win or lose by a result that could also leave them dismayed. Apart from really trivial actions – which we can ignore in this context – it is probably true that what I do or am like affects other people.[18] Any principle which rested on the assumption that other people are not (or may not be) affected would be open to precisely the objections brought against Mill. But deciding whether interests are affected is another matter and a principle that seeks to limit social interference to cases where interests are involved cannot be attacked because it fails to recognize the truth that 'every atom influences and is influenced by every other' or to realize that 'the nature of man is a unity'.

It might be objected at this stage that Mill does not consistently adhere to the term 'interests' and that one is not entitled to assume from its appearance in some passages, coupled with the employment of such phrases as 'conduct which concerns only himself', that there is one unambiguous doctrine running through the entire essay. Our objector might well concede the distinction between a principle based on interests and one based on mere effects, but he feels we are not justified in attempting to produce a coherent theory when, from the variety of the terms used in the relevant passages, there is clearly not one there to extract. My answer to this objection, for the moment at least (whether one can find a single consistent principle running through the whole work I discuss below) is that if Mill is really trying to maintain two (possibly more) principles, and moves from one to the other at different points of the essay without really knowing what he is doing and hence with no warning to his readers of what he is about, then to recognize this fact is at least to notice something which commentators on Mill have, so far as I know, failed to discern in the past. But it need not necessarily follow that because Mill uses phrases like 'conduct which concerns only himself' along with 'conduct which affects the interests of no persons besides himself' this must be regarded as conclusive evidence of an unwitting affirmation of two distinct and potentially incompatible principles. For though the word 'concerns' has sometimes no more force than 'has reference to' or 'affects', with no implication that interests are being referred to or affected, it can also mean 'is of importance to' and could in some contexts carry with it the suggestion that interests are involved. Thus, when Mill says that social control is permissible only in cases when one's conduct 'concerns others' we are not compelled to assume that he means actions which just have 'effects' on others. Hence it may well be that the ambiguity of the word 'concerns' is responsible for concealing a coherent theory based on 'interests' rather than 'effects' and that we can so interpret the passages where the term 'interests' is not specifically used as to yield a single consistent principle.

However that may be, it should be observed that there are statements in the essay suggesting that Mill was quite aware of the manner in which individuals are constantly affecting one another. And so forthright are they that one wonders how it ever came to be thought of Mill that he wished to declare a whole area of human behaviour 'self-regarding' because the actions so named had no 'effects' on others (as opposed to 'affecting their interests'). Thus in the fourth chapter of the essay Mill discusses a possible objection to his principle in these terms:

> How (it may be asked) can any part of the conduct of a member of society be a matter of indifference to the other members? No person is an entirely isolated being; it is impossible for a person to do anything seriously or permanently hurtful to himself, without mischief reaching at least to his near connections, and often far beyond them. . . .
> (p. 95)

And Mill concedes to this objection 'that the mischief which a person does to himself may *seriously affect*, both through their sympathies and their interests, those nearly connected with him and, in a minor degree, society at large' (p. 96, my italics). But he goes on to insist that only when conduct of this sort (i.e. conduct affecting others) violates 'a distinct and assignable obligation to any other person or persons' is 'the case taken out of the self-regarding class, and becomes amenable to moral disapprobation' (p. 96). A little farther on in the same chapter Mill speaks of a person preventing himself 'by conduct purely self-regarding, from the performance of some definite duty incumbent on him to the public' and thus being guilty of a social offence, but where the conduct 'neither violates any specific duty to the public, nor occasions perceptible hurt to any assignable individual except himself; the inconvenience is one which society can afford to bear, for the sake of the greater good of human freedom' (p. 97). It is surely obvious that Mill would be contradicting himself here in the most flagrant manner if we were to interpret 'purely self-regarding' to mean those actions which have no impact (i.e. no 'effects') on other members of society. And the case against this interpretation becomes even more conclusive if we consider Mill's remarks in the opening chapter where he is elaborating the central principle of the essay. He writes:

> there is a sphere of action in which society, as distinguished from the individual, has if any, only an indirect interest; comprehending all that portion of a person's life and conduct which affects only himself . . . when I say only himself, I

mean directly, and in the first instance; for whatever affects himself, may affect others through himself. . . . (pp. 32–3).

Further, in the fourth chapter, Mill talks of the 'self-regarding deficiencies' which a person may manifest and which 'render him necessarily and properly a subject of distaste, or, in extreme cases, even of contempt'. For vices of this kind, he says, a man may 'suffer very severe penalties at the hands of others for faults which directly concern only himself' (p. 92). Here, then, is a clear affirmation that what he calls, perhaps misleadingly, 'self-regarding conduct' can have effects on others. Even to the extent that those affected can retaliate with '*very severe penalties*'!

Mill's critics, Fitzjames Stephen among them, have wondered how the division of human conduct into two spheres could be sustained if self-regarding actions might suffer severe penalties at the hands of others. Mill attempted to maintain the distinction, which is, of course, crucial for the viability of his principle, in these words:

> the inconveniences which are strictly inseparable from the unfavourable judgment of others, are the only ones to which a person should ever be subjected for that portion of his conduct and character which concerns his own good, but which does not affect the interests of others in their relations with him. Acts injurious to others require a totally different treatment . . . these are fit objects of moral reprobation, and, in grave cases, of moral retribution and punishment (p. 93).

And as if to meet the objections of the sceptical Stephen, who could not see how 'inconveniences strictly inseparable from the unfavourable judgement of others' could be differentiated from the 'moral retribution' to be visited when other people's interests were harmed, Mill went on to show why this distinction was not merely nominal, in his eyes at least. In the former case the offender incurs a loss of consideration by reason of his imprudence or lack of dignity, whereas in the latter reprobation is due to him 'for an offence against the rights of others' (p. 94). And, claims Mill, people will react differently if the conduct of which they disapprove is such that they think that they have a right to control the agent. Whether Mill makes his point or not I do not wish to discuss further, but the words 'for an offence against the *rights* of others' raise a very important question and seem to introduce a new

178

element into the principle. Nor is this the sole occasion when 'rights' are mentioned (pp. 78, 93 my italics). In the same chapter from which I have just been quoting, specifically devoted to discussing 'the limits to the authority of society over the individual', and therefore concerned to elaborate and give more detailed consideration to the principle mentioned and briefly treated in the opening chapter – it is in this fourth chapter that we should, I think, look for pointers to Mill's intentions – Mill attempts to demarcate the area of conduct for which we are to be made responsible to society. 'This conduct', he says, 'consists in not injuring the interests of one another; or rather certain interests which, either by express legal provision or by tacit understanding, ought to be considered as *rights* (p. 90, my italics). Nor is this the complete extent of social control, for conduct may harm others 'without going to the length of violating any of their *constituted rights*'. In those cases punishment is inflicted by opinion rather than the law. Then, to sum up, Mill adds: 'As soon as any part of a person's conduct affects prejudicially the interests of others, society has jurisdiction over it', but no such question can arise 'when a person's conduct affects the interests of no persons besides himself. . . . (p. 90, my italics).

The paragraph from which these extracts have been taken, coming as it does at a crucial stage in Mill's argument, is of some significance for the interpretation of his leading principle. It serves, incidentally, as further proof of my claim that it is 'interests' rather than 'effects' with which Mill is concerned. But its main significance for us at this stage is the appearance in it of the term 'rights' and the relationship Mill seems to suppose that term to have to the idea of 'interests'. From Mill's wording it is certain that the rights he has in mind are legal rights ('constituted rights'), for he envisages the law, rather than opinion, protecting some interests and these interests are then to be considered as rights. Other interests will not receive legal protection, though Mill does not exclude the possibility that these might be regarded as rights, though not legal ('constituted') rights. Certainly Mill is not saying that rights and interests are the same things, synonymous terms (and of course they are not), but he does seem to imply that they are very closely related to each other. It would be consistent with what he says here to suppose that when a person can be thought to have interests he is thereby possessed of a right, though not necessarily a right to the unqualified protection of his interests; perhaps only a right to have his interests taken into account. Moreover, by linking interests to rights in this way Mill leaves us with no excuse for confusing the notions of 'interests' and 'effects', which must now be seen as belonging to quite different categories. It may be true that because of the element of vagueness attaching to rights and interests (i.e. as to what a man may legitimately, I do not mean *legally*, account his rights or interests) the concepts would be much more difficult to operate as part of a principle of liberty than the relatively simple notion of effects, but that ought not to blind us to the difference it makes to a principle to have the one rather than the other type of concept as a component.

III

The case I have been trying to make out is that Mill's principle of self-protection rests on a division of conduct into actions which either do or do not affect the interests of other persons rather than on what has generally been supposed to have been the division, namely, into conduct having or not having effects on others. This interpretation does not rely on the evidence of only one or two isolated passages where the word 'interests' appears. In fact the word appears at least fifteen times in the course of the essay and some of the passages where it is used are of the greatest importance in assessing Mill's intentions (pp. 31 [twice], 32, 78, 90 [4 times], 93, 96, 101, 108 [4 times]). Furthermore, there is also the evidence I have already cited which shows how freely Mill admitted that what have commonly been thought of as literally self-regarding actions did have their effects on other persons. But having said that, I would be seriously misleading the reader if I failed to mention a number of difficulties which stand in the way of this interpretation or at least suggest that Mill was not always clear in his own mind as to what he wanted to say. The first difficulty arises out of a passage previously quoted in another context:

> there is a sphere of action in which society, as distinguished from the individual, has, if any, only an indirect interest; comprehending all that portion of a person's life and conduct which affects only himself. . . . When I say only himself, I mean *directly, and in the first instance*; for whatever affects himself, may affect others through himself. . . . (pp. 32–3, my italics).

And we find phrases similar to the one italicized here in other parts of the essay; for example, 'things which do not *primarily* concern others' and 'the part of life in which it is *chiefly* the individual that is interested . . . [as opposed to] the part which *chiefly* interests society' (pp. 73, 90).[19] This seems to me a difficulty because if we are to take this passage seriously (and the repetition of like phrases elsewhere suggests it is not merely a case of careless writing) we should, on the account I have been giving, have to say that when Mill writes here of 'conduct which affects only himself' he means to say 'conduct which affects only his own interests'.[20] Further, since what affects my interests may also affect the interests of others, we should have to allow that 'self-regarding' conduct could affect the interests of others, though not 'directly' or 'primarily'. Hence the distinction Mill was attempting to make in his use of the self-regarding and other-regarding categories would seem to resolve itself into a division between (i) actions which primarily affect the interests of the agent but may affect the interests of others too, and (ii) actions which primarily affect the interests of others, though the agent's own interests may also be involved. It requires little imagination to foresee the immense complications that would be bound to arise in the application of such a formula. Nothing could be less appropriately described as a 'very simple principle' – Mill's own characterization in his opening chapter. Yet we should have to interpret these passages in some such manner or else admit, which is quite possible, that Mill falls occasionally into the language of 'effects', without realizing that he thereby allows a second principle to peep through from time to time while adhering mainly to a doctrine based on 'interests'.

IV

Assuming, then, that Mill's doctrine involves the idea of 'interests' rather than 'effects', is it, interpreted thus, a useful working principle of liberty in the way that the traditional version is patently not? The revised version would read something like this: 'Social control of individual actions ought to be exercised only in cases where the interests of others are either threatened or actually affected.'[21] But how to decide when interests are affected? What are interests? Is there any commonly accepted criterion, or set of criteria, of an interest? Mill's principle, as reformulated, must inevitably provoke questions like these and its value will obviously depend on the answers to be given to them. They cannot be fully treated here and all I shall attempt are some preliminary and tentative remarks.

As it is commonly used, the concept of 'interests' is an elusive one. There is no precise and generally acceptable definition. As Mr Plamenatz observed in this journal, the idea of 'interest', compared with notions like 'right' or 'duty', is extremely vague.[22] But there are many important concepts in our language which evade exact description and they remain none the less indispensable. Failure to bring the notion within the confines of a neat definition ought not to be a sufficient reason for rejecting out of hand a theory to which the concept is central. Moreover, there are sociologists and jurists for whom the term occupies an important place in their theories. MacIver, for example, conceives human activity through the two concepts 'interest' and 'will'. There is, he says, 'no will without an interest and no interest apart from a will'. And by an interest he means 'some object which determines activity', though it is more than mere desire; it has 'a certain permanence and stability'.[23] Another definition of interest he offers is, 'the object of consciousness . . . anything, material or immaterial, factual or conceptual, to which we devote our attention'.[24] Roscoe Pound, too, employs the word with the same kind of wide meaning. For him an interest is a *de facto* claim and he draws up a comprehensive classification of interests which covers a vast field, ranging from individual claims to privacy to the social interest in free science and cultural progress. Among other writers the term is confined to certain kinds of consciousness or a particular class of attitudes such as, for example, those based on needs; and an appropriate list is provided of the bodily and spiritual needs which are to count for this purpose.[25] How are these uses of the word related to the normal sense of the term? Indeed, is it possible to identify an 'ordinary' use of the word? There would seem to be some grounds for saying that in a normal context an interest should not be construed as just a claim, far less any sort of claim. Rather it seems to be the condition in which a person's claim to, or title to, or share in something is recognized as valid by others, or at least is regarded as worthy of consideration. That is to say, there is an objective element about it which precludes any fanciful demand from being an interest. For interests are things we would generally look upon as deserving protection, to be prejudicially affected only by advantages likely to accrue in another direction. Certainly we feel that they ought not to be ignored even if there are compelling reasons for subordinating them to what we think are more important considerations. Interests, then, are not just arbitrary wishes, fleeting fancies, or capricious demands, though some of them may well have developed from forms to which these terms might have been particularly apposite at the time.

Mill does not say much to indicate how he understood the notion of interest, but there is nothing in the essay to suggest that he uses the term in any exceptional manner. There is a passage, however, which points to some of the problems inseparably connected with the idea of interests. The secretary of an association formed to secure prohibition had claimed a right to be protected from the consequences of the liquor trade which, he argued,

> destroys my primary right of security, by constantly creating and stimulating social disorder . . . It impedes my right to free moral and intellectual development, by surrounding my path with dangers, and by weakening and demoralising society, from which I have a right to claim mutual aid and intercourse. (p. 104)

Mill repudiates with indignation such a sweeping claim, amounting, as he saw it, to 'the absolute social right of every individual, that every other individual shall act in every respect exactly as he ought' and conferring on everyone 'a vested interest in each other's moral, intellectual, and even physical perfection' (p. 104). Mill and the prohibitionist are disputing what may legitimately be claimed as rights and what is to count as an injury to a person's interests. According to the standards prevailing in Mill's day, and certainly by those current in our own time, the secretary's claims appear ludicrously excessive and there would be no point in taking his case seriously. But what is of importance is the very fact of disagreement as to what a man may hold to be his interests. The prohibitionist could have submitted the relatively modest claim that a man's interests are prejudicially affected by the noisy behaviour of groups of people gathering outside a public house adjoining, or close to, his home. If the noise became such a nuisance as to lower the value of the property it could not be denied that interests had been affected. But apart from depreciation of value, has a man's interest been adversely affected by the mere fact of disturbance of his privacy? He could be the tenant of the house and suffer no personal pecuniary loss, yet he might find the behaviour of the publican's clients extremely annoying and might set a high monetary value on its cessation. Is it part of a man's interests to be free from interference of this sort? From the noise of the radio in his neighbour's flat or from the machines on the airfield near his house? If we are going to say 'no' to the claim that interests are affected by interference such as noise, as opposed to monetary loss caused by noise, then this would seem to prevent Mill's principle from operating in spheres in which he clearly wanted it to work. But it is obvious that people can differ about what are to be regarded as interests, since standards and values enter into what will be recognized as interests (or what will *not* be recognized) at any given time in a way that they do not in the case of 'effects'.[26] Consequently, whether one takes a wide or narrow view of interests, the principle of self-protection must necessarily harbour value-ingredients which will inevitably render its use a controversial operation. That a drug affects a certain disease is a strictly empirical matter. There are objective procedures for tracing its 'effects'. It is true that there are also cases when it would be a relatively simple matter to decide if my interests have been affected: legal interests, for example. But there are also occasions when, because standards differ, people will disagree about what their interests are. And this is likely to make a principle based on 'interests' rather than 'effects' difficult to apply in many situations. For not only is the concept 'interest' in itself vague: what are to count as interests, even supposing there were a commonly accepted definition, would be an open question in an indeterminate number of cases. Had Mill formulated his principle in terms of rights rather than interests he would have met the same difficulty precisely because what a man's rights are is a question which can be reasonably answered in more than one way.

Mill's principle raises yet another problem. Social interference, he says, is justifiable only when the interests of others are affected but, he adds, 'it must by no means be supposed, because damage, or probability of damage, to the interests of others, can alone justify the interference of society, that therefore it always does justify such interference' (p. 108). Evidently the principle is not intended to absolve us from deciding cases on their merits even when interests have actually been affected. We should have to weigh up the advantages and disadvantages of social interference on each occasion. As Mill puts it: 'the question whether the general welfare will or will not be promoted by interfering with [another person's conduct], becomes open to discussion' (p. 90). One of the examples he gives is the unsuccessful candidate in a competitive examination (pp. 108–9). Others have gained at his expense, but no one would have it otherwise. A recent example would be the publicity given to statements warning of the harmful effects of heavy smoking. No one would wish to suppress information about the relation between smoking and lung cancer merely because it affected the interests of the tobacco firms. However, says Mill, in the case of conduct which affects no person's interests but one's own there can be no question of permitting social control and restraint: 'in all such cases, there should be perfect freedom, legal and social, to do the action and stand the consequences' (p. 90). So the principle provides us with a clear directive only when we can be sure that other people's interests are *not* involved; where interests *are* affected we are left with a margin of discretion and are advised to consider whether the general welfare is or is not likely to be promoted by interference in each particular instance. Hence the range of matters covered by the 'automatic' application of the rule is limited to those occasions on which it can be said that no one's interests have been injured. And it seems to be assumed that the question of interests being injured or not is one that can be readily determined.

It would be uncharitable to reject Mill's principle out of hand merely because it fails to provide an automatic and definite solution in an extensive range of cases (i.e. actions which *do* affect the interests of others). For how many of the principles we constantly wield in everyday life supply us with quick and certain answers? From Mill's point of view the important thing was to check the growing tendency to interfere in cases where intervention should be totally banned and for this purpose what had to be done was to demarcate the area of non-intervention from that in which a prima facie right to control could only be overridden by an appeal to the 'general welfare'. We have seen that with all its indefiniteness Mill's principle is emphatic on one point, namely, that when the interests of others have *not* been affected society should not intervene. But even here a serious doubt emerges. Are there not some actions we should want to control or prohibit which do not seem to injure the interests of others? Take the case of obscenity. It may be that some acts and some kinds of publications which the present law in the United Kingdom prohibits would be permitted in a more enlightened society, but there are certainly many which are, and ought to continue to be, prevented. Mill, too, seems to take this view. He refers to 'offences against decency', acts which, when done publicly, violate good manners, and places them 'within the category of offences against others' and therefore to be prohibited. But he remarks that offences of this nature 'are only connected

185

indirectly with our subject' (p. 112). Why this should be so he does not explain and it is difficult to see what reasons he could have for saying it. Perhaps he realized that to prohibit offences against decency on the ground that they caused harm to other people's interests would involve a dangerous extension of the conception of 'interests'. For whose interests are threatened or injured by the appearance of obscene publications (or the sale of opium, to take an example from a related field)? The interests of those who concern themselves with public morality? Or the social interest in maintaining standards of public decency? But if we are allowed to bring in considerations of this sort, how could Mill have maintained his opposition to a prohibition on the eating of pork in a predominantly Muslim country?[27] Measures against the dropping of litter or the emission of black smoke from chimneys in specified areas are taken in order to protect the *public interest*, not because they affect the interests of particular persons. That Mill recognized the claims of the general interest is clear enough from his discussion of the case of the person who instigates or counsels others to do acts which if done of one's own free and unaided will would be 'blameable' but not subject to social penalties because 'the evil directly resulting falls wholly on the agent'. On the one hand, argues Mill, people must be allowed 'to consult with one another . . . to exchange opinions, and give and receive suggestions', but the question becomes 'doubtful only when the instigator derives a personal benefit from his advice' and is gainfully occupied in promoting 'what society and the State consider to be an evil'; for we would then be faced with a class of persons having an interest 'opposed to what is considered as the public weal'. Mill has in mind such people as the pimp and the keeper of a gambling house. He fails to come to a definite conclusion about the justifiability of prohibiting these activities, remarking that 'there are arguments on both sides' (pp. 112–14). What is interesting in Mill's discussion here is – apart from the confirmation that his principle can yield no clear directive in questions of this kind – his appeal to 'the public weal' as a factor we have to take into account before deciding on the legitimacy of social control. Does he intend that we should classify actions as being harmful to the interests of others if it could be shown that they are contrary to 'the public weal'? We are thus led back to the problem of how widely (or narrowly) we are to construe the notion of interests. Are we to interpret interests so narrowly as to exclude the public interest or so widely as to involve consideration of the general interest and social morality? On the former interpretation we should find ourselves unable to prohibit activity we should want to prohibit; on the latter we should be able to prohibit actions that Mill would certainly wish to be left unrestrained. And if standards and values enter into what we conceive to be a man's interests even in a restricted sense of the term, *a fortiori* they will shape what we take the public interest to require.

NOTES

1 *CW*, 1:259.
2 Mill, *On Liberty*, all page references in the text are to this volume.
3 *CW*, 1:249.
4 F.A. Hayek, *John Stuart Mill and Harriet Taylor* (London, Routledge & Kegan Paul, 1951), 216.
5 Mill, 'Civilization', *CW*, 18:117–49. See also Mill's article on 'Genius' (1832), *CW*, 1:327–41; and my article 'A phase in the development of Mill's ideas on liberty', *Political Studies* 6 (1958), 33–44.
6 Before the publication of the first part of Tocqueville's work in 1835 the American Unitarian preacher and writer William Ellery Channing had uttered warnings similar to Tocqueville's at a number of points. Channing's writings were known in England and there were reviews of some of them in the *Edinburgh Review* and the *Westminster Review* in 1829 and 1830. I argued in a previous article in this journal (February 1958) that Mill was influenced by Channing's views. Apart from the 'Remarks on the formation of associations', which Mill certainly knew, there is the election sermon of 1830. The latter was reprinted in a two-volume edition of Channing's works published in Britain in 1835 (see vol. 2:255). One or two passages are worth quoting. 'The advantages of civilisation have their peril. In such a state of society, opinion and law impose salutary restraint, and produce general order and security. But the power of opinion grows into a despotism, which, more than all things, represses original and free thought, subverts individuality of character, reduces the community to a spiritless monotony, and chills the love of perfection' (268). 'An espionage of bigotry may as effectually close our lips and chill our hearts, as an armed and hundred-eyed police' (271). 'Our great error as a people, is, that we put an idolatrous trust in free institutions; as if these, by some major power, must secure our rights, however we enslave ourselves to evil passions. We need to learn that forms of liberty are not its essence; that whilst the letter of a free constitution is preserved, its spirit may be lost; that even its wisest provisions and most guarded powers may be made weapons of tyranny. In a country called free, a majority may become a faction, and a proscribed minority may be insulted, robbed, and oppressed. Under elective governments, a dominant party may become as truly a usurper, and as treasonably conspire against the state, as an individual who forces his way by arms to the throne' (278).

7 Leading article in *The Times Literary Supplement*, 10 July 1948. Reprinted as part of a pamphlet, *Western Values*, published by *The Times*.

8 'Including some important ones' is necessary here in order to prevent the issue from being trivialized. When Mill's critics say that no action is free from social consequences they must be assumed to be ignoring many petty acts which are obviously free from social effects, or else they are mistaken in refusing to admit their existence. For example, if I shave in a well-lit room before a mirror that reflects the face with uniform clarity and I can, in these conditions, shave equally well no matter which side I begin to shave, then starting with the left or the right side is a matter which cannot be considered to have any effects on other persons. Hence it is of no concern to society how I, or anyone else, begins to shave each morning. The debate between Mill and his critics clearly does not hinge on trivial acts of this kind.

9 Vol. 13, 274.

10 James Fitzjames Stephen, *Liberty, Equality, Fraternity*, 2nd edn (London, Smith & Elder, 1874), x.

11 op. cit., 1st edn (1873), 128. Mill's remarks appear on pp. 103–4 of *On Liberty*.

12 D.G. Ritchie, *The Principles of State Interference* (London: S. Sonnenschein & Co., 1891), 96–98.

13 Bernard Bosanquet, *Philosophical Theory of the State* (New York: Macmillan & Co., Ltd., 1920), 60. Writing about the same time, Frederic Harrison (*Tennyson, Ruskin, Mill*, London: Macmillan and Co., Ltd., 1899) states: 'The attempt to distinguish between conduct which concerns oneself, and conduct that may remotely concern others, is quite fallacious. No distinction can be drawn, for human acts are organically inseparable' (300). See also F.C. Montague's *The Limits of Individual Liberty* (London: Revingtons, 1885), 185–88: Mill's distinction, says Montague, is an offshoot of the doctrine of the social contract and 'is impossible to those who look upon man as receiving from society his whole character and his whole endowment, and as reacting upon society at every moment of his life.'

14 R.M. MacIver, *The Modern State* (Oxford: Oxford University Press, 1926), 457–9.

15 Ernest Barker, *Principles of Social and Political Theory* (Oxford: The Clarendon Press, 1951), 217.

16 R.P. Anschutz, *The Philosophy of J.S. Mill* (Oxford: Clarendon Press, 1953), 48.

17 My italics.

18 See n. 8.

19 It should be noted, however, that 'primarily' and 'chiefly' are not equivalent to 'directly' or 'in the first instance'.

20 In the first draft of this article the words 'to say' did not appear. I have inserted them in response to a remark made by Mr J.M. Brown in some very valuable comments he kindly sent me on the draft. Mr Brown pointed out that to allow 'conduct which affects only himself' to mean 'conduct which affects only his own interests' would undermine the distinction I have sought to make between these two types of statement.

21 I am leaving out the complications connected with 'primarily', 'chiefly', and 'directly'.
22 *Political Studies* 2 (1954), 3.
23 R.M. MacIver, *Community*, 3rd edn (London: Macmillan & Co., Ltd., 1931), 98–101.
24 R.M. MacIver, *Society* (New York: Farrar & Rinehart, Inc., 1937), 20–1.
25 Alf Ross, *On Law and Justice* (London: Stevens, 1958), 358–9.
26 And even if it came to be accepted that a man's interests were affected by the noisy interruption of his privacy there is still the question of whether these interests should be protected against other claims, such as, for example, freedom to converse outside public houses, the demand for air travel, or the desire to listen to music.
27 This is one of Mill's examples (pp. 99–100). 'There are few acts which Christians and Europeans regard with more unaffected disgust than Mussulmans regard this particular mode of satisfying hunger,' says Mill. He goes on to argue that the only good reason for condemning an attempt to ban the eating of pork in a country where the Mussulmans were a majority would be 'that with the personal tastes and self-regarding concerns of individuals the public has no business to interfere.'

MILL'S CONCEPTION
OF HAPPINESS AND
THE THEORY OF
INDIVIDUALITY

John Gray

INDIVIDUALITY, HAPPINESS, AND
THE HIGHER PLEASURES

Mill's Doctrine of Liberty is supported by a view of human happiness which in turn depends on his conception of human nature. Evident in both *On Liberty* and *Utilitarianism* is Mill's belief that the forms of happiness which are most distinctively human are unachievable except against a background of autonomy and security. Human happiness in its fullest expression presupposes a social order in which the vital interests are reliably protected and in which, also, a certain level of cultural and moral development has been generally achieved. I want further to argue that there is an important and largely neglected link between the theory of the higher pleasures in *Utilitarianism* and the account of individuality given in the third chapter of *On Liberty*. The link is found in the idea of autonomous choice which is a necessary ingredient of any higher pleasure and of any form of life or activity expressive of individuality. I want to claim, in fact, that the doctrine of the higher pleasures is not only not the absurdity it has often been represented as, but also a component of the Doctrine of Liberty. According to Mill's theory of qualitative hedonism, the higher pleasures are found in forms of life and activity whose content is distinctive and peculiar in each case, but which necessarily involve the exercise of generically human power of autonomous thought and action. It is these forms of life, distinctively human but peculiar in each case, that Mill sees as expressing individuality and as being open to all only in a society in which the Principle of Liberty is respected and enforced.

Having sketched these links in the Doctrine of Liberty, we are left with a number of puzzles. We need to know how autonomous choice connects in Mill's theory with the development of individuality and the achievement of the higher pleasures, and only then can we command a view of the ways in which the theory of the higher pleasures supports the Doctrine of Liberty. Our task is not an easy one for a number of reasons. Despite his inclination to self-criticism, Mill was rarely explicit about the basic notions deployed in his arguments, and it is rare to come across any formal definition of the terms he employs. Further, 'autonomy' is not a term he employs himself, and I need to support my claim that a conception of autonomous choice is, in fact, central to the argument of *On Liberty*. It is unavoidable that I will use terms and distinctions that would have seemed foreign to Mill, and inevitable that my interpretation must be in the nature of a frankly conjectural reconstruction rather than a literal rendition of Mill's argument. Nevertheless, though it will involve imposing on Mill's writings a terminology that would be unfamiliar to him, I shall claim that it reflects and expresses Mill's underlying commitments and concerns better than any other we have currently at our disposal. The test of its efficacy can only be in whether it yields a plausible and coherent view of Mill's argument. How, then, does Mill's conception of happiness support the Doctrine of Liberty?

We can begin to sort this out if we acknowledge the abstractness and complexity of Mill's conception of happiness. For all his references to pleasure and the absence of pain, Mill never endorsed the primitive view that pleasure is a sort of sensation that accompanies our actions. Mill's departures from Benthamite utilitarianism were in part motivated by an awareness of the inadequacies of the moral psychology of classical utilitarianism. While he continues to adhere to a belief in the uniformity of human nature (in that he never abandons the belief that the way to render human actions intelligible and to explain them is to subsume them under some law-like principles), he breaks with the Enlightenment belief in its constancy. Though he affirms that a science of ethology (the study of the laws of formation of character) will one day ascertain the laws of mind, he goes further than Hume, who acknowledged that variable customs and institutions alter men's motives, in ascribing to human nature a potentiality for unpredictable mutation and for

191

self-transformation. His conception of human nature and his view of happiness accordingly have an ineradicable developmental and historical dimension. His conception of happiness has this historical dimension in that Mill affirms that certain general cultural achievements are indispensable before the fullest happiness becomes achievable by many men. It has a developmental aspect, also, inasmuch as Mill was committed to a view of moral development and personal growth as having several distinct phases. These matters are sketchily treated in Mill, but it is not fanciful to discern such conceptions in his writings. How then does Mill suggest we conceive of human happiness?

Mill's conception of happiness is hierarchical and pluralistic in that it decomposes happiness into the projects, attachments and ideals expressed in an indefinitely large set of happy human lives. If we treat Mill's distinction between the higher and lower pleasures as being between different kinds of activity or forms of life rather than between states of mind, we can see that, though he is far from supposing that the higher pleasures will be the same for all men, he does think they have the common feature of being available only to men who have developed their distinctively human capacity for autonomous thought and action. Mills' view is not, indeed, that highly autonomous men are bound to be happy, but rather that autonomous thought and action is a necessary feature of the life of a man who enjoys the higher pleasures. What more is involved in autonomy, however, than choice-making and an imaginative awareness of alternative forms of life-activity?

Before I attempt to answer that difficult question, it may be worth looking in greater detail at the connections I have postulated between the argument of *On Liberty* and the much-abused doctrine of the higher pleasures in *Utilitarianism*. First, what is the relation between the notion of autonomous choice (which, as I shall argue, is central to the idea of a free man as it is elaborated in *On Liberty*) and the higher pleasures of *Utilitarianism*? Is the connection between autonomous choice and the higher pleasures criterial, or is it merely evidential? If what a man chooses autonomously is the criterion for what is a higher pleasure for him, then he cannot be mistaken as to what are his higher pleasures so long as his choices are autonomous, and, if the pattern of his autonomous choices changes, then so must the content of his higher pleasures. If, on the other hand, the connection between the higher pleasures and autonomous choices is that the latter afford evidence for the content of the former, we need some guidance as to the criteria for the higher pleasures.

I want to argue that this distinction between a criterial and an evidential view of the relations between autonomy and the higher pleasures fails to capture the spirit of Mill's view of the matter. There can be no doubt that Mill does take choice-making to be itself a necessary ingredient of happiness and of any higher pleasure: it is a necessary condition of a pleasure being a higher pleasure that it consist in activities that have been chosen after experience of an appropriate range of alternatives. But the sufficient condition of a pleasure's being a higher pleasure is that it express the individual nature of the man whose pleasure it is, and this, for the man himself as for others, is a matter of discovery and not of choice. Mill's position here is a complex one. On the one hand, like Aristotle, he affirmed that men were the makers of their own characters. On the other hand, there is no doubt that Mill held to the Romantic belief that each has a quiddity or essence which awaits his discovery and which, if he is lucky, he may express in any one of a small number of styles of life. Mill seems, in his complex view, to be treating choice-making as itself partially constitutive of a happy human life and as instrumental to it. How are these different accounts of the role of autonomous choice-making in human happiness brought together in Mill's theory of individuality?

Another question suggests itself. Inasmuch as Mill put autonomous choice at the heart of the higher pleasures and of those forms of individuality or self-development in which the higher pleasures are found, and inasmuch as he denied that there can be a duty to develop oneself, it is clear that the higher pleasures are to be appraised by aesthetic and prudential rather than by moral standards. Moral life may contain higher pleasures, no doubt, but the place of morality is to protect and permit the higher pleasures, not to demand them. Part of the rationale of adopting the Principle of Liberty is that an open space in which the higher pleasures may flourish is thereby guaranteed. But what if men do not converge on the higher pleasures: suppose, after due thought and experiment, they come to prefer forms of life and activity in which autonomous choice is an insignificant ingredient – what then? Does the Doctrine of Liberty presuppose that the condition of freedom is irreversible and the human preference for the higher pleasures unshakeable?

AUTONOMY, AUTHENTICITY, AND CHOICE-MAKING

In order to answer these questions, we need to look more closely at what is comprehended in the notion of autonomy. We may begin our examination by recalling the conception of freedom as self-determination, expressed by the Stoic philosophers. On this view, a man may be said to act freely, if and only if he has engaged in rational deliberation on the alternatives open to him. This conception of freedom as rational self-direction could properly be used of a slave or an agent acting under coercion, providing only that he succeeds in acting in accordance with his own rational policies. The conception of freedom as rational self-direction serves to distinguish the freedom of action of the agent who, though he may act under coercion, yet exhibits powers of rational reflection and possesses strength of will from the freedom of the agent who, possessing neither strength of will nor a rational life-plan, may none the less be said to be free to act in respect of an action in so far as his doing of that action is not prevented by the forcible or coercive intervention of another – who (in other words) possesses negative freedom in respect of that action.[1] My first point, then, is that an agent may possess this negative freedom and yet lack the freedom of rational self-direction, and vice-versa.

A stronger form of freedom to act is denoted by the term 'autarchy'. What is understood by an agent's being autarchic? In its uses in recent discussions,[2] discourse concerning autarchic agency denotes the freedom of action of an agent who, while enjoying (over a wide range of actions) that negative freedom which covers the absence both of force and of coercion, also exercises unimpaired all the normal capacities and powers of a rational chooser by reference to which freedom as rational self-direction is defined. Another form of freedom may now be distinguished – that of the autonomous man. How may we tell an agency which is autarchic from that which is autonomous? Clearly, an autonomous agent will possess all the defining features of an autarchic agent: but, in addition to exercising capacities for rational reflection and strength of will in the objective choice-conditions which are not distorted by the presence of force or coercion, an autonomous agent must also have distanced himself in some measure from the conventions of his social environment and from the influence of the persons surrounding him. His actions express

194

principles and policies which he has himself ratified by a process of critical reflection.

Plainly, even more straightforwardly than is the case with autarchy, autonomous agency must be regarded as something which must be achieved (and which can never be achieved completely) rather than as a natural human endowment or original inheritance.

The distinction between autarchic status and the status of an autonomous agent may become clearer if we look at some of the ways in which an agent may be disqualified from autonomy but not from autarchy. We may begin by noting that an agent falls short of being autarchic if his behaviour is recognisably compulsive, based on delusive ideas which he cannot evaluate critically, and which incapacitate him from making rational choices between real-world options. An agent may fail to be autarchic, also, in so far as his behaviour is governed by someone else by whom he may be dominated, mesmerised or over-awed: of such an agent we may say that he is heterarchic, one governed, not by himself, but by another. We may wish to say of a heterarchic agent that his normal functioning as a chooser has been impaired by the intervention of another, so that his decisions are his own only in a Pickwickian sense – in reality they are the decisions of another. Since the heterarchic agent's conduct is governed, not by any will of his own, but by the will of another, it is plain enough that his freedom of action has been effectively curtailed; but it remains important to distinguish clearly between this kind of loss of freedom and that which occurs whenever an agent acts under coercion. Whenever coercion occurs, one will is subordinated to another: the coerced agent is no longer an independent actor, since his will has been overborne by the will of the coercer. An agent remains self-determining (though not autarchic) even when he acts under coercion: for, in that any instance of coercion involves a conflict of wills, any claim that a man has been coerced presupposes that the coerced agent retains a will of his own, which is not true of the strictly heterarchical agent. (I do not deny that the long-run effect, and in some cases the aim, of coercion may be to destroy or at least impair the capacities involved in being a self-determining agent. This possibility creates complications I cannot go into here, except to say that where coercion does destroy the capacities for self-determination it is plausible to think that the unfreedom of coercion has been replaced by another – and worse – form of unfreedom.) A coerced agent, then, cannot be other than an agent capable of rational self-direction and so of self-determination.

The point that only those capable of rational self-direction can be said to suffer coercion may be brought out again by considering cases in which an agent may be disqualified from autarchy without being heterarchic: such are the cases of 'anomic' or 'wanton' individuals, for example, as Frankfurt[3] has termed them. Individuals who fall into this class satisfy the conditions of human agency: they are individuals whose desires are not ordered into any stable hierarchy, and who lack any standards by appeal to which they may judge and perhaps repress the inclinations of the moment. An anomic or wanton individual, then, is one who possesses no ideal image of himself by reference to which he may assess his own performances. Frankfurt has stated[4] that the defining feature of a wanton is that he does not care about his will, and so has none of the second-order desires and volitions the possession of which serves to distinguish persons from animals and from some human beings: the class of wantons includes all (or, more cautiously, almost all) non-human animals, all human infants, and some adult human beings. Since an anomic individual lacks a will of his own of the kind we ordinarily attribute to persons, there can be no implication of any ascription of anomic status that his will has been overborne by that of another (as in cases of coercion), or that the will of another has been substituted for it (as in cases of heterarchy). Manifestly, in so far as coercion always involves a conflict of will, it is no more possible to coerce a wanton than to coerce an animal or an infant (though all three may be subject to force). Only a very restricted conception of negative freedom as the absence of force, then, is applicable to the class of wantons: the wanton cannot be said to have that kind of freedom (of which self-determination, autarchy, and autonomy are instances) the possession of which would warrant ascribing to him responsibility for his actions and the absence of which in his case acts as a permanent excusing condition.

I have observed that one of the most important ways in which an agent may be disqualified from autarchy is by being heterarchic. It is evident, also, that an agent who is not heterarchic may yet be heteronomous. For a man may have all the attributes of a rational chooser (including a will of his own) and yet be wholly under the sway of custom, habit, or the expectations of his peer group. In David Riesman's useful terminology,[5] he may be 'other-directed'

– he may act unreflectively on standards and principles which he has taken over from his social and cultural environment without ever subjecting them to a critical evaluation. Such an agent, though not properly speaking heterarchic, is yet heteronomous in that his conduct is governed by a law (*nomos*) which he has taken over from others, without due thought, and which is not his own in the required sense. One of the crucial differences between autarchy and autonomy may be located in the fact that an autonomous agent is one who, in Rousseau's expression, acts in obedience to a law he has prescribed for himself. In Frankfurt's idiom,[6] an autonomous agent is one who has a will of his own, who has subjected his volitions to a sustained critical evaluation, who has the opportunity to translate his will into action, and whose will is free. It is important to note that the last two of these four conditions are not equivalent, but distinct. For the question of whether a person's will is free is not the question of whether he is in a position to translate his first-order desires into actions; the latter question is the question of whether an agent is free to act as he wants to act; it is the question of whether coercive interferences (for example) prevent him from acting as he wants to act. By contrast, freedom of will means here rather that an agent is free to want that which he wants to want. To act freely in the formal sense means to act as an autarchic agent; while, if an agent enjoys both the freedom of action of an autarchic agent, and also freedom of will, then he may qualify as an autonomous agent proper. The dual aspect of autonomous agency, which I have expressed by saying that an autonomous agent acts freely and has freedom of will is happily captured by Joel Feinberg, when he says: 'I am autonomous if I rule me, and no-one else rules I.'[7]

It is evident that the four conceptions of freedom which I have tried to elucidate – negative freedom, rational self-direction, autarchy, and autonomy – have been characterised in such a fashion that autonomy embraces the previous three, inasmuch as anyone who may be said to enjoy the freedom of autonomy will possess these other modes of freedom too. A society of autonomous agents, then, would be a society whose members enjoyed legal immunity in the exercise of certain important powers and of whom it was also true that they had developed these capacities and abilities up to at least a minimum level. The Janus-faced aspect of the concept of autonomy is disclosed in the fact that every application of it must make reference at once to a range of legal liberties and to a span of personal powers to act in ways characteristic of those of whom autonomous agency is predicated. It is worth emphasising that autonomy is abridged not only when actions are prevented by some external obstruction such as forcible restraint or the threat of legal punishment, but, more fundamentally, when the pressure of public opinion is such that certain options are not even conceivable, or, if conceivable, not treated as genuine candidates for viable forms of life. Mill argues for liberty, not because he believes that, once liberty is protected, there will be a society of free men; rather, he seeks to promote a society of free or autonomous men, and argues that this is impossible of achievement if liberty is curtailed beyond the domain circumscribed by his principle.

The reader may reasonably doubt if the apparatus of terms and distinctions I have sketched has any basis in Mill's writings but, though the reservation is not unreasonable in that these distinctions are not in any sense derived from Mill's work, it is groundless if it implies that nothing in Mill's writings corresponds to them. Mill's exclusion of children, the mentally unbalanced, and backward peoples from the sphere of application of the Principle of Liberty suggests strongly that he regarded the autarchic status as a necessary condition of the application of the principle. What evidence is there, though, of Mill's holding to an ideal of personal autonomy? Much the clearest evidence occurs in the famous third chapter of *On Liberty*. Consider the following passage:

> The human faculties of perception, judgement, discriminative feeling, mental activity, and even moral preference, are exercised only in making a choice. He who does anything because it is the custom makes no choice . . . The mental and moral, like the muscular powers, are improved only by being used. (p. 74)[8]

Again:

> A person whose desires and impulses are his own – are the expression of his own nature, as it has been developed and modified by his own culture – is said to have a character. One whose desires and impulses are not his own, has no character, no more than a steam-engine has a character. (p. 76)

We find here unmistakable traces of a Kantian conception of autonomy, absorbed by Mill (in a neo-Romantic variant) from

198

Humboldt. Despite the absence in his writings of any explicit use of the jargon of autonomy and authenticity, I think we are on firm ground if we include an ideal of personal autonomy among Mill's most fundamental commitments. A man failed to be a free man in Mill's view, if he was subject to force or coercion in the self-regarding area, or if the pressure of public opinion were brought to bear in that area. Human beings failed to be autonomous if – as was the case of women in traditional marriage arrangements, according to Mill – they lacked the opportunity to develop wills of their own and to act on them. In this latter case, which Mill examines at length in *The Subjection of Women*, it is the condition of heterarchy that thwarts autonomy. The more widespread condition of heteronomy which Mill attacks in *On Liberty* is that in which human beings constantly defer to the pressures of social convention and public opinion, submitting their own tastes (if they have any tastes of their own) to the anonymous arbitration of the mass. There is no doubt that Mill saw much of the importance of the Principle of Liberty in its disfavouring this latter sort of heteronomy (even if the adoption of the principle by society could not itself positively promote autonomy). But, further, there can be no doubt either that Mill saw the striving for autonomy as a permanent part, though an easily thwarted part, of the human striving for happiness. It is fair to say, indeed, that Mill would have represented this ideal as an adaptation of the Benthamite conception of happiness to the realities of human psychology. I will return to this point in the last section of this chapter.

We may now return to our original question: what more is involved in being autonomous than making choices based upon an imaginative appreciation of alternative forms of life? We come now to a fundamental aspect of Mill's theory of individuality, namely his claim that a man who attains or displays individuality will have desires and projects of his own – he will, in the idiom I have adopted, exhibit authenticity. A crucial question, now, is how authenticity is related to autonomy. On some accounts, such as Ladenson's, authenticity is collapsible into autonomy. As Ladenson puts it, 'For Mill . . . the cultivation of individuality is the development of reason.'[9] Though that claim captures an aspect of Mill's theory of individuality, it neglects an aspect, too. For Mill, as I have pointed out, a man displays individuality only if his desires and projects are his own. No doubt, reason – self-criticism, careful thought, and so on – will typically be an indispensable means for any agent to determine what are his projects and desires; but the point is that for Mill, this is partly a matter of discovery. On Mill's account, autonomy and authenticity are not equivalent, since a man could display autonomy in a very high measure, and yet (in virtue of false beliefs, perhaps) be mistaken as to where his unique endowments and potentialities lie. Part of the rationale for encouraging experiments in living, after all, is that they are aids in attaining self-knowledge (which may, in turn, be useful to others). If there were not a cognitive dimension to judgements about which desires and projects are my own, if such judgements were in the end in the nature of sheer groundless commitments, the argument for liberty would no longer have the instrumental aspect which it must retain if it is to be in any relevant respect a utilitarian argument. It would be an argument appealing primarily or simply to the value of choice; and, to that extent, a less complex, less persuasive, and less interesting argument than Mill's.

It is not hard to find in the text of *On Liberty* itself passages lending support to the interpretation I have advanced. Mill asserts:

> Human nature is not a machine to be built after a model, and set to do exactly the work prescribed for it, but a tree, which requires to grow and develop itself on all sides, according to the tendency of the inward forces which make it a living thing. (p. 75)

Here we have a form of expression suggesting, in Aristotelian fashion, that there is a natural tendency in men to self-realisation which social arrangements may nurture or thwart. Admittedly, Mill's conviction of the oppressive force of custom and tradition led him to take a deeply pessimistic view of the capacity of the great majority of men to assert their inborn tendencies against established traditions and conventions. Still, the teleological language which Mill uses, and the whole context of his discussion, suggest the thesis that each man has a unique range of potentialities, expressible in a relatively small range of possible lives, and that the actualisation of these potentialities is indispensable for any man's greatest well-being. This thesis is one of the hinges on which the argument of *On Liberty* turns.

There are, it is true, a number of obscurities in Mill's account, all of which centre on the relationship between choice and the knowledge of what makes for happiness or the good life in one's own case. So far I have written as if there were a univocal notion of autonomy, which Mill's writings exemplify. Such an impression could only be seriously misleading. Rather, we discover in a range of writers, and even within the writings of a single thinker, a whole continuum of conceptions. At one extreme, we find in Spinoza a conception of autonomy which might be called 'closed', in that it implies that the fully autonomous agent (if such there could be) could find uniquely determinate solutions to all practical questions. On this view, moral and practical dilemmas are each of them susceptible to resolution through the application of reason, which (at least in principle) is fully capable of yielding a specification of the good life for man and, presumably, for each man. At another extreme, there is in the writings of the early Sartre an 'open' view of autonomy, in which the idea that reason may settle practical questions is itself dismissed as expressive of a heteronomous 'spirit of seriousness'.

Mill's own conception of autonomy, I suggest, is most nearly akin to that adumbrated by Aristotle. As a number of commentators have observed,[10] Mill's account of character as a cluster of 'habitual willings', closely resembles Aristotle's account in the *Nicomachean Ethics*. One major difference between the two accounts, however, is found in Mill's radical pluralism. Though, like Aristotle, he thinks that all human excellences will be informed or characterised by the exercise of generic human capacities, he differs from Aristotle in insisting on the uniqueness which will characterise any man's happiness, when it is taken as an 'organic whole'. A happy man will not, then, be simply a very distinct instance of a general type; rather, one part of his happiness, a necessary part, in Mill's view, will be that he has fulfilled the peculiar demands of his own nature. Note that Mill is not insisting on the truism that circumstances and accidents of individual endowment will limit or constrain any man's opportunities for the attainment of excellence. More, he is insisting that the nature that awaits actualisation has unique features. It is this latter claim which some writers have ridiculed as expressing a doctrine of 'the Sanctity of Idiosyncrasy'.[11] Apart from the pejorative tone of such an expression, those who use it are surely correct that it is Mill's view that autonomous men, each of whom is in search of his own nature, will be more different from one another the closer they come to responding to the demands of their individual natures. Clearly, given Mill's emphasis on a pluralism of individual natures, there are epistemological problems both in determining their outer boundaries of variation and in determining the narrow range of life-styles within which any man may hope to attain excellence.

A second area of difference between Mill's account of individuality and Aristotle's account of human flourishing is located in Mill's insistence that choice-making is a necessary ingredient of the good life for any man. On some interpretations of Aristotle's view of practical deliberation, at any rate, the role of choice would be that of a means to the good life: it would not be even partly constitutive of it. There is indeed a tension in Mill between the cognitivist overtones of his talk of 'experiments in living' and the moral voluntarism intimated in some parts of his exposition of the elements of individuality. Some hard questions suggest themselves. Must a man whose desires and projects are his own, who displays authenticity, be autonomous? (Might he not just stumble on a form of life which fulfils his unique nature?) True, a man in whom the generic capacities of choice-making and so on are undeveloped will not attain the full happiness of which he is capable as a human being. On the other hand, certain kinds of self-knowledge connected with autonomy might actually obstruct the flowering of a man's unique capacities and gifts. (Think of the creative artist whose work withers after psychoanalysis.) There is here a significant area of difficulty for Mill's conception of happiness and of the place of individuality in it.

Again, at times, Mill moves bewilderingly between the perspective of the practical agent and that of the detached observer. On some views of practical knowledge, it might seem that an experiment in living could yield knowledge only to the committed partisan, the agent actively involved in its undertakings. On other views, just the opposite would be true.

Unsurprisingly, we find no explicit treatment of these problems in Mill. We may conjecture that the role of choice-making for Mill derives in part from his conviction that many goods are such only if they are chosen, and, also, perhaps, from a conviction that, whereas the unique elements of any individual's character are given to him by nature, their achieving any kind of organic unity can only be the product of recurrent choice-making.[12] We may express what was perhaps Mill's view on these questions in the idiom of open and closed conceptions of autonomy I adopted earlier, by saying that Mill's own conception was probably only partly a closed one. Given the absence in Mill's writings of any sustained consideration of these questions, such an interpretation is reasonable, but it is not the only one supportable by the evidence.

The preceding discussion may enable us to restate more precisely the relationship between Mill's theory of individuality, his philosophical psychology, and his argument for liberty. Mill always emphasises the presence of an active element in the mind: both in the formal discussions of pyschology, and in the occasional writings, such as the essays on poetry, Mill rejected the view of the mind as purely receptive of external impressions. Similarly, according to Mill, happiness was to be found in activity: it was not, as he put it, 'a collective something' which might be considered as 'swelling any aggregate',[13] but rather the form of life expressing each man's own nature. Again, recall Mill's argument that to suppose that men can be happy without the exercise of their active faculties is to confuse the two ideas of happiness and contentment.[14] On occasion, Mill comes close to embracing a kind of moral individualism, in which the notion of well-being or happiness loses all sense except as an abstract term applied to the objects of any sort of human striving. It is not, indeed, wholly an abstract term, since Mill thinks it to be a fact that individuals will tend to converge on forms of life which have some shared characteristics. It is, indeed, this latter belief which creates some difficulties for Mill. For, if I have described his utilitarianism as hierarchical and pluralistic, it is plain that Mill needs some account of how conflicts are to be settled, when the various elements of utility make competing demands; and this is not to be found in his writings. What is clear, however, is that Mill denies that anyone can achieve happiness or the good life, unless he has his own conception of happiness; and the diversity of legitimate conceptions of happiness is grounded in the plurality of individual natures.

A major question for the Doctrine of Liberty has to do with the authority Mill claims for his view of human nature. As an empiricist, Mill is compelled to build his theory of men on the evidences of observation and experiment. In the *System of Logic* Mill had advanced the project of an empirical science of ethology, which would uncover the laws of development of human character. Mill's own failure to contribute to this science (which we recognise now as an earlier version of social psychology) was a source of disappointment and embarrassment to him, and not without reason. It was on the basis of the laws of ethology that the various precepts of the Art of Life were to be grounded, and scepticism about the possibility of a progressive science of morals and politics founded on human nature – a scepticism to which Macaulay had given biting expression in his attack on James Mill's *Essay on Government* – at last confounded. Unfortunately, Mill came up with no candidates for laws of ethology, so that the Doctrine of Liberty (along with the rest of the Art of Life) lacks the empirical foundation in scientific knowledge of man and society he wanted to give it.

Mill was not himself successful, then, in linking the Art of Life with the laws of ethology, and in our assessment of the plausibility of Mill's view of man we must draw on whatever theoretical and commonsensical beliefs about human nature we put our store in. The absence in Mill's larger philosophy of a scientific foundation for the Art of Life does not show that such a basis cannot be supplied. A fundamental objection to the consistency of Mill's philosophy and, indirectly, to the utilitarian credentials of the Doctrine of Liberty, concerns the question whether the view of human nature presupposed by *On Liberty* is empiricist at all. It might be urged that, not only Mill's affinities with Aristotle on the nature of happiness, but the teleological language of *On Liberty* and the *a priori* character of much of Mill's moral psychology, show him to be working with an essentialist rather than an empiricist conception of man. This is to say that Mill did not take the evidences of human behaviour as decisive for a statement of man's essential attributes, which might be more or less revealed in human conduct. The difficulty, of course, is that Mill's empiricist theory of knowledge seems to close this option for Mill. How might this difficulty be coped with?

In part, the idea that there are human essences or natures poses no problem for Mill, even though his empiricist outlook is uncongenial to essentialist language. I have already suggested that Mill absorbed the Romantic belief that each man possessed a peculiar and in-born endowment which might or might not be realised in the course of his life. This belief does not overthrow Mill's empiricism, so long as the identification of any man's essence or nature remains a matter of observation and experiment. But can the notion of an individual nature or essence itself be given an empiricist interpretation? I cannot see that the difficulty here is fatal for Mill. As Stuart Hampshire has observed, discussing Spinoza's idea of freedom:[15]

The notion of an individual nature or essence may be found altogether obscure. We can, I think, still attach a sense to the notion of the essential characteristics of a species, and to the judgement of individuals as more or less perfect specimens of their kinds. But can we intelligibly speak of an individual or particular thing becoming more or less of an individual? Spinoza provides a criterion by which the approach to perfection of an individual qua individual is to be judged: the criterion is the degree to which the individual is active and self-determining.

My argument here is that, so long as we allow Mill the notion of an individual endowment open to discovery by observation and experiments in living, the rationalist or essentialist idiom of individual essences or natures can be given an empiricist translation. Whether or not empirical investigation bears out the claims of the theory of higher pleasures, and thereby supports the Doctrine of Liberty, is a further question. I wish here only to remark that, apart from the claim that individuals have natures or essences, Mill makes no claim about the general properties of human nature. The psychological laws he mentions are, in fact almost wholly abstract and formal, all of them being reducible to the law of association of ideas itself. Much of Mill's informal discussion of questions in morals and politics suggests that he thought human nature to be susceptible to almost unlimited variation and modification, so that the idea of a species–nature for man (apart from that given by his biological constitution) had little application for Mill. At times, though, Mill was attracted by a paradoxical version of essentialism, according to which the indefinite alterability of human nature is itself to be explained by the power, rooted in reflexive thought, which men have to make experiments on themselves. It is this view of human nature, more than any other, that is consonant with the argument of On Liberty. The obvious question is whether this essentialist thesis about man can be given an empirical defence.

The theory of human nature presupposed by On Liberty can be restated, then, as follows: according to this theory, human beings are understood to be engaged in recurrently revising the forms of life and modes of experience which they have inherited, and by which 'human nature' itself is constituted in any given time and place. In this account of man as a creature engaged in an endless process of self-transformation, what distinguishes human beings from members of other animal species is only their powers of reflexive thought and deliberate choice by which indeterminacy enters into human thought and action (together with the properties involved in having a more or less unalterable biological constitution). In such an account again, no statement claiming universal validity can be made about the attributes of human nature, save that it is essentially indeterminate, and so open to improvement in indefinitely many divergent directions. It is this conception of man, in which radical uncertainty of human nature constitutes the human species, that coheres most naturally with *On Liberty*. If this conception of human nature is imputed to Mill, it becomes intelligible why Mill saw progress, not in terms of the mass manufacture of any one type of human being, but, as the promotion of the growth of the powers and capacities of autonomous thought and action. It is the growth of these powers which allows the cultivation of diverse excellences or forms of self-development, elevates the character of human wants, and fosters cultural and social development in 'innumerable divergent directions' by facilitating 'experiments of living'.

As I have reconstructed it, the argument of *On Liberty* is that social freedom (which I have taken to comprehend both legal liberty and immunity from the penalties and pressures of public opinion) is to be ranked over other goods because the promotion of a diversity of styles of life and modes of thought is partly constitutive of man's development as an autonomous agent. In *On Liberty*, then, social progress cannot be conceived of apart from the promotion of liberty. As Mill puts it:

> The spirit of improvement is not always a spirit of liberty, for it may aim at forcing improvements on an unwilling people; and the spirit of liberty, insofar as it resists such attempts, may ally itself locally and temporarily with the opponents of improvement; but the only unfailing and permanent source of improvement is liberty, since by it there are as many possible independent centres of improvement as there are individuals. (p. 86)

So, if it is true that man's powers of reflexive thought prevent anything in man's social life from ever being fixed, finished or closed, then progress will consist in the open-ended transformation of the forms of man's social life along with a search (equally interminable) for the weaknesses, incoherences and other inadequacies in his understanding of the forms of his life. This is an essentialist view of human nature according to which, paradoxically, the essence of man is identified in the discovery that man lacks any determinate generic nature such as is possessed by material objects and by unreflective creatures. It is a paradoxical version of essentialism, also, in that the indeterminacy characterising mankind as a species is qualified by the discoverable essence in which Mill believes each member of the human species to be peculiar. Mill's theory of individuality, then, combines the claim that man is his own maker with the claim that, for each man, a nature exists which awaits discovery. Mill's thesis is that a happy human life requires the recurrent making of choices because only choice-making can weld into an organic whole the diverse and possibly competing demands of a man's nature. A fundamental question arises here as to whether this view of human happiness is not thoroughly ideal-regarding and, if so, whether this opens a fatal breach with anything recognisable as utilitarianism.

WANTS AND IDEALS IN THE DOCTRINE OF LIBERTY

Many of Mill's critics have accused him of bolstering the doctrine of liberty with an aprioristic moral psychology for which there is little independent justification. Certainly, a measure of circularity would enter his doctrine if it could be shown that his conception of happiness merely encapsulates his moral ideals in other terms. So far as his own view of the matter is concerned, Mill's position is reasonably clear. There can be little doubt that Mill believed that, given an appropriate range of relevant experience, men would in fact prefer activities involving the exercise of their best powers of discrimination and judgement over activities that do not. Mill is not committed to the view that men always display this preference – he is not bound to hold to the absurd view that, as between beer-drinking and wine-bibbing, men who know both always favour the latter on the ground of its greater demands of discrimination on the palate; but he is committed to the view that a preference for activities involving the exercise of autonomous thought and of capacities of imagination and discrimination will dominate the lives of experienced judges.

Mill's position in this area may still seem unpersuasive or unclear to many readers. Indeed, many of Mill's more recent critics have found it so. In his able critique of Millian liberalism, Haksar has argued that Mill cleaves to a high-minded conception of the good dependent on a certain ideal of the person: Mill's doctrine, he maintains, 'does not commit him to giving equal status to all forms of life', even though the identification of higher forms of life involves Mill in making perfectionist judgements which his official utilitarian theory disallowed.[16] Again, Mill's conception of happiness may still seem open to the objection, urged by Finnis,[17] against all forms of consequentialism, that it entails making comparable what are strictly incommensurable goods: it is bound to try to rank along a single scale values for which there is no common measure. Most crucially, perhaps, it might be urged that Mill's belief that there is a determinate class of higher pleasures is in conflict with his belief in the indefinite diversity of human nature: he cannot have it both ways. Either his doctrine of the higher pleasures supports his theory of liberty only because it already embodies a liberal preference for certain kinds of personality (in which case it gives no independent reason in favour of the Principle of Liberty) or else it rests on assumptions in empirical psychology and sociology which may well be false. What is there to be said in response to these criticisms?

The first of these objections, best put by Haksar, submits that Mill's underlying moral theory is perfectionist. By this is meant (following Rawls) that it is concerned primarily with the promotion of a certain type of human excellence, and only secondarily with want-satisfaction. The perfectionist theory is a species of maximising consequentialism, but not a want-regarding sort. If the attribution to Mill of this sort of ideal-regarding conception[18] were sound, it would indeed be a serious blow to his Doctrine of Liberty, which aims to have persuasive force even for those attached to illiberal ideals of character. But I cannot see that it has force. In the first place, the perfectionist character of a moral outlook is a matter of degree. A perfectionist moral code (one which attached great weight to considerations to do with personal excellence) may incorporate very specific precepts about behaviour, or else it may be more or less open-ended. No doubt Mill himself favoured persons of an adventurous, generous, open-minded disposition over timid, mean-spirited and narrow-minded types, but his argument as to the value of liberty is intended to have force for both. Mill's conception of the good life may be perfectionist in the sense that it ranks lives which are in large measure self-chosen over those that are customary, but this is a procedural perfectionism rather than a full theory of the good life. In weighting autonomy and security heavily in any scheme of human welfare, and giving priority to autonomy once certain conditions have been satisfied, Mill does work with what Rawls has termed a thin theory of the good – a minimalist conception of human welfare expressed in terms of a theory of vital interests or primary goods.[19] Operating with such a reference to the minimum conditions of the full achievement of human well-being does not by itself go any distance towards making Mill a perfectionist. Indeed, Mill's own claim is that those who are used to making their own choices will not easily or lightly abandon this practice, and this is an empirical claim, a wager of sorts, rather than an affirmation of an ideal. If Mill never faced the possibility that men would freely give up their liberty, this is because he thought he had good reason to believe the advantages of liberty were self-reinforcing. To argue that Mill was mistaken about this, even if the argument were incontrovertibly sound, would not support the very different claim that his real moral theory is perfectionist.

The two latter objections are in several respects more substantial. Mill acknowledged that each man's conception of his own happiness would most likely include competing elements, but he offered no guidance as to how these conflicts were to be settled: this is a point to which I shall return when I come to appraise his doctrine taken as a whole. Is his conviction of the diversity of human nature in conflict with his account of the higher pleasures? I cannot see how: Mill's criteria of a higher pleasure were that it be chosen after a process of autonomous thought and choice and that it express the unique demands of the individual's own nature. This pair of conditions excludes many pleasures while still leaving an infinite variety of intellectual and other pleasures in the field. There is nothing inconsistent in Mill holding that some pleasures can be known to fail the two tests I have mentioned whereas there may at the same time be novel pleasures, as yet unknown, which pass them. Some pleasures, it is true, may conceivably be autonomously chosen as in accordance with the individual's own nature and yet involve a relinquishment of autonomy. Mill's view on this possibility, I take it, is not an *a priori* one: he does not seek to defeat it as a possibility, but rather to suggest its improbability or rarity. This may be a modest position, but it is not an absurd one. Mill is committed to the proposition that men who have tasted the advantages and pleasures of liberty will not trade them away for other benefits: he holds, as an empirical matter, the belief that the condition of liberty is in this respect irreversible.

It is not immediately clear what sort of evidence Mill would accept as overturning his beliefs in this area. Nor, indeed, is it at all clear what evidence it would be reasonable for Mill to accept in this connection. However, provided Mill's prediction holds up in the generality of cases, there is nothing ideal-regarding in his conception of happiness. Mill is not holding to a perfectionist ethic in which the promotion of an ideal of human excellence is to be undertaken even if it competes with want-satisfaction. His view is, rather, that human happiness depends upon a certain sort of stability of character. The crucial question is, however, whether Mill holds to an ideal of personality independent of its contribution to general want-satisfaction. There is no historical or textual evidence that he did, and conjectures about what he would think were his expectations about human development confounded are excessively speculative. Though it is not the case that Mill's doctrine could be overturned by the odd case of a contented sloth, it is avowedly vulnerable to the test of human experience. Thus it can claim for itself only that it represents a not unreasonable wager, defeasible by experience and criticisable by the evidence of life.

NOTES

1 I have discussed negative freedom in my 'On negative and positive freedom', *Political Studies* 28 (December 1980), 4:507–26.
2 See S.I. Benn's 'Freedom, autonomy and the concept of a person', *Proceedings of the Aristotelian Society* 76 (1976), 109–30.
3 I adopt the terms 'anomic' and 'wanton' from H.G. Frankfurt's discussion in 'Freedom of the will and the concept of a person', *Journal of Philosophy* 68, 78 (1971), 5–20.
4 See ibid., 11–12.
5 See David Riesman, *The Lonely Crowd* (New Haven, Yale University Press, 1950), for an elucidation of this idiom.
6 See Frankfurt again, 'Freedom of the will'.
7 Joel Feinberg, *Social Philosophy* (Englewood Cliffs, New Jersey, Prentice-Hall, 1973), 15–17.
8 Mill, *On Liberty*; all page numbers in the text refer to this volume.
9 Robert F. Ladenson, 'Mill's conception of individuality', *Social Theory and Practice* 4 (1977), 2:167–82.
10 For example, F.R. Berger, *Happiness, Justice and Freedom: the moral and political philosophy of John Stuart Mill* (Berkeley, University of California Press, 1984).
11 Robert Paul Wolff, *The Poverty of Liberalism* (Boston, Beacon Press, 1968), 19.

12 See, especially, Antony Thorlby, 'Liberty and self-development: Goethe and J.S. Mill', *Neohelicon* 3–4 (1973), 91–110.
13 Mill, *CW*, 10:235.
14 Ibid., 212.
15 Stuart Hampshire, *Freedom of Mind* (Oxford University Press, 1972), 193–4.
16 V. Haksar, *Liberty, Equality and Perfectionism* (Oxford University Press, 1978), 233.
17 John Finnis, *Natural Law and Natural Rights* (Oxford, Clarendon Press, 1980), 111–18.
18 Brian Barry attributes this view to Rawls and, by implication, J.S. Mill, in his *The Liberal Theory of Justice* (Oxford, Clarendon Press, 1973), 28.
19 Rawls discusses his use of the term 'thin theory of the good' in *A Theory of Justice* (Oxford, Oxford University Press, 1972), 395–9.

MILL'S DEFENCE OF LIBERTY

C.L. Ten

I

Mill's defence of liberty is uncompromising. In certain areas the liberty of individuals should be absolute and indefeasible. 'The only part of the conduct of any one, for which he is amenable to society, is that which concerns others. In that part which merely concerns himself, his independence is, of right, absolute.'[1] (p. 31) He treats the case of religious toleration as a model of the way in which individual liberty should be defended. So his remarks here are instructive: 'The great writers to whom the world owes what religious liberty it possesses, have mostly asserted freedom of conscience as an indefeasible right, and denied absolutely that a human being is accountable to others for his religious belief.' (p. 29) There is no doubt that Mill himself endorses this view.

So Mill's conclusion on the absoluteness of individual liberty is firm and clear; the question is how he arrives at it. As everybody knows, Mill is officially a utilitarian, and he seems to reiterate his commitment to this doctrine when he writes:

> It is proper to state that I forgo any advantage which could be derived to my argument from the idea of abstract right, as a thing independent of utility. I regard utility as the ultimate appeal on all ethical questions; but it must be utility in the largest sense, grounded on the permanent interests of man as a progressive being. (p. 31)

It is not immediately clear what Mill means by 'utility in the largest sense', and how he sees liberty as promoting utility in this sense. But let us begin at a simpler level by considering whether Mill's conclusion can be adequately defended within the framework of the two most common forms of utilitarianism – hedonistic and preference utilitarianism.

Both these versions of utilitarianism are clearly distinguishable from non-utilitarian doctrines. According to hedonistic utilitarianism the only thing intrinsically desirable is pleasure, and all forms of pleasure are intrinsically desirable. Right acts are those which maximize happiness, interpreted as pleasure and the absence of pain. Preference utilitarianism, on the other hand, seeks to maximize the satisfaction of desires. Both doctrines are consequentialist and aggregative, judging acts solely in terms of their total utility or their total consequences in producing happiness or the satisfaction of desires. The value of liberty is therefore wholly dependent on its contribution to utility in these senses. But if that is the case, how can the 'right' to liberty be absolute and indefeasible when the consequences of exercising the right will surely vary with changing social circumstances?

II

Let's begin with the suggestion that Mill arrives at his conclusion by balancing the utility of interfering with liberty against the utility of non-interference and by discovering that the latter always outweighs the former. On this view then the distress of the 'religious bigot' at the 'abominable worship' of others, or that of the Sabbatarian at Sunday amusements and entertainments, or other similar forms of distress occasioned by the knowledge that others are engaging in activities which one regards as wrong, perverse, or otherwise unacceptable, are all to be taken into account in the utilitarian calculation. But this kind of distress, which includes what Honderich calls morality-dependent distress, is always relatively small compared with the undesirable consequences of abridging individual liberty.[2]

For a variety of reasons, the above suggestion cannot possibly represent Mill's view. First, Mill believes that morality-dependent distress can be very great. He cites the strength of the Muslim's disgust at the eating of pork as an example.

> There are few acts which Christians and Europeans regard with more unaffected disgust than Mussulmans regard this particular mode of satisfying hunger. It is, in the first place, an offence against their religion; but this circumstance by no

213

means explains either the degree or the kind of their repugnance; for wine also is forbidden by their religion, and to
partake of it is by all Mussulmans accounted wrong, but not
disgusting. (pp. 99–100)

Yet Mill rejects out of hand the prohibition of the eating of pork
even in a society in which the majority were Muslims. Neither the
intensity of the distress nor the number of people who share it seem
to affect the conclusion that it is illegitimate for the majority to
impose its values on the rest of society.

Secondly and more importantly, Mill's rejection of these forms
of distress as a proper basis for social interference with the liberty
of individuals is stated with a peremptoriness which would be
inexplicable if his case for liberty were dependent on the contingencies and uncertainties of the balancing process. Thus in spite of
the acknowledged intensity of the Muslim majority's abhorrence of
pork-eating, Mill points out that 'with personal tastes and self-
regarding concerns of individuals the public has no business to
interfere'. (p. 100) Again a little later on he expresses the same
attitude towards Sabbatarians:

> How will the remaining portion of the community like to
> have the amusements that shall be permitted to them regulated
> by the religious and moral sentiments of the stricter Calvinists
> and Methodists? Would they not, with considerable peremp-
> toriness, desire these intrusively pious members of society to
> mind their own business? This is precisely what should be
> said to every government and every public, who have the
> pretension that no person shall enjoy any pleasure which they
> think wrong. (p. 101)

In telling intrusive members of the public to 'mind their own
business' and in pointing out that they have 'no business to
interfere', Mill is setting up a principle of non-interference which is
deliberately insensitive to such utilitarianly relevant considerations
as the intensity and extent of the distress experienced by members
of the public as a result of activities which fall within the 'self-
regarding concerns' of individuals. His intention is to reshape the
whole framework within which issues of individual liberty are to
be discussed. He deplores the existing state of affairs in which,
'Wherever the sentiment of the majority is still genuine and intense,
it is found to have abated little of its claim to be obeyed.' (p. 29)

A balancing of utilities would hardly require a change of the fundamental framework of discussion and the adoption of 'the higher ground' which rules out an appeal to the 'likings and dislikings' of society. The balancing approach cannot explain why Mill evidently discounts morality-dependent and other forms of distress.

Finally, Mill does indeed adopt the balancing approach in cases where conduct harms others, and *contrasts* that approach with the requirement that 'there should be perfect freedom' to perform actions not harmful to others.

> As soon as any part of a person's conduct affects prejudicially the interests of others, society has jurisdiction over it, and the question whether the general welfare will or will not be promoted by interfering with it, becomes open to discussion. But there is no room for entertaining any such question when a person's conduct affects the interests of no persons besides himself, or needs not affect them unless they like (all the persons concerned being of full age, and the ordinary amount of understanding). In all such cases, there should be perfect freedom, legal and social, to do the action and stand the consequences. (p. 90)

There is a threshold to be crossed before the balancing of utilities, to determine whether the general welfare will be promoted, can be applied. The threshold is that the individual's conduct *harms* others, or 'affects prejudicially the interests of others'. We know from Mill's other remarks that conduct does not harm others simply because they dislike or abhor it and are thereby distressed by it. Thus in pleading for 'liberty of tastes and pursuits', Mill rules out interference from others 'so long as what we do does not harm them, even though they should think our conduct foolish, perverse, or wrong' (p. 33). Mill's notion of harm is quite complex, and I have tried to explain it elsewhere,[3] but it is sufficient to point out that if the balancing of utilities is required at all levels where interference with liberty is contemplated, it would make no sense for Mill to insist on 'perfect freedom' in 'tastes and pursuits', and contrast this with the qualified acceptance of freedom in cases where there is harm to others.

So we have reached a stage of the discussion where we have to explain why, from the point of view of either hedonistic or preference utilitarianism, the morality-dependent and other forms of distress may be discounted from the utilitarian calculation. The balancing approach fails, but there are at least two other types of explanations which we should now consider. The first is indirect utilitarianism in which, on utilitarian grounds, it is argued that *direct* appeals to utility (or to certain kinds of utility) should not be made. The second type of explanation seeks to show that there are reasons internal to utilitarianism for discounting certain forms of distress. Each type of explanation is susceptible of too many refinements to be all discussed here. But an examination of a few representative accounts would be sufficient to assess the general strengths and weaknesses of these types of approach.

III

Indirect utilitarianism may be supported by a variety of considerations including the belief that in certain areas direct appeals to utility (or to some aspects of utility) would be self-defeating. Thus Mill's exclusion of certain forms of distress from the utilitarian calculation can be justified as a utilitarian strategy which will ensure the maximization of utility in the long run. For example, in practice utilitarians would support absolute non-interference with self-regarding conduct if in the majority of cases non-interference with such conduct will maximize utility, and the attempt to identify the minority of cases when interference is justified will be unsuccessful and costly in utilitarian terms.[4] In such a situation there would be utilitarian reasons for not directly appealing to utilitarian considerations in deciding what one should do. Utilitarianism is primarily a principle for evaluating actions. It does not require that people should always aim to promote maximum utility. What is important is that actions, however motivated, should maximize utility. In some situations it may be that the best way to maximize utility is to aim not to maximize it but to adhere instead to some non-utilitarian rules.

But the simplest form of indirect utilitarianism involves the adoption of non-utilitarian rules as rules of thumb. Rules of thumb are convenient tools for facilitating the utilitarian calculation. Through lack of information or time, or the likelihood of mistakes in calculation, or through various human weaknesses which make us favour the interests of some more than the similar interests of others, or through other similar considerations, utilitarian agents may fail to maximize utility if they try to do so directly. So the solution is to adopt rules which experience has shown to be generally useful. But the value of these rules is entirely derivative from their contribution to the maximization of utility. They are simply means to the promotion of the utilitarian end. They do not rule out direct appeals to utility under propitious circumstances. Whenever such direct appeals reliably show that following a generally very useful rule of thumb on a particular occasion will not maximize utility, the rule will be broken. The fact that the same rule is maximally useful even in all other cases will not make a difference.

Some sophisticated utilitarians have not been satisfied with the treatment of non–utilitarian rules as merely rules of thumb. Rules of thumb will not generate sufficient commitment to certain values, or lead to the cultivation of the right dispositions. For example, suppose that love and friendship are conducive to the promotion of utility. But if utilitarians adopt the rule that one should be loyal to one's beloved and friends merely as a rule of thumb to be set aside when the pursuit of utility demands, then their personal relationships will be too hedged in by contingency plans for them to take deep roots. On the other hand, once deep loving and friendly relationships have been cultivated, lovers and friends do not value one another merely as resources for the maximization of utility. They will value love and friendship for their own sakes and will develop associated dispositions. These dispositions make it very difficult for them to be disloyal to their friends even when they know that such disloyalty is warranted by utilitarian considerations, and will lead them to experience guilt and shame if they succeed in being disloyal. When this stage is reached, they have cultivated dispositions which make them adverse to being disloyal for whatever reasons. The rule that they should be loyal to their beloved and friends ceases to be a mere rule of thumb to be broken, without remorse or compunction, or a deep sense of reluctance, when utility demands.

A version of this new form of indirect utilitarianism is provided by R.M. Hare's two levels of moral thinking.[5] At the intuitive level, we apply fairly general moral principles, like those enjoining us to tell the truth and to keep our promises. These general principles will cover situations that we confront typically in our daily lives. By accepting these principles we are saved from the necessity of making frequent utilitarian calculations under the stresses and temptations with which we are confronted. The

217

intuitive level principles are relatively simple and easy to follow and teach. They sometimes conflict and these conflicts will have to be resolved at another level of moral thinking which Hare calls the critical level. At the critical level, moral thinking is conducted free from the constraints and limitations of the rush hour. Hare believes that reasoning from the logical properties of moral concepts will lead us to accept utilitarianism as the rational method of critical moral thinking. The form of utilitarianism that emerges is preference utilitarianism. I shall not be concerned with Hare's derivation of preference utilitarianism, but shall assume, for the purposes of argument, that it is successful. For Hare the intuitive level moral principles are prima facie principles applicable to most situations, but overridable. Utilitarianism will be the basis for evaluating the intuitive level principles and for resolving conflicts between them. But because these intuitive principles have been inculcated in us in our moral education, we not merely follow them, but have also developed firm dispositions to follow them and deeply engrained feelings about the importance of acting in accordance with them. These feelings cannot be switched on and off easily, and that is why we react strongly whenever the principles are violated. The association of these dispositions and feelings with the intuitive level moral principles makes the principles more than rules of thumb, even though, like rules of thumb, they are selected by utilitarians for their contribution to the maximization of utility.

Hare does not apply his account of moral thinking to Mill's defence of liberty. But recently John Gray has given an analysis of Mill's argument which explicitly invokes Hare's indirect utilitarianism.[6] According to Gray, Mill's principle of liberty identifies as wrong only those acts which harm the vital interests of others in security, and it presupposes the equal distribution of moral rights to security and autonomy. The principle is adopted by Mill as a utilitarian strategy which will best promote the goal of maximizing happiness. The principle of liberty is therefore an intuitive level principle. It differs from Hare's intuitive level principles in that it is absolute or quasi-absolute. But this testifies to its practical importance and does not affect the formal structure of the indirect utilitarianism. Gray gives a complex and non-hedonistic account of Mill's concept of happiness about which I shall say nothing at this stage. My present concern is whether the principle of liberty can be firmly established as an intuitive level principle on the basis of its contribution to the promotion of utility. The issue here has to be settled in the light of empirical considerations. Gray argues that, according to Mill, the direct pursuit of utility will produce social instability because it sometimes requires people to sacrifice their vital interests, a sacrifice which they would regard as unreasonable. On the other hand, the principle of liberty, by protecting the vital interests, sets reasonable terms of social co-operation. Mill's distinction between the higher and lower pleasures is a distinction between different kinds of activities or forms of life. Autonomous choice is an ingredient of the happy human life of those who enjoy the higher pleasures by expressing their different individual natures. Liberty is valuable partly as a constitutive element of autonomous choice and partly as an instrument for the discovery of the variety of individual natures. Mill's argument for liberty relies on the empirical claim about the irreversibility of liberty, namely that those who are used to making their own choices would want to continue to do so. As Gray puts it, 'Mill's utilitarianism reposes on the wager that civilised men will in fact prefer the life of free men because it is in such a life that they find their happiness'.[7]

Gray ably charts the complex relationship in Mill's theory between the central concepts of happiness, autonomy, and liberty. As he tries to effect the reconciliation of liberty with utility, Gray's arguments are sometimes compelling, and always illuminating. But, in the final analysis, I doubt that the attempted reconciliation succeeds.

According to indirect utilitarianism, direct appeals to utility must be ruled out once the principle of liberty is accepted. So at that stage the preferences of those who wish to suppress non-harmful acts may be ignored. But the argument about whether the principle of liberty should be adopted in the first place must be an argument about whether its adoption is the best strategy for maximizing happiness. At *this* level, all preferences are relevant. Since Mill's arguments for the principle of liberty are conducted at this level, he cannot discount the strong anti-liberal preferences of the majority. Of course, some support for the principle of liberty is provided by the alleged irreversibility of liberty. But, as Gray concedes, the claim of irreversibility is for Mill only a conjecture lacking in the certainty that, for Mill, only a science of ethology, or character formation, could have provided. Against the uncertainty of the conjecture about future liberal preferences, we are confronted with the certainty of widespread and deep-seated illiberal preferences. So if Mill were carrying out a purely utilitarian calculation on the best strategy for maximizing happiness, the arguments which Gray attributes to him are by themselves too speculative to explain the strength of his liberal convictions in the face of those anti-liberal sentiments whose presence he fully acknowledges.

In any case, Mill does not subscribe to the version of the irreversibility of liberty thesis that is required in order to sustain a utilitarian defence of liberal beliefs. Even if it were certain that those who have experienced liberty would never wish to give it up, there is massive evidence that many of them show no similar tenderness towards the liberties of others. Mill is aware of such evidence, and indeed his plea for liberty is made in the context of the intolerance of religious and moral majorities who themselves already enjoy the very freedoms which they seek to deny others. No doubt some utilitarians underestimate the depth and durability of illiberal preferences. But Mill is not guilty of this, and his case for liberty is accordingly fought on 'the higher ground' of principle where 'intrusively pious members of society' have to 'mind their own business'.

So an indirect utilitarian defence of Millian liberty, although formally sound and logically coherent, fails on the basis of dubious empirical assumptions.

IV

There are also more general problems with an indirect utilitarian defence of liberty. If liberty is an intuitive level principle, utilitarians would not want it to be so deeply entrenched in our moral thinking that we are unable to adapt ourselves to changing circumstances when liberty ceases to be the best means of maximizing utility. But if the principle of liberty is to have the force of an absolute moral principle which debars direct appeals to utility, we must not only act in accordance with it, but must also cultivate in ourselves the relevant dispositions and feelings. However, once these dispositions and feelings have developed and have embedded themselves in our character, purely utilitarian considerations will lose their appeal. We lose the flexibility to respond to the requirements of utility.

Consider an analogy. Some students may initially have a purely instrumental interest in a certain subject, studying it only because acquiring a proficiency at it is a means to getting a good job. But suppose they become convinced, as a result of the propaganda spread by their teachers, that the only way in which they can acquire proficiency is to be thoroughly immersed in the subject and to forget for the time being the fact that it is only important for them as a passport to a good job. Once they succeed in involving themselves deeply in the subject, they are caught up in its internal demands and momentum. The sorts of problems which interest them are no longer identified in terms of their contribution to a good job, but as problems which have a place in the subject. At this stage they will choose to pursue the subject even at the cost of getting a good job.

The case for the utilitarian defence of absolute rules is strong if it is possible for people to follow those rules in a 'clinical' sort of way without developing the associated dispositions and feelings. But often this is not possible. For example, granted that loyalty to one's beloved and friends will maximize utility, utilitarians will choose to act loyally. But loyalty to one's friends involves showing partiality to them and their interests at least in some contexts, and this goes against the normal utilitarian requirement of giving equal weight to the similar interests of all. Loyalty here is based on personal relationships of friendship and love which are built round strong dispositions not only to act, but also to have deep feelings and sentiments. Once the dispositions take root we do not treat, and are incapable of treating, our beloved and our friends simply as instruments for the promotion of utility.[8] There are two related points here.

At the conceptual level, it may be argued that the very nature of a loving or a friendly relationship involves showing a certain degree of partiality towards one's beloved or friends. Thus, as Newton-Smith has argued, when confronted with a choice between saving a total stranger and one's beloved, 'If the putative lover elects to save the stranger, then, all things being equal, the relation is not one of love'.[9] A person's love is partly constituted by the way he or she chooses in certain contexts. Love, like lovers, has to prove itself in the performance.

But the second point is that love and friendship have certain causal powers which lead lovers and friends to show partiality to one another even in contexts when other things are not equal. So even if it were clear that greater utility would be promoted by rescuing the stranger, lovers and friends are still likely to act otherwise. E.M. Forster's famous remark illustrates the extent to which loyalty to one's friends can be taken, 'if I had to choose between betraying my country and betraying my friend, I hope I should have the guts to betray my country'.[10] In his essay 'Reflections on Gandhi', George Orwell attributes to Gandhi the view that 'for the seeker after goodness there must be no close friendships and no exclusive loves whatever'.[11] 'Close friendships, Gandhi says, are dangerous, because "friends react on one another" and through loyalty to a friend one can be led into wrong-doing.'[12] This view recognizes the causal powers of love and friendship and seeks to avoid them, and it is a view that utilitarians may have to endorse. Confronted with the choice presented by Godwin between rescuing Archbishop Fénelon or his valet who is also one's father, a person with filial love will find it impossible to rescue the Archbishop even if the utilitarian benefits are clearly greater.[13] This would not matter from the utilitarian point of view if such occasions were rare, for then the overall utilitarian benefits of love and friendship would be sufficient to swamp the few acts of wrongdoing, which it is impossible to fine-tune out of existence. But in fact there are numerous less dramatic occasions in daily life when love and friendship will lead us into what utilitarians would regard as wrongdoing. In such a world utilitarians cannot afford to be good lovers or friends.

I have strayed from the discussion of Millian liberty. But the problems there for the utilitarian are essentially the same. If utilitarians give full weight at the critical level to illiberal preferences and sources of distress, they would not, at the intuitive level, accept Mill's principle of liberty. But even if they are led to Mill's principle in certain social situations, they would not want to cultivate dispositions and feelings which are necessary for the application of the principle in an absolute manner. To do so would give the principle an independence from utilitarianism which makes it practically impossible, or extremely difficult, for new intuitive level principles to be adopted in changed circumstances.

I conclude therefore that indirect utilitarianism does not provide a firm enough basis for Millian liberty. Mill discounts certain types of distress and certain types of pleasure, and indirect utilitarianism does not seem to be able to account for this.

V

Let us now turn to various other attempts to show that Mill

provides a utilitarian defence of liberty. These involve claims that the notion of utility must be reinterpreted so that certain kinds of pleasures or pains do not even enter into the utilitarian calculation at any level of moral thinking. They are excluded not because that is required by utilitarian strategies for maximizing utility, but because they are not the relevant kinds of utilities which a reconstructed utilitarianism would take account of in the first place. Now this kind of approach does seem to be very close to Mill's position. However, the interesting question is whether the reconstruction of utilitarianism is dictated by considerations that are external to utilitarianism, as I believe, or whether it is required in order to preserve the internal coherence of utilitarianism. It is a characteristic of the accounts I shall now discuss that they all seem to think that the reconstruction is dictated basically by considerations internal to utilitarianism. They are all mistaken.

The first account is that of Ronald Dworkin who distinguishes between personal and external preferences, and argues that what a reconstructed utilitarianism seeks to maximize is the satisfaction of personal preferences. My personal preference is my preference for my own enjoyment of some goods or opportunities, whereas my external preference is my preference for the assignment of goods and opportunities to others.[14] One pair of illustrative examples used by Dworkin refers to the different preferences for the consequences of racial segregation which a white applicant for a place in a law school may have. If he prefers the policy of segregation because it will improve his own chances of admission, then his preference is a personal one. But if he prefers it because he is contemptuous of blacks and disapproves of their mixing with whites, then this is an external preference. Dworkin argues for the exclusion of *all* external preferences, whether they are malevolent or altruistic. Elsewhere I have discussed his arguments as they were originally presented in *Taking Rights Seriously*.[15] Here I wish to concentrate on the exclusion of illiberal or 'non-utilitarian' external preferences in the light of Dworkin's more recent elaboration of his view.[16] Dworkin points out that the attractiveness of utilitarianism lies in its promising a basis for treating people as equals by giving equal weight to the similar preferences of different people. But suppose we live in a society in which many people love a particular person, Sarah, very much, and they have strong external preferences that Sarah's preferences should be given twice as much weight as the similar preferences of others. Utilitarianism's egalitarian character would be undermined if these external preferences were counted. Utilitarianism is supposed to be neutral between the similar preferences of different people. But the external preferences of the Sarah-lovers are distinctly unneutral and utilitarianism would be self-undermining if it included these external preferences in its calculation.

Utilitarianism must claim the truth of its doctrine that equal weight should be given to the similar preferences of all people, and so it must reject as false any theory which contradicts this claim. For example, the Nazis' preferences that Jews count for less than Aryans must be rejected. The Nazi morality, on which the Nazis' external preferences are based, is a political morality which is in competition with utilitarianism, seeking to occupy the same space. So whereas utilitarianism can and must be neutral between the personal preferences of different people, it cannot be neutral between itself and a rival political morality like Nazism.

Dworkin's arguments are unconvincing. Utilitarianism is *not* neutral between itself and Nazism when it includes Nazi preferences in its calculation. Utilitarians are simply applying their doctrine that all preferences of the same intensity should be given the same weight irrespective of their content. It is not in virtue of the content of the Nazi's external preferences that they are taken into account. On the other hand, Nazism as a political morality is defined in terms of the content of the Nazis' preferences. Nazism gives no weight to preferences of the same intensity but with a different content. The utilitarian's neutrality is towards the content of *preferences*, and this does not commit it to the equality of *persons* if by this is meant that no person's major interests may be sacrificed for the minor interests of others. Since utilitarianism is an aggregative doctrine the addition of the minor interests of many individuals can outweigh the major interests of one individual. Dworkin claims that utilitarianism is 'neutral toward all people and preferences'.[17] This is misleading if the neutrality towards persons is additional to, and independent of, its neutrality towards preferences: the only sense in which utilitarianism is 'neutral towards all people' is that it is neutral towards the similar preferences of all people.

Dworkin points out that if a constitution provides that Sarah's preferences are to carry twice as much weight as those of others this would be unacceptably unneutral. But suppose now we replace the unneutral constitution with an apparently neutral utilitarian constitution which gives equal weight to the similar preferences of all, including Sarah. If external preferences are counted, the weight of the preferences of many Sarah-lovers would lead to Sarah receiving more goods and opportunities than others. The apparently neutral constitutional provision would be self-undermining. However, Dworkin's argument is unsuccessful because the fact that the two constitutions will both favour Sarah does not mean that they are both unneutral in the same sense. The lack of neutrality towards Sarah in the first constitution is entrenched, and is not sensitive to variations in social circumstances. On the other hand, the fact that the second constitution favours Sarah is dependent on there being a large number of Sarah-lovers. If Sarah loses all her lovers to Sam the constitution would now favour Sam in the distribution of goods and opportunities. The second constitution, unlike the first, remains neutral towards different people's preferences. The neutrality towards preferences is not undermined, and there is no neutrality towards persons which is not derivable from, or reducible to, the neutrality towards preferences.

However, Dworkin's arguments are interesting because they raise the issue of how utilitarians are to treat the preferences or desires of non-utilitarians. This is an issue that is discussed at length by Richard Wollheim.[18] Wollheim interprets Mill as discounting morality-dependent distress as the basis of social intervention. Thus, if homosexuality between consenting adults causes no distress except to those who are affected simply because of their moral belief that homosexuality is wrong, then homosexuality is a self-regarding act which should never be interfered with. As an interpretation of what Mill means by self-regarding conduct, this comes close to the truth. But Wollheim also believes that the exclusion of morality-dependent distress can be justified by the adoption of utilitarianism. Elsewhere[19] I have argued at length against his view, and here I shall only sketch some of my reasons for thinking that Wollheim is wrong. If an act causes no distress independently of its being thought wrong, then there can be no utilitarian reason for the belief that it is morally wrong. The only distress arises after one has formed the belief that it is wrong, and so cannot be the basis of that belief. So, Wollheim points out, utilitarians will regard the moral belief about the wrongness of the act as false. But even if we accept this argument, so far no reason has been given as to why the utilitarian should never interfere with a self-regarding action. Utilitarians are not required to restrict interference to acts which are wrong by the utilitarian standard. For whether interference with an act is justified depends not simply on the consequences of the self-regarding act, but also on the consequences of interference. So utilitarians may consistently justify interference with an act which is not wrong, just as they may consistently justify non-interference with a wrong act. One of the utilitarian benefits of interference with self-regarding conduct is that such interference may eliminate the morality-dependent distress. So the falsity of the moral belief about the wrongness of self-regarding conduct does not in itself provide a utilitarian reason for ignoring the morality-dependent distress.

The real reason why, according to Wollheim, utilitarians may ignore morality-dependent distress is simply that the distress depends on a *moral belief* about the act. Wollheim maintains that 'the Utilitarian calculation must be made as if in a world prior to the adoption of moral attitudes'.[20] If by 'moral attitudes', he means utilitarian moral attitudes then he is of course right because utilitarian moral attitudes are the outcome of the utilitarian calculation. But if the moral attitudes are non-utilitarian, then there is no reason why the utilitarian calculation should not include the pleasures and pains caused by the adoption of these attitudes. It is a fact about the world as it is that there are numerous non-utilitarians in it. If utilitarians are to remain neutral between different preferences, then it should not matter what the content of these preferences is.

Wollheim assumes that the moral belief about the wrongness of self-regarding acts must be false. If this were so then the morality-dependent distress has to be excluded, for otherwise the morality of the acts may change if a sufficient number of people strongly believe the acts to be wrong, and are distressed by the knowledge that others are engaging in them. Right acts would then be transformed into wrong acts simply because a sufficient number of people believe them to be wrong. But the inclusion of the morality-dependent distress of non-utilitarians in the utilitarian calculation does not in fact generate this kind of transformation because the utilitarian calculation is incomplete in the first place without the inclusion of such distress. Wollheim is therefore too quick to conclude that, from the utilitarian point of view, the non-utilitarian's belief in the wrongness of self-regarding acts is false. The only legitimate conclusion is that the non-utilitarian's belief is not based on any distress caused by those acts, as there are no forms of distress independent of the moral belief.

So at best the only type of distress that the utilitarian may discount is the morality-dependent distress of irrational utilitarians, who believe that self-regarding conduct is wrong even though they know that it causes no distress. As most of those who are likely to suffer from morality-dependent distress are non-utilitarians, the exclusion from the utilitarian calculation of the distress of these irrational utilitarians will not have much effect on the outcome of that calculation.

Is there some way by which the utilitarian can further discount all forms of irrationally based distress? Bernard Williams makes some relevant comments on this issue.[21] Williams tries to show that there is a strong argument for the utilitarian to give no weight at all to certain kinds of feelings because they are, for the utilitarian, irrational. Williams' discussion is interesting because if he is right, then the utilitarian can avoid having to embrace some apparently illiberal conclusions.

Williams discusses the example of Jim who, while on a botanical expedition, accidentally finds himself in the central square of a South American town, where twenty Indians are about to be killed for protesting against the government. Jim is treated as a guest of honour, and is invited to kill one of the Indians. If he accepts the offer, then the other nineteen Indians will be released. But if he rejects it, then someone else will kill all twenty Indians, as originally planned. What should Jim do? Williams argues that, according to the utilitarian, the obviously right answer is that Jim should kill the Indian and thereby save the nineteen others. However, Williams then considers the utilitarian's reply that there are other remoter effects of Jim's killing the Indian that must also be taken into account. It is only the first of these remoter effects that is relevant to our present discussion, and this relates to the psychological effect on Jim of killing the Indian. If he kills the Indian he would feel very bad about the act, and given that these effects are bad enough, they may tip the utilitarian scales against the act. But Williams points out that if the bad feelings arise simply because Jim thinks that he has acted wrongly, then they are, from the utilitarian point of view, irrational. For, if indeed the balance of good and bad outcomes, excluding these bad feelings, were in favour of Jim's killing the Indian, then Jim would not have done the wrong thing in killing. It is therefore irrational to have bad feelings, and the utilitarian would not want to encourage such feelings. Hence he would give Jim's bad feelings only small weight.

But Williams goes on to argue that there is a case for the utilitarian attaching not just small weight, but no weight at all, to Jim's bad feelings, and it is here that his argument becomes directly relevant to the promotion of liberal values. He considers the case of a racial minority which does no harm nor any good to the ordinary interests of the other citizens in the society. But the majority is so prejudiced against the minority that it finds even the mere knowledge of the minority's presence in the community very disagreeable. Given that the majority's feelings cannot be easily changed, and given that these feelings are intense, a utilitarian calculation might result in recommending the deportation of the minority. But Williams argues that if the utilitarian counts these feelings merely as such, then the result might be self-defeating. For these feelings are irrational from the utilitarian point of view. Utilitarians would therefore not have them, or if they had them, they would be discounted. Similarly, utilitarians would discount these feelings in calculations about what should be done in their society.

Now these feelings of the majority may be irrational from various points of view, but what is unclear is why they are irrational *from the utilitarian point of view*. The only argument Williams provides applies to those bad feelings, like Jim's, which are based on the belief that what has been done is wrong. Jim's bad feelings are irrational from the utilitarian point of view because he has not done anything wrong. But the racially prejudiced majority does not hold any view that is irrational in the same sense. Indeed it just finds the 'sight' of the minority, and 'even the knowledge of its presence' very disagreeable.

But perhaps the argument is that, if one probes deep enough, there is always some irrational belief of the majority which is the cause of the strong feelings. So let us assume that the majority is against the minority because it believes that the minority take up most of the well-paid jobs in the community. This belief is clearly false, and therefore in one sense, irrational. But the utilitarian standard does not justify us in completely ignoring the distress caused by false beliefs.

But now, suppose that the minority is largely immigrant. Its presence will then very likely give rise to new types of restaurants, places of worship, styles of dress, entertainment, etc. The social environment of the majority will be altered, and this may be the source of the hostility towards the minority. But now there is not even a false belief to which one can point. For it is the case that the majority is distressed by these social changes, or the prospect of these changes. Moreover, it is trivially true that the mere presence of the minority changes the society. And if *this* is what distresses the majority, then it *is* distressed, and that is as brute a fact as any that the utilitarian will find. The feelings of the majority are independent of any belief about what social policies are right or wrong by the utilitarian standard. So they should form part of what the utilitarian would take into account in deciding what to do.

Williams maintains that 'a utilitarian might be expected to take into account certain other consequences of the prejudice, as that a majority prejudice is likely to be displayed in conduct disagreeable to the minority'.[22] So, in deciding whether the racial minority should be deported, the utilitarian will presumably take into account the following considerations: the majority will unfairly discriminate against the minority in the getting of jobs and accommodation, and sometimes members of the minority will be harassed and even assaulted. All these are 'consequences of the prejudice', and they may be counted by the utilitarian, and indeed, given the situation Williams depicts, they will count in favour of the deportation of the minority. On what ground then can the utilitarian totally disregard the strong feelings themselves, when these feelings are not based on any view about the rightness or wrongness of deportation, but are instead one of the utilitarian considerations which argue for deportation, in the same way as the discrimination, the harassments, and the assaults?

But, finally, the utilitarian might argue that the irrationality of the majority's feelings is shown by the fact that the minority causes no particular harm to the ordinary interests of the majority. Hence the strong feelings of the majority are not based on anything that can be rationally justified from the utilitarian point of view. But if this is the argument, then it begs the whole issue. For surely the question is precisely whether these feelings in themselves are what the utilitarian would count as a type of harm. If they are, then the majority has been harmed by the mere presence of the minority. There is no need to show that any *further* harm has occurred. And to say that these feelings, to be counted, must be based on the fact, or the belief, that the minority is harming the *ordinary* interests of the majority, is to assume that these feelings are in themselves utilitarianly irrelevant. But that is precisely what is in dispute.

The classical utilitarians, as Williams points out, take the world as it is, counting every type of pleasure and pain, no matter what their source might be. However, Williams has argued that there is a case for giving little, and perhaps even no weight at all, to the distress which arises solely from the false belief that the act under consideration is wrong. But there is nothing in what he says to show that the utilitarian is justified in totally disregarding the distress caused by *all* false beliefs, or the distress of deeply prejudiced people. It may, in some sense, be profoundly irrational for people to be distressed by self-regarding conduct, but none the less their distress is part of what is, as it were, there to be counted before the utilitarian moral judgement is arrived at.

VI

I shall consider one more attempt, in some respects similar to Wollheim's, to explain why Mill's discounting of certain pleasures and pains can be explained within the utilitarian framework. This is the view presented in the late John Rees' excellent book *John Stuart Mill's On Liberty*.[23]

A central theme of the book is that the framework of Mill's ideas on liberty had to a large extent been shaped by his father and Bentham. In particular, Rees argues that both James Mill and Bentham are of the view that penalties, in the form of legal punishment or moral sanctions, should not be imposed on conduct that causes no injury. What counts as injury and when injurious acts should be legally prohibited are determined by the principle of utility. But Rees tries to show that the painful feelings experienced by those who have 'unfounded' or 'groundless antipathies' are not regarded by James Mill and Bentham as injuries. James Mill argues that since these antipathies are excited by actions 'from which no evil ensues', they should not be the basis for limiting a person's 'sphere of innocent enjoyment'. The examples he gives of such groundless antipathies include the Muslim disapproval of the drinking of wine.

Rees sees similarities between the views of James Mill and Bentham and those of John Stuart Mill. John Stuart Mill restricts interference with the conduct of individuals to cases where there is harm to others, and his concept of harm seems to resemble his father's and Bentham's notion of injury. Again, the younger Mill strongly opposes the appeal to the mere 'likings and dislikings of society' as the basis for moral judgement and legal intervention. He also uses the term 'antipathies' to describe the outraged feelings of Muslims excited by someone eating pork. But Rees warns that John Stuart Mill's notion of harm needs to be understood in connection with his defence of individuality and self-development, which takes him 'far beyond his Utilitarian inheritance'.[24] James Mill and Bentham, on the other hand, do not show particular concern about the dangers to individuality from the pressures of public opinion.

It is of course impossible to determine the depth of the influence of James Mill and Bentham on John Stuart Mill unless one has more detailed accounts of their views on liberty. For just as John Stuart Mill's appeal to 'utility in the largest sense' differs from Bentham's principle of utility, so too the remarkable similarities between them in the language and key expressions used to formulate their respective cases for liberty may well conceal fundamental disagreements about how individual liberty is to be defended. Conscious of this possibility, Rees returns in the final chapter of the book to discuss John Stuart Mill's doctrine of liberty and its dependence on his analysis of justice.

Mill wants to secure individual liberty within 'the limits imposed by the rights and interests of others'. According to Rees these limits are set by rules of justice which protect the essential interests of others, and in particular their interest in security. The observance of these rules is necessary in order to preserve peace among human beings. The obligations of justice are more stringent than other moral obligations, and they are correlated with moral rights. Individuals cause harm to others by acts of injustice that violate their rights and damage their essential interests. So although he acknowledges some difficulties for his interpretation, Rees concludes that for Mill harm consists in the violations of the rules of justice. On the other hand, Bentham and James Mill link the notion of harm and injury to that of pain.

Rees is deservedly well known for his very effective refutation of the traditional interpretation of self-regarding conduct, according to which such conduct does not affect others. In a paper originally published in 1960, and included in this book, Rees argues that Mill makes a crucial distinction between merely affecting others and affecting the interest of others, and that, whereas self-regarding actions affect others, they do not affect their interests. Rees maintains that interests 'depend for their existence on social recognition' and are 'closely connected with prevailing standards about the sort of behaviour a man can legitimately expect from others'.[25] This account of interests has been criticized, and Rees himself became dissatisfied with it. In the concluding chapter of the book, Rees holds on to the general distinction between effects and interests, which rests on the view that, whereas interests depend on an appeal to standards of evaluation, the painful effects of a course of action can be established by a simple empirical procedure. But now he maintains that the interests Mill wants to protect are the essential interests. Self-regarding conduct can therefore painfully affect others, and can presumably also adversely affect their non-essential interests. The identification of the relevant interests to be protected no longer depends on the variable prevailing social standards, but rests instead on the rules of justice that are common to different societies since they are necessary for the preservation of peace and security.

Rees is therefore able to explain why Mill disregards the pain experienced by those who merely dislike a form of conduct, or who hold groundless antipathies. But, somewhat surprisingly, he maintains that James Mill and Bentham, in spite of the link between their concept of harm and pain, also ignore the distress felt by such people. In order to assess Rees's view, we must distinguish between two different ways in which a hedonistic utilitarian like Bentham might try to ignore a certain type of pain.

First, as was pointed out earlier, it could be argued that in practice certain types of pain ought to be totally discounted as part of a utilitarian strategy to ensure the maximization of happiness in the long run. Bentham and James Mill can, in this manner, quite consistently ignore the distress caused by groundless antipathies. For example, they might believe that such distress would always be outweighed by the pains caused by attempts to interfere with conduct giving rise to antipathies. Much of James Mill's discussion of groundless antipathies, to which Rees refers, is in the context of determining whether actions that arouse such antipathies should be reported or exposed by the press. There is of course a powerful utilitarian case for not exposing actions which provide innocent enjoyments without causing any pain, apart from those associated with groundless antipathies. Groundless antipathies would not be excited but for the knowledge of the actions. So in this context ignorance is truly bliss.

But Rees seems to think there is another way in which Bentham and James Mill ignore the distress of those holding groundless antipathies. These pains do not even enter into the utilitarian calculation at all. Rees rightly points out that to adopt this position is to abandon 'pain as such as the criterion of a right action'.[26] But how can this be consistent with Benthamite utilitarianism? Bentham is quite explicit that pleasure is in itself a good and pain is in itself an evil, and this is 'true of every sort of pain, and of every sort of pleasure'.[27] It is therefore clear that what Bentham calls 'the pleasures of antipathy' and 'the pains of ill-will, of antipathy' must be included among the pleasures and pains to be taken into account in the utilitarian calculation. Whereas John Stuart Mill appeals to his doctrine of Individuality in order to exclude certain pains, Bentham and James Mill do not seem to have any basis for such exclusion.

But Rees presents an argument on behalf of the utilitarian for ignoring the pains that are inseparable from the belief that an action is wrong. Pains of this type are not caused by an action in an 'objective' manner 'to be settled by empirical observation in the same sort of way that, say, we settle the question of smoking and lung cancer or whisky and liver disease'.[28] Rees believes that this argument is implicit in Bentham and the two Mills. Earlier in the book he also places great weight on the fact that in the case where disapproval of an act arises out of an antipathy, there is no 'external' consideration by which the act is judged to be harmful. There would be no pain except for the antipathy. On the other hand, in the case of arson or assault there is harm independently of 'the pain to be identified with feelings of moral disapprobation'.[29]

Rees relies for his argument on Bentham's rejection of 'the principle of sympathy and antipathy', which 'approves or disapproves of certain actions, . . . merely because a man finds himself disposed to approve or disapprove of them'.[30] This principle is a rival to the utilitarian theory and obviously cannot be accepted by a utilitarian. It makes an action wrong simply because it is believed to be wrong. Rees is right that Bentham and both the Mills would agree that, for example, drinking wine cannot be wrong if it produces no pain independently of the belief that it is wrong. But the question of whether, from the utilitarian point of view, the state should ever interfere with the act is a different issue. For the pain associated with groundless antipathy is 'external' to, and independent of, the moral judgement about the rightness or wrongness of *interference*, and would now have to be taken into account. At least there is nothing in his rejection of the principle of sympathy and antipathy that commits Bentham to the exclusion of the pains of antipathy from the utilitarian calculation. To conclude otherwise is to assume that utilitarians would not only reject non-utilitarian criteria of moral wrongness, but would also leave out from their calculations the distress of non–utilitarians who become aware of violations of their moral belief. But the fact that non-utilitarians are distressed by conduct they believe to be wrong is as much an 'objective' fact about the world, to be settled by empirical observations, as the fact that assault causes physical injury.

So Rees's argument does not convince me, and I do not think that the views of his father and Bentham are as close to Mill's position as Rees sometimes suggests.

VII

We have seen that Mill's defence of liberty does not seem to be based on an appeal to the most common forms of utilitarianism, namely hedonistic and preference utilitarianism. But it has been suggested that Mill's defence is none the less still utilitarian in character, relying on a concept of happiness that is 'hierarchical, pluralistic, and essentially non–hedonistic'.[31] This view is highlighted by Robert Hoag in his recent lucid and sympathetic exposition of the complex arguments to be found in the books by John Gray and Fred R. Berger.[32] I have already discussed some aspects of Gray's argument which is shared by Berger, and in particular the subscription to indirect utilitarianism. Berger's work is subtle and ranges widely and illuminatingly over the whole range of Mill's moral and political philosophy. With much of what he says I am in agreement, but I shall focus on just those aspects of his view which Hoag thinks has established the utilitarian foundations of Mill's liberalism.

Berger believes that freedom and individuality (or autonomy) are valuable even when they do not promote pleasure, because happiness, and not pleasure, is Mill's ultimate standard of value. Mill's concept of happiness is related to the development of people's 'higher faculties', and there is a diversity of different ingredients of happiness. Autonomy is one element of human happiness, and living an autonomous life requires freedom to choose one's life-plans and to develop one's capacities. Freedom is therefore one of the essential interests of persons, and, like the other essential interests, is protected by rules of justice which confer rights to liberty and autonomy.

So far two features of Mill's concept of happiness have been sketched: happiness is pluralistic and non-hedonistic. But these features are insufficient to provide an adequate defence of Millian liberty. Mill wants to defend *each person's* right to liberty and autonomy (or individuality). But if his standard of value, like other forms of utilitarianism, is purely aggregative, then there are two ways in which a particular individual's right to liberty and autonomy may be overridden. First, it may conflict with the similar rights of others, and it is overridden in order to minimize the violations of such rights, or to maximize the sum of intrinsic value. Rawls points out that in a purely aggregative doctrine, if individuality has intrinsic value, the maximization of such value may lead to the sacrifice of the individualities of some in order to promote a greater increase in the individualities of the rest.[33] The second way in which a person's right to liberty and autonomy may be overridden is when it conflicts with the lesser interests of many individuals. Again, if utilities are additive, many small utilities can add up to a big sum. The general point is that the liberty and autonomy of a particular individual may be sacrificed in conformity with what Nozick calls the doctrine of 'utilitarianism of rights' in which the desirable goal is to minimize 'the total (weighted) amount of violations of rights'.[34] Nozick contrasts this doctrine with his own view that rights are moral side-constraints which one is forbidden from violating even in the pursuit of desirable goals.

But Berger and Hoag also focus on a third feature of Mill's concept of happiness: it is hierarchical. The non-essential interests of even numerous individuals can never outweigh the essential interests in liberty and autonomy of a single individual. Berger also adds a distributive dimension to Mill's view when he states that for Mill 'freedom and equality imply one another, in this context, it means that living an autonomous life entails that one enjoys the status of an equal with others'.[35]

What emerges then is a form of utilitarianism which does not have the distinctive features which are shared by hedonistic and preference utilitarianism. It is a form of utilitarianism that is not purely aggregative but has a distributive dimension, that is not neutral between people's desires or preferences, and that is not monistic in recognizing only one thing as intrinsically valuable – pleasure or the satisfaction of people's desires.

I argued in *Mill on Liberty* that there are substantial non-utilitarian elements in Mill's defence of liberty. Hoag disagrees with me, and cites my claim that Mill's notions of individuality and harm are non-utilitarian as being at odds with Berger's account of Mill. I believe that Mill is a consistent liberal whose view is inconsistent with hedonistic or preference utilitarianism. But I have not argued that Mill is an inconsistent hedonistic utilitarian, which is the view Hoag tries to foist on me. Again, in contrasting my view with Berger's, Hoag fails to notice close similarities between the accounts of happiness and individuality which both Berger and I attribute to Mill. On the other hand, Berger himself points out the similarities, and indeed goes so far as to describe our accounts as 'indistinguishable'.[36] Finally, in my elucidation of Mill's non-utilitarian notion of harm I too invoked Mill's discussion of the rules of justice in a manner that is not substantially different from the account of harm as injury to people's vital or essential interests which Berger and Gray attribute to Mill. So Hoag has been misled, because, although Berger and I are in considerable agreement about Mill's view, I call it substantially non-utilitarian, whereas both Berger and Hoag insist on calling it utilitarian. But this is so far only a verbal difference.

However, Berger and Hoag use a very broad interpretation of utilitarianism, according to which it refers to 'any moral theory that takes consequences (of acts, rules, and so on) as the criterion of right and wrong action',[37] and they point out that 'a utilitarian need not ascribe intrinsic value to pleasure, for example, but can consistently ascribe "value to whatever he thinks is valuable"'.[38] But if this is the case utilitarianism ceases to be a distinctive doctrine, and can, by suitable choices of intrinsically desirable things and suitable adjustments of their respective weights, be made extensionally equivalent to moral theories which are non-consequentialist. For where a non-consequentialist will regard the distribution of happiness as morally relevant, the utilitarian can treat a particular distribution as intrinsically valuable. The utilitarian can attach weighted intrinsic value to any feature of an act which others regard as morally important.

However, I find attractive the particular 'hierarchical, pluralistic, and essentially non-hedonistic' doctrine that has been attributed to Mill. I had not recognized it as a version of utilitarianism, and would prefer to treat it as a non-utilitarian view. But if others insist that this is truly a form of utilitarianism, then I am still prepared to embrace it, a little cautiously at first as I look back to its uncertain parentage, but with a great deal of hope as I look forward to using it in order to build a sound political morality for the better defence of Millian liberty.

NOTES

1 J.S. Mill, *On Liberty*, all references to the essay are to this volume, 23–128.
2 Ted Honderich, ' "On Liberty" and morality-dependent harms', *Political Studies* 30 (1982).
3 C.L. Ten, *Mill on Liberty* (Oxford, Oxford University Press, 1980), ch. 4.
4 See, e.g., Rolf E. Sartorius, *Individual Conduct and Social Norms* (Belmont, Dickinson, 1975), 144–61.
5 R.M. Hare, *Moral Thinking* (Oxford, Oxford University Press, 1981), especially chs. 2, 3, 8, 9 and 10.
6 John Gray, *Mill on Liberty: A Defence* (London, Routledge & Kegan Paul, 1983). My discussion of Gray is drawn from my review of his book in *Canadian Philosophical Reviews* (1984).
7 Gray, *Mill on Liberty: A Defence*, 46.
8 For a very subtle and elegant exploration of this issue, see Bernard Williams, 'The point of view of the universe: Sidgwick and the ambitions of ethics', *Cambridge Review* 7 (1982). See also Bernard Williams, *Ethics and the Limits of Philosophy* (London, Fontana, 1985), 106–10. Williams also provides instructive general discussions of indirect utilitarianism in J.J.C. Smart and Bernard Williams, *Utilitarianism: For and Against* (Cambridge, Cambridge University Press, 1973), 118–35; and in Bernard Williams, *Morality* (Harmondsworth, Penguin, 1972), 104–12.
9 W. Newton-Smith, 'A conceptual investigation of love' in Alan Montefiore, ed., *Philosophy and Personal Relations* (London, Routledge & Kegan Paul, 1973), 120.
10 'What I believe' in E.M. Forster, *Two Cheers for Democracy* (London, Arnold, 1951), 78.
11 G. Orwell, 'Reflections on Gandhi' in Sonia Orwell and Ian Angus, ed., *The Collected Essays, Journalism and Letters of George Orwell*, vol. 4 (London, Secker, 1968), 466.
12 Ibid.
13 See D.H. Monro, ed., *A Guide to the British Moralists* (London, Fontana, 1972), 187–92. The extract is taken from William Godwin, *Enquiry Concerning Political Justice*, book 2, ch. 2.
14 Ronald Dworkin, *Taking Rights Seriously* (London, Duckworth, 1978), 234.
15 See Ten, *Mill on Liberty*, 30–3.
16 R. Dworkin, 'Do we have a right to pornography?' in Dworkin, *A Matter of Principle* (London, 1985), especially 359–65.
17 Ibid., 361.
18 Richard Wollheim, 'John Stuart Mill and the limits of state action', *Social Research* 40 (1973) 1–30.

19 Ten, *Mill on Liberty*, 19–29.
20 Wollheim, 'John Stuart Mill and the limits of state action', 12.
21 See Smart and Williams, *Utilitarianism: for and against*, 93–107, especially 104–6. Williams himself is of course an acute critic of utilitarianism.
22 Ibid., 105.
23 John C. Rees, *John Stuart Mill's On Liberty* (Oxford, Clarendon Press, 1985). My discussion of Rees is taken from my review of his book in *The Mill News Letter* 21 (1986).
24 Rees, *John Stuart Mill's On Liberty*, 49.
25 This volume, p. 175.
26 Rees, *John Stuart Mill's On Liberty*, 167.
27 *An Introduction to the Principles of Morals and Legislation* in J.H. Burns and H.L.A. Hart, eds, *The Collected Works of Jeremy Bentham* (London, Athlone Press, 1970), ch. 10, sect. 10.
28 Rees, *John Stuart Mill's On Liberty*, 167.
29 Ibid., 44.
30 Bentham, *An Introduction to the Principles of Morals and Legislation*, ch. 2, sect. 11.
31 Robert W. Hoag, 'Happiness and freedom: recent work on John Stuart Mill', *Philosophy & Public Affairs* 15 (1986), 189.
32 John Gray, *Mill on Liberty: A Defence*; Fred R. Berger, *Happiness, Justice, and Freedom: The Moral and Political Philosophy of John Stuart Mill* (Berkeley, University of California Press, 1984).
33 John Rawls, *A Theory of Justice* (Oxford, Oxford University Press, 1972), 210.
34 Robert Nozick, *Anarchy, State, and Utopia* (Oxford, Blackwell, 1974), 28.
35 Berger, *Happiness, Justice and Freedom*, 238.
36 Ibid., 337, n. 61.
37 Ibid., 5.
38 Hoag, 'Happiness and freedom: recent work on John Stuart Mill', 189, n. 4.

SOCIAL LIBERTY AND FREE AGENCY
Some ambiguities in Mill's conception of freedom

G. W. Smith

PRINCIPLES AND CONCEPTS OF LIBERTY

'The sole end for which mankind are warranted, individually or collectively, in interfering with the liberty of action of any of their number, is self-protection' (p. 30).[1] So goes Mill's deceptively crisp formulation of the animating idea of *On Liberty*, the celebrated 'one very simple principle', the Principle of Liberty. Two preliminary points about the principle are worth noting. First, it is a normative rule of liberty invoking a logically distinct and independent concept of freedom, that is to say, it prescribes an area within which individuals ought to be free, and by freedom Mill means 'liberty of action'.[2] Second, Mill is often regarded as an exponent of 'negative' freedom on the grounds that the Principle of Liberty is a negative principle defining an area of non-interference. This is unhelpful: the classic statement of the principle above is clearly positive rather than negative, in that it warrants interference with others' freedom on the condition that it is only for self-protection.[3] Of course, it may equally well be formulated negatively, but that merely indicates that the issue is basically a verbal one. The substantive question of whether Mill is a negative libertarian or not hinges upon the kind of *concept* of freedom applied *within* the Principle of Liberty. Hence the question cannot be limited to the essay *On Liberty* (1859). For Mill discussed the conditions for, and the nature of, freedom extensively in other places too, especially in chapter 2 of Book 6 of the *System of Logic* (1842), in chapter 26 – on punishment and responsibility – of *An*

Examination of Sir William Hamilton's Philosophy (1865), and throughout the lengthy critique of classical economic theory in his *Principles of Political Economy* (1848). Indeed, I shall argue that the polemical power of *On Liberty* tends to draw the eye away from these (apparently) less immediately relevant texts, with the result that Mill comes over as a thinker of far less originality, in respect of the philosophical development of the notion, than he really is. Though, as will become apparent, he pays a price in clarity for his philosophical originality, and this in turn reflects a fundamental ambiguity in his liberalism.

We need to begin our investigation with *On Liberty*, however, and particularly with the Principle of Liberty, if only to vindicate the importance of attempting to determine precisely what concept of freedom Mill deploys. A great deal of effort has been expended in trying to attach a definite sense to 'self-protection' (and to its corollary 'harm to others') in the conviction that ambiguity here means unclarity in the scope of application of the principle itself. And this must be right, for how can we know how far Mill wishes people to be left free if we are given no sure guidance about what is to count as harming others? But, in general, critics have been less alive to the fact that clarity at this point (even if attainable) is of limited avail if we cannot discriminate with reasonable confidence between free and unfree agents in the first place. A false confidence that there can be no real problem here tends to be raised by two considerations. First, there is the predisposition to read Mill as a negative libertarian, applying a pretty straightforward liberal concept of freedom, because he is apparently situated so obviously in the tradition of nineteenth-century British liberalism which (save for the deviancy of T.H. Green and Bernard Bosanquet) cleaves to an empiricist and negative concept of liberty almost as the ark of the covenant of its political faith. Second, what Mill explicitly says about freedom when he lays down his principle reinforces the view that, however unconventional his liberalism might be in other respects, on this issue he is fundamentally orthodox. For, in almost the same sentence in which he formulates the principle, he mentions, as impediments to 'liberty of action', 'compulsion', 'physical force in the form of legal penalties', and 'the moral coercion of public opinion', (p. 30) all suggesting that freedom of action is to be construed (roughly) as 'absence of external impediments on an agent's doing what he wants to do'. Hence, it seems reasonable to conclude that if Mill goes beyond the rigorously narrow Benthamite conception of freedom at all it is only by extending intentional impediments on wants to include the informal and diffuse sanctions of public opinion.

The important question, however, is not: what does Mill say 'freedom' is?, nor even: what concept of freedom does Mill take himself to be deploying?, but rather: what kind of notion is presupposed by the use to which Mill puts the Principle of Liberty in the essay, and by the overall pattern of argument therein? In other words, what sense of 'freedom' is implied in consistency by Mill's position in *On Liberty*? H.J. McCloskey, for example, argues that though Mill sets out with 'doing what one wants' as his 'official' definition of liberty he in fact slides pretty quickly into a much more positive notion of freedom as self-determination.[4] In a similar vein, R.B. Friedman maintains that the typical liberal idea of freedom, according to which 'the agent's own desires are taken as given data, and he is understood to be free if no one restrains him from giving effect to them', is accompanied by a thoroughly positive conception of freedom embodying a moral ideal of unservile self-assertion.[5] The reason for such scepticism about Mill's adherence to his definition is not far to seek. One of his major preoccupations in the essay is with the rise of democratic conformism, yet how can mass conformity be depicted as perhaps the most insidious modern threat to liberty if freedom is construed simply as a matter of unfrustrated want-satisfaction? For, is the conformist not precisely someone who always wants to do whatever he happens to be permitted to do?

The issue arises in a particularly acute form in Sir Isaiah Berlin's sympathetic and highly influential interpretation of Mill's liberalism. In a remarkably eloquent and persuasive exposition of liberal values, Berlin locates the nerve of Mill's political position when he says:

> Mill believes in liberty, that is, the rigid limitation of the right to coerce, because he is sure that men cannot develop and flourish and become fully human unless they are left free from interference by other men within a certain minimum area of their lives, which he regards as – or wishes to make – inviolable.[6]

If there is any single theme running through the complex web of argument and rhetoric in *On Liberty* it is surely this – that 'self-development' (or, as Mill usually calls it in the essay, 'individuality') cannot possibly be realized without 'freedom, and variety of situations' (p. 73 and p. 88). Berlin's 'rigid limitation of the right to coerce' refers, of course, to the Principle of Liberty; it is freedom in this normative sense which, for Mill, is a necessary condition of individuality. But what concept of freedom does Berlin think the Principle presupposes? He mentions 'freedom from interference', and in his 'Two concepts of liberty' he attributes to Mill a 'definition of negative liberty as the ability to do what one wishes'; but he goes on immediately to insist that, as a concept for use by genuine liberals, 'this will not do'.[7] For, 'if the tyrant (or "hidden persuader") manages to condition his subjects (or customers) into losing their original wishes and embrace ("internalize") the form of life he has invented for them, he will, on this definition, have succeeded in liberating them.'[8] By the same token, if this were indeed what Mill meant by 'freedom', the Principle of Liberty could not possibly function as Berlin claims Mill intends, for it would clearly be worthless as a guarantee of the possibility of individuality precisely because it would embody a concept of freedom permitting us to describe anyone whose desires had been ironed into conformity as not being unfree.

Berlin is, of course, much too acute a reader of Mill to be unaware of the problem, though the solution which he suggests, or implies, carries with it peculiar difficulties for a thinker who, more than anyone in recent years, has set the categories within which the question of freedom is raised. Prefacing his claim that Mill believes in the individual's right to a sphere of freedom, he emphasizes Mill's profound conviction that 'man differs from animals primarily neither as a possessor of reason, nor as an inventor of tools and methods, but as a being capable of choice . . .'[9] And indeed one of the great strengths of Berlin's method in 'Two concepts of liberty' lies precisely in his recognition of the importance of views about human nature in determining conceptions of freedom: different concepts of freedom are, he argues, fully intelligible only against the context of the particular view of man presupposed in each. Mill's view of man, as Berlin quite rightly says, is of man as a chooser. The implication is surely clear. Whatever Mill might say, whatever tidy definition he might propose, Berlin's position must be that the effective notion of freedom actually at work in the essay reflects Mill's distinctive convictions about human nature and human needs. Hence, it is freedom *qua* freedom of choice, not freedom as merely unfrustrated want-satisfaction – a notion applicable to animals as well as to men – that (on Berlin's own principles) makes crucial sense of Mill's claim that the Principle of Liberty is a necessary means to individuality. Undoubtedly we have here a more adequate reading of Mill than that suggested by either McCloskey or Friedman in that it implicitly recognizes the absurdity of a narrow negative notion of freedom in the context of Mill's actual purposes in *On Liberty*, but without attributing to him a precipitous slide, or wild oscillation, between two diametrically opposed ideas of liberty. What is particularly intriguing about this idea, however, is that, prima facie at least, it undermines the categorial framework of the 'Two concepts of liberty', because it implies that Mill is operating with a concept of freedom which is neither clearly negative nor clearly positive.

It might be replied, and perhaps Berlin would be prepared to argue, that freedom *qua* freedom of choice is fundamentally a negative conception of liberty, no less unambiguously so than freedom as absence of want-frustration, on the grounds that someone who enjoys freedom of choice is simply someone faced with a range of uncoerced opportunities, and the larger the range, the greater his freedom. This, however, ignores the complications introduced by the idea that options are available only (to use Berlin's own words) to 'beings capable of choice'. It is indeed possible for the liberal to accommodate this 'subjective' dimension of free agency by simply stipulating that all human beings, except extreme cases such as infants, the certifiably insane, or the mentally subnormal, are to be assumed to enjoy powers of rational judgement and decision, so that the question of freedom remains restricted to manifestly visible and external impediments on chosen actions. And indeed Berlin sometimes speaks as though this is his position.[10] Yet, as we have already seen by the way in which he deals with the threat of manipulative tyrants and hidden persuaders, he remains very much alive to invasions of freedom by way of the alteration of a subject's desires, and the most obvious way to effect this is, of course, to undermine his capacity rationally to appreciate and to choose alternatives upon which to act.

Berlin's reluctance explicitly to incorporate considerations of rationality into his concept of freedom as choice is explicable, of course, in terms of the way in which he draws the major dividing line between negative and positive liberty: positive libertarians, he argues, identify freedom with 'rational self-mastery' and this with doing what is morally right, with the (to his mind) entirely inevitable result that the purportedly immoral, and hence irrational, may be 'forced to be free'. It has been suggested that there is nothing in Berlin's position which would prevent him in principle from adopting a conception of freedom as opportunity for choice embodying a notion of rationality other than the strong meta-physical version which, by asserting that all values are rationally coherent, entails the illiberalism to which Berlin objects.[11] As he appears to be imputing just some such weaker notion to Mill, it is perhaps not without interest to pursue the implications of this interpretation in more detail in order to discover whether Mill succeeds in broadening the traditional 'mechanical' negative liberal notion of freedom whilst avoiding the pitfalls of positive liberty so influentially depicted by Berlin. However, to this end, we need to begin rather obliquely by addressing a question about freedom which many students of Mill have held to be strictly irrelevant to an understanding of liberty in his social philosophy.

LOGIC AND LIBERTY

In the *System of Logic* Mill concludes his proof of the possibility of human freedom in a causally determined world with the words, 'And hence it is said with truth, that none but a person of confirmed virtue is completely free'[12] – an unqualifiedly moralistic and positive notion of freedom. What should we make of the claim that only those who choose rightly are really free, especially in the light of the purportedly libertarian doctrines of *On Liberty*? John Rees takes a strong line: what Mill says about freedom in the *Logic*, or elsewhere in his metaphysical works, may simply be ignored if we are interested in what he means by liberty in his social writings: 'No conclusions about the free-will problem entail any particular theory of civil or political liberty. Questions about human actions being determined by unalterable laws are not questions about legal or social restraints', and he continues, 'There is every sign that Mill, too, was fully aware of the distinction. Guilty of many logical blunders, he can escape the charge of failing to differentiate civil liberty from the freedom of the will.'[13] After all, Rees continues, Mill makes the point in the very first sentence of *On Liberty*: 'the subject of this Essay is not the so-called Liberty of the Will . . . but Civil, or Social Liberty: the nature and limits of the power which can be legitimately exercised by society over the individual.'[14]

But, if we bear in mind the elementary distinction between the principle and the concept of liberty, Rees's interpretation can be seen to be manifestly misguided. In the opening sentence of the essay Mill is distinguishing two *topics*: by 'civil', or 'social' liberty he obviously intends the principle and its implications, and though he announces this, rather than the 'Liberty of the Will', to be his topic of discussion in the essay, he neither says nor implies that the two topics involve distinct or incommensurable concepts of freedom.[15] Moreover, Mill's choice of target in his discussion in the *Logic* of 'the so-called Liberty of the Will' clearly indicates that the division between metaphysics and politics, emphasized by Rees and taken almost as an axiom by many philosophers of the linguistic school, means nothing to him.[16] For he elects to address the 'social fatalism' of the reformer Robert Owen, in part because he is convinced that it is philosophically misguided, but also because he believes its effects to be politically and socially pernicious.[17]

The intimate connection for Mill between metaphysical and social freedom can be seen if we consider his response to Owen. Owen is a social determinist, that is to say, he holds that we cannot be responsible for what we do nor for what we are, because our desires (and actions) are caused by our characters and our characters by social circumstances beyond our control. Now, if Mill were an orthodox negative libertarian who took freedom simply as the absence of external coercion, he clearly could have no cause for quarrel with Owen. After all, Owen's socially manufactured men, whose wants are not determined by themselves but by society, may from the orthodox liberal point of view be just as free (or unfree) as any other kind of human being – it simply depends upon whether the wants they happen to have are frustrated by others or not. But Mill is adamant: if Owen were right, human freedom would be impossible. Where, then, does Mill differ from Owen? It is not on the question of determinism. For, like Owen, he accepts that human actions are natural events, in the sense that they are (at least in principle) causally explicable and perfectly predictable. Spurred on, however, by the picture of human impotence depicted in Owen's doctrine of social fatalism, Mill sets himself the stiff challenge of reconciling universal determinism with human freedom, where the latter connotes not simply absence of external frustration but, more positively, human self-determination.

The germ of the conception of freedom which implicitly informs the argument of *On Liberty* may be revealed if we are prepared to attend rather more carefully than is usually the case to some of the details of Mill's refutation of Owenite social passivism. The first point to note is that his aim is, as has already been suggested, in one respect somewhat limited. It is to modify, rather than to reject, the traditional empiricist solution to the free-will problem offered by Hobbes and Hume.[18] The traditional line is to argue that freedom must be compatible with universal determinism, because the causal history of an agent's wants is strictly irrelevant to his liberty. The Compatibilist holds that though human actions are caused they are not thereby compelled, for the causal relation is merely one of constant conjunction of events, not a relation of necessity. Human actions are necessitated, and hence unfree, only when they are coerced, and they are coerced only by external impediments imposed intentionally by other persons. Hence an agent is free when he does what he wants, even though his desires figure as occurrences in a causal chain stretching before and beyond him.

Mill's position is significantly different. He accepts the Humean analysis of causality, but rejects the claim that the causal history of the agent's desires is irrelevant to his freedom. On the contrary, he argues, the way in which his desires originate is crucial to his liberty. This does not mean that he is going back on his position and embracing some version of Indeterminism: an agent's desires flow from his character rather than arising spontaneously from an act of arbitrary will, but the circumstances which causally account for his character are not to be ascribed simply to his social conditioning. The nub of Mill's modified Compatibilism lies in his suggestion that causal laws are hypothetical rather than categorical in form. Instead of stating impossibilities or inevitabilities, they merely lay down what will, or will not, occur if intervening causes do not apply. We are all familiar, says Mill, with how the course of events is often changed by human intervention – as when someone who would otherwise necessarily die from poisoning is saved by the timely application of an antidote. We intervene all the time in other people's development – by law, public opinion, and so on. Whether we do so, and if we do, how, is of course itself determined, but this does not affect our being able to do what we do. And, he concludes, what we can do for others, we can do for ourselves. It would be impossible for us to control our own characters, and thus make our wants genuinely 'our own', only if the causal conditions for so doing could never be realized; but amongst the most important causal antecedents of what Mill calls in the *Logic* 'self-development', 'self-amendment', and 'self-mastery' (all close synonyms of the 'individuality' of *On Liberty*) is the desire on our part to do so. As there is nothing about the truth of universal determinism which necessarily precludes the occurrence of this desire, Mill concludes 'this feeling, of our being able to modify our own character, *if we wish*, is itself the feeling of moral freedom we are conscious of'.[19] He is prepared to concede that some people cannot determine their own characters, and thereby make their desires their own, even if they wish. They experience 'intractable compulsions', or suffer from 'inveterate habits', which frustrate the aim of self-reform. But it is only they who find themselves in the predicament of unfreedom which Owen misguidedly imputes to us all.

In this 'conditional' or 'hypothetical' notion of freedom we find the essence of Mill's idea of liberty, both metaphysical and social, for clearly his central concern is not merely with bodily freedom to satisfy wants; he is instead anxious to show how men can be free as agents capable of claiming, and admitting, autonomous responsibility for their desires, and hence for their actions. The practising individualist of *On Liberty*, who develops his character to the point where his desires are peculiarly, perhaps even uniquely, 'his own', because he has moulded it more thoroughly than others, exemplifies precisely the type of agent-freedom whose possibility Mill strives to demonstrate in his attack on Owenite social fatalism.

CONDITIONAL FREEDOM AND THE PRINCIPLE OF LIBERTY

Before examining the adequacy of Mill's position as a solution to the traditional problems of freedom and determinism, let us consider the implications of construing the liberty invoked in the principle along these lines. The idea is positive in four main respects:

1 It involves what Berlin holds to be a crucial element in all positive versions of freedom – that of self-mastery or self-determination.

2 Rather than mere absence of impediments to action, it is a matter of the possession of abilities and powers for self-development.

3 Self-development is clearly for Mill a prized achievement – there is nothing 'value-neutral' about the notion, as there is about freedom *qua* uncoerced satisfaction of wants, whatever they might be for.

4 The impediments to self-mastery explicitly mentioned by Mill are 'internal' rather than 'external' – psychological defects of character such as weakness of will or subjection to habit, not coercion by others. On the other hand, it remains negative in two important respects:

1 The actual achievement of self-mastery is not a condition of freedom. The conformist, the lazy, even the vicious, may still on this definition be free. Mill insists that we may 'yield to temptation' and remain free – just so long as we could resist, if we wished. Freedom thus remains basically liberal in that it is a matter of enjoying opportunities rather than of actual positive achievements.

2 Because the actual attainment of Mill's ideal of personality development is not presented as a necessary condition of freedom, he manages to sustain a distinction, often held particularly dear by orthodox liberals, between liberty – the opportunity to do something arising from the possession of the requisite powers – and what makes freedom useful or valuable: the actual doing or achieving of that thing.[20]

Clearly, the dichotomy of *either* negative *or* positive freedom is simply misleading when applied to such a notion. Yet conditional freedom is precisely the idea at work when Mill makes the points he does about the value of a sphere of 'self-regarding' action, as it captures just those persons whom he is usually understood particularly to want to protect, namely those who may be presumed to be capable of forming their own personalities, and who may also be taken to want to do so, but who are likely to feel inhibited by the prospect of social disapproval from expressing themselves in the way in which they feel they need to do. These likely exponents of individuality are to be guaranteed 'liberty of action', that is to say, the Principle of Liberty ensures them a sphere of freedom within which they may, if they wish, take the opportunity to exercise their powers of self-development by practising 'experiments in living', where these do not harm others. This conception of freedom also squares with liberty *qua* 'letting people alone to pursue their *own* good in their *own* way', (p. 33) as well as with the orthodox liberal view of the proper function of the state, with which Mill is usually associated, that is, as protecting or conserving a freedom which individuals are presumed already to possess.

However, though the conditional notion of free agency undoubtedly represents the core of Mill's understanding of liberty, additional complexities are revealed by considering the implications of a common criticism of his Compatibilist solution to the problem of freedom and determinism. It is often argued that, strictly speaking, Mill has no right to a notion of freedom as self-development because his empiricist theory of personal identity, which resolves the self into a Humean 'bundle of impressions', cannot account for the possibility of an enduring self maintaining a persisting identity through a series of developmental changes.[21] Mill is in fact rather less dogmatic about associationism, at least as far as its implications for self-identity are concerned, than is sometimes represented.[22] But it cannot be denied that this represents a void at the centre of his philosophical system, in that his official epistemology commits him to precisely that attenuated conception of personality which gives plausibility to the standard liberal notion of freedom as non-frustration of wants. For, if the self is nothing more than a bundle of perceptions and desires, nothing more than their unhindered satisfaction can properly be demanded in the name of liberty. However, the criticism which raises philosophically more promising issues for Mill is connected not so much with his theory of personal identity as with his ideal of personal autonomy. It is contended that the basic flaw in Mill's theory of freedom lies in his admission that 'the will to alter our own character is given us, not by any effort of ours, but by circumstances we cannot help: it comes to us from external causes, or not at all'.[23] An admission that any clear-minded determinist can scarcely avoid, yet the fallacy seems manifest: if we cannot *actually* determine our character unless we *actually desire* to do so, and if the desire for self-mastery cannot (as Mill admits) be self-induced, are we not all ultimately heteronomously motivated, and hence by his own criterion unfree?

Mill makes no direct response to this challenge, and perhaps there is none to be made, though there may be more to his position than some critics have been prepared to allow.[24] There is something of an irony here, however, in that the deficiencies of his answer to Owen at the purely metaphysical level point him in a potentially very fruitful direction in his social philosophy. It is simply that, if the desire for self-reform cannot be self-induced, the external (i.e. social) circumstances which either stimulate or inhibit its occurrence take on crucial significance for the individual's actual engagement in the process of self-development – even if this latter cannot, in strict metaphysical terms, lay claim to being a fully or genuinely autonomous condition of character. Though there is no explicit evidence that Mill clearly registers the implications of his position, the way in which he treats Owenite social fatalism as a real threat to freedom (and not simply as a misguided intellectual position) suggests that he implicitly slides from taking the desire for self-development as merely a hypothetical requirement of freedom to invoking it categorically, at least in the sense that anyone prevented from conceiving the wish for self-reform is to be classed with those whose desire is frustrated as being unfree *tout court*. The context of this vital elision is to be found in Mill's comments upon the deplorable effect, as he sees it, of swallowing Owen's account of human impotence. On the one hand, it might 'depress' or 'paralyse' the will of someone who already wants to engage in character self-reform, as do uncontrollable impulses and inveterate habits. But it can also prevent someone who could reform himself if he wished from even desiring to do so, by encouraging him falsely to think that he could not succeed even if he tried.[25] On a strict construal of Mill's original conditional formulation the former is, of course, unfree whereas the latter remains free. Mill, however, treats them as being essentially similar: in both cases individuals who might otherwise successfully amend their own characters are prevented from so doing by the influence of a false ideology. Though the impediments to self-reform operate by way of different psychological routes, they originate in the same social phenomenon and eventuate in the same effect. Hence Mill's implicit elision of two conditions which, according to his preliminary account of conditional freedom, are quite distinct.

By implicitly broadening the concept in this way Mill is, of course, enabled to embrace a far wider set of social circumstances as possible threats to liberty than could his liberal predecessors. It cannot, however, be over-emphasized that Mill's mind remains far from clear as to the precise logical contours and implications of the revolutionary idea of freedom which he develops as a response to social fatalism – a fact which, as we shall see, bears important consequences for an understanding of the central doctrine of *On Liberty*. Nevertheless, Mill in effect is operating with a three-factor conception of freedom, one positive, two negative. 'Complete freedom', as he calls it, presupposes:

(a) Possession of the capacity to alter one's character, if one wishes.
(b) Absence of impediments upon the exercise of this capacity when one does wish to exercise it.

(3) Absence of conditions inhibiting the occurrence of the desire so to do.[26]

The logical kernel of the idea lies in (a), and it is developed by Mill in response to Owen's social fatalism and offered as a form of modified Compatibilism as a solution to the metaphysical problem of 'free will'. When considering the kinds of constraints – (b) – upon the exercise of powers of self-development, Mill alludes in the *Logic* to internal psychological defects of character; but external impediments are mentioned in connection with the threat of Owenite fatalism, and everything Mill says in *On Liberty* about the dangers of coercive public opinion to freedom implies that he takes external constraints as relevant too. But it is in regard to (c) that Mill's worries about the peculiarly modern threat to freedom really take form. And it is this condition which bears fundamentally upon the Principle of Liberty in the essay.

HUMAN NATURE: MILL'S STRATEGIC OPTIMISM

First, an obvious point. As well as embracing victims of Owenite fatalism, the notion of freedom developed by Mill in the *Logic* is ideally suited to capture the condition of just those persons who Mill believed, following Tocqueville, presently constitute perhaps the most worrying feature of democracy, namely, those whose 'souls' have been 'enslaved' by modern society: abject conformists are at once the victims of the democratic ethos of undifferentiated equality and uniformity, and represent its most dangerous threat. They are essentially Owenite socially manufactured men who have been trained to want only what society is prepared to permit them to do or to get; and they have been so well drilled in their psychological responses that, as Mill says, 'it does not occur to them to have any inclination, except for what is customary' (p. 77). The threat they pose lies in part, of course, in the way they are prone to mobilize themselves into a coercive public opinion designed to frustrate the aspirations of individualists, or potential individualists, who are already free in respects (a) and (c). But their influence is particularly insidious because of the way in which their very existence and numbers bear upon condition (c). By imposing a pall of deadening conformity over society, they succeed in shortening the personal horizons of all but the most

251

robust individualists. For where there is no variety in life-styles, and where variety when it occurs is frowned upon, there can be no emulation of individuality, and hence *no stimulation of the desire* for self-development. And yet, as we have seen, there is for Mill no essential difference between the social inhibition of the desire for self-mastery (as the result, for example, of a widespread acceptance of the inevitability of social fatalism) and someone's lacking the power of self-reform, or being prevented from exercising it by some specific interfering condition. The power (a), the opportunity for its exercise (b), and the desire so to do (c) are severally necessary and jointly sufficient conditions for 'complete freedom' as Mill understands it. Hence the effect of blanket social conformity and the effect of an unchallenged Owenite ideology is the same – both constitute conditions which by criterion (c) are inconsistent with individual freedom.

What, then, are the implications of this for the Principle of Liberty? The first point to note is the way in which the application of condition (c) brings Mill's view of human nature to the forefront. For much of the time in *On Liberty* Mill's attitude is unreservedly optimistic. That is to say, he simply assumes that it is quite natural for human beings to want actively to shape and mould their own personalities to meet a personal vision of ideal living. From this perspective the behaviour of anyone who might happen to display an indifference to self-reform demands an explanation. And the spread of Owenite fatalism, or the rise of democratic *mores*, are obvious explanatory candidates. For the assumption is that, in the absence of impediments of this kind, people would naturally aspire to freedom. On the other hand, Mill from time to time qualifies his optimism. In this mood the desire for active individuality is thought to appear only under unusually propitious social circumstances which serve to stimulate the average individual out of a condition of relative apathy. Optimism, whether of the one kind or the other, of course, dominates in *On Liberty*. Indeed, the coherence of Mill's position depends vitally upon it, for it represents the psychological axiom by which he manages to square his far from orthodoxly liberal concept of freedom with the liberal orientation of the Principle of Liberty. As was pointed out earlier, the Principle applies most naturally as a basically conservative instrument, designed to preserve the freedom assumed to be already enjoyed by the great majority of citizens. According to the unqualifiedly optimistic Mill, the 'freedom of action' thus protected is freedom to pursue and to satisfy the desire for self-development or individuality. In other words, the logic of the operation of the principle is fairly limpid when it is assumed that agents already fulfil conditions (a) and (c), for then the principle simply serves to guarantee the fulfilment of (b). But where we cannot assume that people generally do desire freedom, the principle clearly cannot function in this straightforward liberal manner as a liberty-conserving device. For, where condition (c) cannot be assumed to obtain, a prior problem for freedom arises: namely, to create the appropriate social atmosphere for the pursuit of freedom by countering conditions productive of apathy.

This might be thought, with some justice, to be a radical rather than a liberal programme. So what place is there in Mill's theory for a conservatively orientated principle, once unqualified gives away to qualified optimism about human nature and the problem of stimulating people to freedom appears? Mill's answer involves a supplementary piece of optimism. Idiots, lunatics, colonial races, and minors apart, people must be assumed to be generally capable of being influenced by reason and persuasion. So, though they might now be prevented by the influences of social uniformity from even wanting to develop their own characters, and hence strictly speaking fail to count as free agents under (c), they still qualify for protection under the principle. They must be allowed to pursue their own desires (where this does not harm others), but under the stimulating examples of successful practitioners of individuality, always backed up where necessary by firm, but non-coercive, direction by way of argument and exhortation (p. 31). In this way Mill manages to turn the principle in a radical direction to cover a passive and conforming majority who cannot of their own accord come to want to engage in personality expanding 'experiments in living'. That he is able to do this is, of course, most important for Mill, as his predominant attitude is that of qualified rather than unqualified optimism about human nature – a conviction not that men aspire naturally or easily to individuality, but that they can be socially stimulated and educated so to do by a minority who, rather unnaturally, are spontaneous individualists.

We have now arrived at a point where it is possible to dispel a common misapprehension. Typically Mill is read as arguing that freedom is valuable as a (or the best) means to individuality. Certainly he maintains that the Principle of Liberty is a means to freedom, that is to say, it is a rule or institutional device for preserving or acquiring freedom. But it should be clear by now that Mill cannot mean that the freedom thus protected is merely the uncoerced opportunity to satisfy the widest range of desires – conceptually distinct from individuality and merely the instrumental means thereto. Three considerations may be borne in mind here. First, Mill has already explicitly repudiated such a negative conception of liberty in his passage with Owen in favour of freedom *qua* self-development, of which the individuality of *On Liberty* is obviously a variant. Second, if the freedom secured by the principle were simply a matter of the uncoerced opportunity to satisfy desires it would apply even in a society of contented Owenite social zombies, in which case the significance of the principle for Mill becomes entirely problematical (*vide* Berlin's worries about 'manipulation'). Third, unlike the idea of freedom as self-development, which (as we have seen) is able to embrace as threats to liberty conditions bearing upon an agent's conceiving the desire for self-reform, condition (c), negative freedom simply cannot accommodate the kinds of diffuse and subtle influences undermining liberty exemplified by the Owenite ideology and by the ethos of democratic conformism – precisely the conditions which most disturb Mill in *On Liberty*.

In response to the first point it might be replied (in the spirit of Rees) that, however convenient the conception Mill develops in his metaphysical writings about freedom might be to his social philosophy, he nevertheless, when he comes to write the latter, shifts back to the more elementary liberal notion of liberty and sharply distinguishes (negative) freedom from self-development and individuality. But this is surely entirely unconvincing, as it involves imputing to Mill a peculiarly perverse line of thought. For in his campaign against the threat of social conformism in *On Liberty* he manifestly displays a preoccupation almost identical with that informing his attack on the effect of Owenite social fatalism in the *Logic*. Is it then really plausible to maintain that he must abandon in the former a concept he found so necessary and eminently serviceable in the latter? Why, then, the persistent reluctance to recognize that, for Mill, freedom is identical with individuality and not a separable means to it? Leaving aside the elementary confusion between the Principle of Liberty and the concept of freedom, the reason is surely to be found in the general tendency of commentators to ignore the fundamental strategic significance to Mill's position of his qualified optimism about the social educability of human nature.

Certainly, the claim that people should be permitted the widest possible arena of action to do what they wish is a passionately argued theme in *On Liberty*. But this can be taken as a commitment to a conventional liberal conception of freedom only if it is forgotten that Mill simply takes it for granted most of the time that – at least in the long run and for the great majority of people – a policy of tolerance, encouragement of social variety, and concerned non-coercive intervention will trigger, not any arbitrary range of self-regarding desires, but a very specific desire: that for individual self-improvement, whereby otherwise passive subjects will become agents desiring to make their characters 'their own'. It is because he believes that most people are capable of being educated up to individuality by way of example and exhortation by practising individualists that Mill gives the misleading impression that, like unreconstructed liberals, he takes freedom to be a matter of doing what one wishes without coercive interference. To this it might be replied that, since Mill deploys the Principle of Liberty on these assumptions to guarantee a sphere in which people are permitted to do as they wish, this is what freedom must in effect amount to, irrespective of any further conceptual elaboration which Mill might or might not attach to it. Hence the strict irrelevance of his conceptual innovations in the *Logic*, even if he does intend to carry them over to *On Liberty*. The fundamental problem with this line of argument, however, is that it takes it for granted that Mill remains at least a qualified optimist about the educability of human nature, whereas in fact he oscillates between optimism and the most profound pessimism concerning the prospects for human development.

Thus, for example, at one point in *Utilitarianism*, Mill considers the objection to his proposed inductive test designed to distinguish between 'higher' and 'lower' pleasures 'that many who are capable of the higher pleasures occasionally, under the influence of temptation, postpone them to the lower'.[27] In the light of his fears in *On Liberty* about the dangers posed by modern democracy, his reply is surely significant:

> But I do not believe that those who undergo *this very common* change, voluntarily choose the lower description of pleasures in preference to the higher . . . Capacity for the nobler feelings is in most natures a very tender plant, easily killed, not only by hostile influences, but by the mere want of sustenance; and in the majority of young persons it speedily

dies away if the occupations to which their position in life has devoted them, and the society into which it has thrown them, are not favourable to keeping that higher capacity in existence.[28]

Individuals who are both capable of discriminating between higher and lower pleasures and who choose the former are, of course, the self-mastered persons of the free-will discussion in the *Logic* and the individualists of *On Liberty*. And it is evident, here at least, that Mill regards the achievement of self-development as no common or easy thing. Many will fail entirely in the face of the difficulties; many who manage to develop the 'nobler feelings' will do so only to lose them; and the debasing effect of modern society is clearly, to Mill's mind, a major cause of failures of both kinds.

The consequences of this shift to pessimism are worth dwelling upon. It is not simply that the prospects for freedom, as Mill understands that term, are dim. Berlin has been most influential in insisting that a central and most objectionable feature of positive conceptions of freedom is the way in which free choice becomes implicitly identified with choosing what is rational, or right, or good. Hence liberty comes to be equated with the practice of rational virtue, and the morally (or aesthetically) unorthodox are simply classified as psychological defectives or mental incompetents with no freedom to lose.[29] We have already seen how Mill identifies the free with the virtuous agent in the *Logic*, and he again implicitly inclines to this position when he says that those who give in to 'temptation' never do so 'voluntarily', for someone who opts for push-pin rather than poetry reveals by his preference, in Mill's view, that he is suffering from an 'infirmity of character' or has lost his 'sense of dignity'.[30] It should not require stressing that such a position, carried through consistently, would imply that only those capable of 'virtue' (however Mill wishes to define it) are really free, and hence only they strictly qualify as falling under the protection of the Principle of Liberty. This is a highly authoritarian outcome which only Mill's reluctance (or inability) to carry his theory of freedom to its logical conclusion prevents.[31]

Although nothing quite so ominous appears in *On Liberty*, even Mill's qualified optimism falters significantly in places, particularly in his discussion of the 'hostile influences' which smother prospects for individuality by imposing a blanket of mindless conformity over society as the democratic personality develops its characteristic Tocquevillian features:

society has now fairly got the better of individuality; and the
danger which threatens human nature is not the excess, but
the deficiency, of personal impulses and preferences . . . the
mind itself is bowed to the yoke . . . by dint of not following
their own nature they have no nature to follow: their human
capacities are withered and starved: they become incapable of
any strong wishes or native pleasures, and are generally
without either opinions or feelings of home growth, or
properly their own. (p. 77)

It is worth noting that such persons must be thoroughly unfree in
the minimal and central sense (a) of Millian freedom: we may
expect their powers to be so atrophied from lack of use that
they could not alter their own characters, even if they wished.
They have in effect been reduced to the status of Owenite men:
irretrievably abject conformists entirely proof against self-reform
through example and persuasion.[32] And the corollary should be
registered too. Mill intends the Principle of Liberty to protect
men's interests as 'progressive beings'. As the abject conformist
neither is, nor has any real prospect of becoming, 'progressive'
in the fundamental Millian sense of having an interest in the
opportunity to develop and exercise his human potentialities and
powers, he must in all consistency fail to qualify for the protection
of the principle which is designed to protect those capable of
human freedom.

Consistently drawn out, then, the implications of Mill's pessimism about human nature suggest a picture significantly different
from any recognizably liberal view of the proper nature and scope
of freedom. For, from this perspective, the function of the Principle
of Liberty must be basically that of protecting the fundamental
interest in freedom of the fortunate minority who still have liberty
to lose by curbing the activities of the majority who have none.
Of course, pessimism enters On Liberty only sporadically. By a
mixture of optimism about human nature and vagueness as to the
precise logical implications of his conceptual innovations Mill
manages to sustain a fragile coherence between his complex and
ambiguous concept of freedom and his genuinely liberal instincts.[33]

Nevertheless, it is surely somewhat ironic to find Berlin's
eloquently expressed suspicions about the dangers of abandoning a
strictly negative conception of freedom vindicated in the thought of
a philosopher who is so often taken to be an exemplary liberal. For

the inevitably authoritarian outcome of Mill's shift of philosophical allegiance from a Benthamite notion of liberty is avoided only by the imposition of a highly contingent, and on his own admission somewhat unlikely, view of human nature. When Mill's confidence in the educability of human nature falters, the illiberal conclusions follow of necessity. This is an embarrassment of which he remains essentially unaware, largely because he never entirely succeeds in clarifying to himself all the implications of the complex and ambiguous conception of freedom which figures centrally in his novel and inventive response to the challenge of Owen's social determinism.

NOTES

1 Mill, *On Liberty*, all page references in the text are to this volume.
2 I shall use 'liberty' and 'freedom' interchangeably, as Mill does.
3 Warranted, of course, only if the general utility of so doing outweighs the utility of non-interference.
4 H.J. McCloskey, *John Stuart Mill: a critical study* (Macmillan, London, 1971), 104–5.
5 R.B. Friedman, 'A new exploration of Mill's essay *On Liberty*', *Political Studies* 14 (1966), 281–304: 'men are thought of as unfree not essentially because of the coercive interference of *other men*, but instead because they "do not desire liberty", and servility is not, in this view, a feature of the relations among men, but rather an attribute of character . . .' ibid., 289.
6 Isaiah Berlin, 'John Stuart Mill and the ends of life', this volume, (pp. 146–7).
7 Isaiah Berlin, *Four Essays on Liberty* (Oxford, Oxford University Press, 1969), 139.
8 ibid,. 139–40.
9 Berlin, 'John Stuart Mill and the ends of life', this volume, (p. 135).
10 This is, in effect, Berlin's 'revised' idea of negative freedom, presented as a solution to the problem of the 'contented slave'. See Berlin, *Four Essays on Liberty*, xxxvii–xl. For its adequacy, see G.W. Smith, 'Slavery, contentment and social freedom', *Philosophical Quarterly* 27 (1977), 236–48, and John Gray, 'Freedom, slavery and contentment' in M. Freeman and D. Robertson, eds., *The Frontiers of Political Theory* (Harvester, Hassocks, 1980), 76–100.
11 John Gray, 'On negative and positive liberty', *Political Studies* 28 (1980), 507–26.
12 Mill, *CW*, 8:841.
13 J. Rees, *Mill and his Early Critics* (University College Leicester, 1956), 48–9.
14 ibid., 49.

15 The issue is discussed in more detail, in connection with Rees' views about the authorship of 'On social freedom', a piece invoking a highly moralistic positive concept of liberty, and at one time attributed to Mill, in G.W. Smith, 'J.S. Mill on Edgar and Réville: an episode in the development of Mill's conception of freedom', *Journal of the History of Ideas* 41 (1980), 433–49.

16 See Alan Ryan, Introduction to Mill's *An Examination of Sir William's Philosophy*, *CW*, 9:xi–xii.

17 Mill, *CW*, 8, book 6, ch. 2.

18 The argument here is drawn from G.W. Smith, 'The logic of J.S. Mill on freedom', *Political Studies* 28 (1980), 238–52.

19 Mill, *CW*, 8:840. Italics original.

20 See, e.g. Berlin: The freedom of which I speak is opportunity for action, rather than action itself. If, although I enjoy the right to walk through open doors, I prefer not to do so, but sit still and vegetate, I am not thereby rendered less free.' *Four Essays on Liberty*, xiii.

21 See Alan Ryan, *John Stuart Mill* (New York, Random House, 1970), ch. 6.

22 Mill, *CW*, 9:206–9.

23 ibid., 8:840.

24 Ryan, op. cit., ch. 8. The desire for self-change is in essence a second-order desire directed at first-order wants typical of various character ideals, etc. Mill's free man who, in desiring to alter his character, shows himself capable of acting on such a second-order want, displays the capacities and volitions which H.G. Frankfurt, for example, sees as distinguishing free from unfree agents. 'Freedom of the will and the concept of a person', *Journal of Philosophy* 68 (1971), 5–20.

25 'It is of no consequence what we think forms our character, when we have no desire of our own about forming it, but it is of great consequence that we should not be prevented from forming such a desire by thinking the attainment impracticable, and that if we have the desire, we should know that the work is not so irrevocably done as to be incapable of being altered.' Mill, *CW*, 8:841.

26 These are worked in more detail in Smith, 'The logic of J.S. Mill on freedom'.

27 Mill, *CW*, 10:212.

28 ibid., 212–13. Italics mine.

29 Berlin, *Four Essays on Liberty*, 132–4.

30 Mill, *CW*, 10:212.

31 It is only at the price of carrying this argument through consistently that Mill is able to conclude, in his proof of freedom in the *Logic* that 'none but a person of confirmed virtue is completely free'. See Smith, 'The logic of J.S. Mill on freedom'.

32 This mood is particularly evident in his comments upon the uselessness of attempting to persuade a confirmed wife-beater out of his habit: 'It is like preaching to a worm who crawls on the ground how much better it would be for him if he were an eagle.' Mill, *CW*, 19:444.

33 cf. Maurice Cowling, *Mill and Liberalism*, 2nd edn (Cambridge, Cambridge University Press, 1990); B. Knights, *The Idea of the Clerisy in the Nineteenth Century* (Cambridge, Cambridge University Press, 1978), ch. 5.

JOHN STUART MILL AND ISAIAH BERLIN
The ends of life and the preliminaries of morality

Richard Wollheim

I

In the introductory chapter of *On Liberty* John Stuart Mill claimed that for him utility was the ultimate appeal on all ethical questions, and that he renounced any advantage that might accrue to his argument from considerations of abstract right (p. 30)[1]. In 'John Stuart Mill and the ends of life' Isaiah Berlin challenges Mill's claim.[2] He puts it forward as his view that, though Mill avowed a commitment to utility, the commitment is not real. In support of the avowed commitment Mill was compelled to stretch the notions of happiness and pleasure to the point of vacuity. Meanwhile, his real commitment was to various distinct values such as individual liberty, variety, and justice. These values may at a number of places make demands that coincide with those of utility – in so far, that is, as these themselves are coherent – but they cannot be given a consistently utilitarian interpretation.

In many writings Berlin has urged upon us a single message of great power and moment. It is that human values are necessarily many, not one, and that of the many values there is not one to which the others are properly subordinate. Values come in systems, and systems of value possess the kind of complex structure that allows the different constituent values to interact. What morality rejects is monism, and the pluralism within which it can find accommodation is a pluralism of a loose kind or pluralism without hierarchy.

It is worth pointing out that this message, which has profound and subversive implications for both practical and theoretical thinking yet to be absorbed, relates exclusively to the internal nature of an individual's morality. It says nothing about the relations between the moralities of different individuals, and specifically it does not say that there must or even can be a multiplicity of such moralities. Berlin himself, who has always held to a version of voluntaristic meta-ethics, probably believes in this kind of pluralism too. But the pluralism here under discussion is perfectly compatible with the belief in a single system of values, to which the different systems of value held by different individuals ought to conform and upon which they may be expected to converge. The message that I have attributed to Berlin is consistent, as far as I can see, with ethical objectivism and even ethical realism.

Now, once Berlin's message is clearly before us, it is plausible to think that his reading, or re-reading, of Mill derives from it. The derivation would take roughly the following course: Berlin finds Mill a sympathetic thinker with many of whose views on moral and social topics he finds himself in deep agreement; he finds it impossible to believe that these views could be arrived at on the basis of the monistic morality that utilitarianism must insist on; therefore, whatever he may profess, Mill is not really committed to utilitarianism; rather he is committed to a pluralistic morality, moreover to a loosely pluralistic morality, and it is from this that his best thinking depends.

In this chapter I want to tread a narrow path. I accept whole-heartedly Berlin's strictures upon moral monism and indeed upon anything other than a loose form of pluralism in morality. I share his high opinion of Mill, who for me also is a sympathetic thinker on moral and social topics. However, I reject Berlin's reading of Mill and I accept Mill's claim about himself. In other words, I believe that Mill did remain a utilitarian and I think that he certainly continued to think of utility as he said he did: that is, as the ultimate appeal on all ethical questions. But the crucial qualification here is, to my mind, provided by Mill himself when he goes on to say that he intends utility 'in the largest sense' or utility 'grounded in the permanent interests of man as a progressive being' (p. 31). For it is central to my way of thinking about Mill that this significantly extends the notion of utility, that it is vital to the understanding of Mill's revision of utilitarianism, and that it does not, as Berlin thinks, stretch the notion of utility to the point of vacuity. For me it is just this qualification, properly understood, which explains simultaneously how Mill remained a utilitarian and how he emerged as an interesting and sympathetic thinker. And, by qualifying the notion of utility as he does, Mill, to my mind, produces not only a more plausible morality, but a morality that can be more plausibly regarded as utilitarian, than that constructed upon the cruder notion or notions of utility held alike by his immediate predecessors and many of his numerous successors.

A residual question remains: Berlin insists upon the diversity of human values. Mill ascribes complexity to the single value to which he subscribes. Given that Mill in talking of complexity succeeds in doing justice to everything that Berlin has in mind by diversity, given that Mill shows that utility, properly understood, can lay claim to the appropriate complexity, is he still right to think of utility as the complex value appropriate to occupy the central place in morality? I shall not attempt an answer to this residual question.

II

In 1826 John Stuart Mill underwent a severe mental crisis, to which so much of his earlier life contributed, and from which so much of his later life was to draw benefit. Mill himself wrote of the crisis as an event in his intellectual development. It was clearly more than this, but it was also this, and it is solely as an event in his development as a moral philosopher that I wish to consider it.

One day Mill found himself putting to himself the following question:

Suppose that all your objects in life were realised; that all the changes in institutions and opinions which you are looking forward to, could be completely effected at this very instant: would this be a great joy and happiness to you?[3]

He did not have to wait long for an answer. The question was posed, and

an irrepressible self-consciousness directly answered 'No!' At this my heart sank within me: the whole foundation on which my life was constructed fell down. All my happiness was to have been found in the continual pursuit of this end. The end had ceased to charm, and how could there ever again be any interest in the means? I seemed to have nothing left to live for.

One striking detail about the incident, or about Mill's telling of it, is the way in which Mill frames the original question. For he does not ask, as one might expect: Do I still find the utilitarian ideal a good ideal? Am I in accord with it as a moral or political objective? Instead he asks whether the realisation of utilitarian objectives will give him pleasure, whether the satisfaction of the utilitarian ideal will in turn satisfy him, and at first this might strike the reader as a peculiarly personal or poignant touch, showing how deeply this crisis of belief affected his whole being and how it had shaken the more drily abstract way of looking at things which had been natural to him. The briefest reflection will show that this is a misinterpretation of Mill. In framing the question as he did, just what Mill shows is how firmly he still stood within the utilitarian framework. For, according to utilitarianism, it is a constraint upon morality that, for any given moral judgement, general or particular, there should be a precise match between the content of the judgement, or what it obliges an agent to do, and its motivational force, or its capacity to incite the agent – the agent, that is, who has fully understood it – to act in conformity with it. Further, utilitarianism prided itself on being a morality – indeed the only morality – which could meet this constraint. By assigning content to the moral judgement in the way in which it did – that is, as what would result in the greatest net balance of pleasure over pain for its recipients – it claimed to provide the agent with a uniquely good motive for putting it into practice: that is, the prospect of the greatest net balance of pleasure over pain for him too. Accordingly Mill was accepting one cardinal tenet of utilitarianism and using it to challenge another when he began to suspect that the fulfilment of the utilitarian ideal would not bring him happiness. As this suspicion hardened into certainty, his mental crisis peaked.

Mill's recovery from depression coincided with the attempt he made over the subsequent years to bring the content and the motivational force of utilitarianism back into line. Or – as it might more realistically be put, for Mill never really took altogether seriously the idea that there could be a morality which, once properly grasped, would prove irresistible – with the attempt he made to recapture motivational appeal for utilitarianism. Reflection must have shown that there were in principle two ways of doing this. Starting from the simple Benthamism with which he had become so thoroughly disillusioned, either he could rethink the content of utilitarian morality, so as to enhance its appeal, or he could put forward a revised account of human motivation with the aim of showing that utilitarian morality, content unchanged, had after all the capacity to move to action.

There was an evident difficulty for Mill in pursuing the second course. It would have required him to deny the most crucial experience of his life. In rewriting human motivation he would have had to rewrite his own motivation, and he would have had to say that, at the very moment when he was utterly convinced that the ideals in which he had been brought up no longer moved him, he did in fact have a motive, however best described, for acting on them, the deliverances of self-consciousness notwithstanding. In other words, Mill would have extricated himself from his mental crisis only at the expense of unlearning the lesson it seemingly had taught him, and it is no surprise that, in his attempt to recapture motivational appeal for utilitarianism, he chose the first course.

Mill's revision of the content of utilitarian morality can most conveniently be considered if it is looked upon as falling into two stages. The two stages are not chronological stages, and there are good reasons for thinking that Mill's thought is ill-suited to chronological study – which, it is no accident, his detractors greatly favour.[4] Mill was a very perceptive thinker, and he often ran ahead of himself in grasping the conclusions to which his current thinking would lead him. At the same time he was very preoccupied with the impression that his words might make on a reader, and sometimes, in order to dispel the suspicion that he had abandoned the leading ideas of his earlier years, he would use phraseology which no longer consorted well with his actual thinking. To consider then, as I propose to do, the shift that Mill effects in utilitarian morality as falling into two stages – one of which is the shift from a morality that employs a monistic conception of utility to one that employs a conception of utility that is pluralistic but with hierarchy, and the other is the shift from a morality that employs a conception of utility that is pluralistic but with hierarchy to one that employs a conception of utility that is pluralistic and without hierarchy – is not to advance a historical thesis. Evidences of the later stage are already to be found in the essay on Bentham (1838), while the earlier stage still leaves its mark on *Utilitarianism* (1861).

In explicating the revision that Mill effects upon the content of utilitarian morality, I shall do so with an eye to the two questions that may be raised about it. The first is: does this shift in content succeed in restoring appeal to utilitarianism? The second is: is this shift really a shift within utilitarianism, or isn't it, rather, a shift out of utilitarianism?

Finally, with Mill's revision of utilitarianism fully before us I shall draw attention to a corollary that Mill appended to utilitarianism. Its effect is to show that utilitarian morality may be set within a larger framework of ordinances. This larger framework I shall call an ethic, and that Mill proposed a three-tiered ethic is, I shall suggest, one of the most interesting, as well as one of the more neglected, aspects of his work as a moral philosopher.

III

In our consideration of Mill's revision of utilitarianism, there is one problem, which might be expected to have priority for someone out to revise utilitarianism, which we do not have to trouble ourselves with. For reasons whose adequacy need not detain us, Mill took the problem as solved. The problem is that of the transition from a purely egotistic morality, which is the form in which, according to a well established tradition, utilitarianism initially proposes itself, to a non–egotistic morality: that is, to a morality which enjoins the maximisation of pleasure but is indifferent to whom it is to whom the pleasure accrues, and, specifically, is blind to the distinction between agent's pleasure and the pleasure of others.[5] For the purposes of this paper this transition is assumed.

The first stage in the shift that Mill effects in the content of utilitarian morality consists in the move from a monistic conception of utility to a conception of utility that is pluralistic but with hierarchy. Alongside the primary principle of hedonism, or the maximisation of pleasure, secondary principles make their appearance. Examples of such secondary principles would be the education of the mind, the cultivation of sexual love and family affection, patriotism, the maintenance of personal dignity, or the attachment to beauty, and, of course, it must be appreciated that these secondary principles, like the primary principle, may be non-egotistic. Secondary principles fix the agent's ends – their ends are his ends – but there is no reason why his ends should be self-interested or exclusively for him. However, what is characteristic of this stage of Mill's thinking, and what defines it, is that secondary principles are strictly subordinate to the primary principle, and it is because of this subordination that the pluralism brought about by the introduction of secondary principles is hierarchical.

In order to see how hierarchy manifests itself, let us take as the central case – for it is the clearest case – that in which a moral agent invokes utilitarian morality in order to decide how he ought to act.[6] Once we have grasped how hierarchy manifests itself here, we can use this understanding in order to grasp the effects of hierarchy in what may be regarded as derivative cases: that is, where a moral agent decides whether he has acted as he ought to have, or where a moral critic decides how others ought to act or whether they have acted as they ought to have.

Now, in the central case, the moral agent in reaching a decision may consult the primary principle; alternatively he may consult one or other or more of his secondary principles. Let us suppose that he consults secondary principles. He does so, and he arrives at a decision. Then it is open to him to consult the primary principle and arrive at a decision on the basis of it. It is not required of him to do so, but, other things being equal – that is, the costs not being prohibitive – it is a rational course of action. It is so just because, should the two decisions diverge, then what he ought to do is given by the decision arrived at on the basis of the primary principle. The original decision must be abandoned. Of course, if the secondary principles have been at all carefully thought out, such divergences will be a rare thing. Nevertheless, should they occur, the primary principle operates in the agent's reasoning as though it were the only principle in the field, and this is one way in which secondary principles show themselves to be subordinate to the primary principle, or in which hierarchy manifests itself.

This way is the straightforward way, and to see the oblique way let us now suppose that the agent, in reaching a decision on how he ought to act, consults the primary principle. In such a case what he will do is that he will survey the various actions that are practicable for him, he will assign to each the consequences that it is most likely to have for himself and for others, and he will calculate for each of these consequences the net balance of pleasure and pain that it is likely to produce, and then arrival at a decision will be a matter of selecting that action whose consequences maximise pleasure or produce the greatest net balance of pleasure over pain. Non-egotism is preserved by indifference to whom it is to whom the pleasure accrues. Now, in computing the pleasure and pain for each action, the agent will have to consider how his action interacts with the actions of others, and therefore he will need to know the courses of action on which those others who are affected by the action are embarked. However, these courses of action will themselves have been decided upon in one or other of two ways: either on the basis of the primary principle or on the basis of some one or more of the secondary principles of the person embarked on it. Let us now suppose that all the courses of action on which those others affected by the agent's action are embarked have been decided upon on the basis of secondary principles, and that this is known to the agent. All persons affected by his action are acting on secondary principles. In that case in computing the pleasure and pain that action is likely to produce the agent will surely find it natural to equate, for each person, pleasure with the achievement of the end or ends fixed by the secondary principle or principles on which that person is acting. This determines the way in which, at any rate in the first instance, the agent will consider the interaction of his action with the actions of others. But, once again, this calculation having been made, though it is not required, it is, other things being equal, rational for the agent to make a complementary calculation. This time, in computing the pleasure and pain that his action is likely to produce, the agent, one allowance apart, ignores the fact that those others whom his action affects have decided upon the courses of action on which they are embarked on the basis of secondary principles. He assumes all persons affected by his action are acting on the primary principle, and in consequence, for each person, he equates pleasure, not with the achievement of the end or ends fixed by the secondary principle or principles on which that person is in point of fact acting, but just with whatever the primary principle enjoins for him – the one allowance that the agent makes being that he still has to count as pain for each person any disappointment he might experience from frustration of the secondary principle or principles on which he is actually, if misguidedly, acting. On this new assumption the agent will arrive at a fresh decision on how he ought to act, and should the two decisions diverge, it is the second decision that he should prefer. He should, in other words, act as though the primary principle operates, this time not in the agent's reasoning, but in the reasoning of others, as the only principle in the field. Here we have the other way in which secondary principles show themselves to be subordinate to the primary principle, or in which hierarchy manifests itself.

The subordination of the secondary principles to the primary principle at this stage in Mill's thinking has, as a consequence, that the ends fixed by the various secondary principles stand to the end fixed by the primary principle in a special relationship: they stand as means to end. The agent's ends are, and are to be assessed as, means to pleasure. This means–end relationship totally coheres with the motivation that prompts this first shift in the content of utilitarian morality. This motivation is essentially practical, and is best expressed by Mill when he talks of utility as 'too complex and indefinite an end'[7] for a moral agent always to have had to take stock of in calculating what he ought to do or what would be best for himself and others. Such a calculation remains a calculation about utility, but it might be more practical to arrive at an answer by working it out in terms both simpler and more definite than utility. These terms are just what secondary principles provide through fixing subsidiary aims.

If Mill's first revision of utilitarian morality makes it easier for the agent to operate, it also does more than this, and it is this additional thing it does that enhances the appeal of utilitarian morality. For the revision brings it about that an agent, in deciding what he ought to do, has no longer to regard as irrelevant a whole body of thoughts, and also the attitudes and feelings connected with these thoughts, had by him or had by others, and which must be reckoned by any sensitive person as amongst the most interesting that either he or they are likely to entertain. I refer, of course, to those thoughts which define either his ends or the ends of others, for these thoughts must now enter into his calculations in so far as he thinks of pleasure accruing to himself or to them through the satisfaction of secondary principles upon which they act. So far, but no further. This body of thoughts acquires relevance for his calculations, but the relevance is merely provisional. Once it seems to the agent that pleasure is less likely to accrue this way, once the ends of the secondary principles no longer convince him as being the best means to the end of the primary principle, then these thoughts cease to have a claim upon his attention. He may, indeed he must, put them out of his mind.

The purely provisional way in which these thoughts enter into the agent's calculations, and, correspondingly, the way in which they can be appropriately displaced by the direct thought of pleasure or utility, attest, of course, to the hierarchy that at this stage constrains the new-found pluralism of utilitarian morality.

But they attest to something else as well. They attest to the degree to which the concept of pleasure, or happiness, or utility – and so far I have not found it necessary to distinguish between them – is itself found quite unproblematic. More specifically, the concept is not felt to require any of the interesting thoughts I have just referred to, or the ends fixed by secondary principles, for its elucidation. All this, however, is to change as utilitarian morality undergoes its second revision, to which we may now turn.

IV

The second stage in the shift that Mill effects in the content of utilitarian morality consists in the move from a conception of utility that is pluralistic but with hierarchy to one that is pluralistic and without hierarchy. Not merely do secondary principles appear alongside the primary principle but now they are not subordinate to it. The ends fixed by the secondary principles no longer stand to the end fixed by the primary principle in the means–end relationship. Or at least they no longer stand to it exclusively in this relationship. They also serve to elucidate it.

That the ends fixed by the secondary principle now serve to elucidate the end fixed by the primary principle has the implication that by now the latter end, or utility, has ceased to be unproblematic. And this is so. It is characteristic of utilitarianism under its second revision that utility is found problematic, but it is important to grasp how. The point is not that – or is not merely that – Mill, the moral philosopher, finds utility problematic. Rather, in his moral philosophy Mill reconstructs the fact that the moral agent finds, indeed must find, utility problematic. It then goes on to represent how the moral agent tries to resolve the problem for himself. He is represented as trying to make utility unproblematic by subscribing to secondary principles.

Why the moral agent finds utility problematic is to do with the highly abstract nature of the concept. Grasping this highly abstract concept, the agent finds that it doesn't contribute, in the way that utilitarianism leads him to believe that it should, to a decision how he ought to act. Even with all requisite information at his disposal, he will still have an inadequate grasp of what he should do to maximise utility. The abstract concept utility needs to be filled out, and this filling out can be thought of in two parts. In the first instance, the moral agent is required to have what might be thought of as a conception of his own utility. Only then can he consider how his utility is to be advanced. This conception is, however, not something that can be given to him or that he can learn. It is something that has to be formed, and it is formed through the process of trial and error. He tries out various secondary principles and finishes by subscribing to those whose ends give him or teach him what he wants. But, in the second instance, the moral agent requires that others have – that is, others form – a conception of their own utility, for only then can he consider how he is to advance their utility. And, once again, this conception is one that they have to form, they form it through trial and error, and it is codified in their secondary principles.

But it is one thing to believe that utilitarian morality cannot be successfully pursued unless each forms a conception of his own utility and that such a conception is formed through subscribing to secondary principles, and another thing, and evidently unjustified, to equate the subscription to just any set of secondary principles with the formation of a conception of one's own utility. Surely there must be some constraint upon the secondary principles subscribed to. More specifically, there must be some constraint upon the ends that these principles fix. To put the point another way: it may very well be that the pursuit of morality requires the subscription to secondary principles; but what has to be true of the secondary principles for the morality that they permit to be truly thought of as a utilitarian morality?

Actually it is an exaggeration to say, as I have said, that at this stage of Mill's revision of utilitarian morality utility is found problematic, if this is taken to mean that utility is found altogether problematic. There remains an unproblematic aspect of utility, and to mark the distinction that is at stake here it would be useful to employ the traditional distinction between pleasure and happiness. Unproblematically utility connotes pleasure, where pleasure is thought of as a kind of sensation or adjunct of sensation, and so long as utility is given this highly restricted interpretation, the moral agent may arrive at utilitarian decisions about how he ought to act without either his forming for himself or others' forming for themselves conceptions of their own utility. Such decisions are decisions about the maximisation of the privileged sensation or adjunct of sensation. It is only when the moral agent appreciates that utilitarian decisions cannot be circumscribed in this way that utility becomes problematic for him. Any issue from this problematic situation is possible only if two conditions are met. In the first place, utility must be recognised to connote more than just pleasure. It also connotes, and it must be perceived to connote, happiness. Secondly, for the concept of utility in its broader connotation to gain application, it is required that the agent and others form conceptions of their own utility. This they do, as we have seen, through subscribing to secondary principles. If, however, we now ask what these secondary principles must be like, or what is the constraint laid upon the ends fixed by secondary principles if the conception to which these principles contribute is to be regarded as a conception of the person's utility or if the morality that they help to constitute is to be regarded as a utilitarian morality, the answer is easier to find. The constraint appears to be this: the ends fixed by the various secondary principles must be systematically related to pleasure.

But to say that the ends of the secondary principles must be systematically related to pleasure if utilitarianism is to be safeguarded does not say enough. There are various ways in which the ends of secondary principles may be systematically related to pleasure. For instance, some moral philosophers would argue that the systematic relationship is to be of a conceptual kind. The ends must derive from the concept of pleasure. I wish to suggest that the systematic relationship must be of a genetic kind. And I also wish to suggest that this is how Mill thought of the matter. In other words, utilitarianism as revised by him requires that it is possible to arrange pleasure and the ends fixed by the secondary principles of a moral agent on one and the same dendrogram, where the ends lie on the branches, pleasure is at the base of the tree, and the diagram as a whole represents the emergence of the moral agent according to the best available theory of human nature.[8]

From this last point an important consequence follows. To be able to say what it is for a morality that consists in a primary principle enjoining the maximisation of utility and various secondary principles not subordinate to the primary principle to be overall a utilitarian morality presupposes that one has in one's possession a developmental psychology of a certain richness. It is only through such a psychology that one can tell whether the secondary principles appropriately relate to the primary principle. It is unnecessary to observe that Mill did not have such a psychology. He conceded the point – notably in the essay 'The subjection of women' – and in at least one place he gave it as his opinion that the lack constituted the biggest single gap in contemporary knowledge.[9] However, there is a passage where he clearly recognises just what has to be the internal structure of a morality that is pluralistic and without hierarchy and also utilitarian, and how this structure presupposes a theory of human nature. I refer to the passage in *Utilitarianism*, widely ridiculed, in which Mill talks of higher and lower pleasures.[10] To see how this passage bears upon the present issue, the reader needs to orientate himself appropriately. For, generally, this passage is read for what Mill has to say about the difference between higher and lower pleasures, or how it is that one pleasure can vary qualitatively from another. But the passage can also be read for what Mill has to say about what higher and lower pleasures have in common, or why it is that both are kinds of pleasure. Roughly, Mill's view is that higher and lower pleasures are both kinds of pleasure because they are functionally equivalent at different levels of a person's psychological development – which, of course, is also, to the same degree of roughness, just the reason why one kind of pleasure is qualitatively superior to the other. Thereby Mill throws everything on to the question of psychological development and how its levels are to be identified and what lies on each level. Given his lack of a psychological theory, Mill is naturally unable to answer these questions, but what is crucial for the proper interpretation of Mill is that he saw just what it was that was necessary if such answers were to be produced or where they were to come from.

I shall call utilitarianism under its second revision, or where its content is given by the primary principle of hedonism and various secondary principles not subordinate to but elucidatory of it, 'complex utilitarianism', and I turn to the question how, or how far, complex utilitarianism restores appeal to utilitarianism.

The crucial way in which complex utilitarianism restores appeal to utilitarianism is that it compels – it doesn't just permit, it compels – the moral agent, in deciding what he ought to do (or in coming to any related decision), to take account of what I have already called thoughts that are amongst the most interesting that human beings entertain: that is, thoughts definitive of the ends fixed by secondary principles, whether the agent's own or of others. And in taking account of these thoughts the agent is also required to take account of the feelings and attitudes that group themselves around those thoughts. And the account that he is required to take of these mental constellations is something that is by now ineliminable. It is not merely provisional, and it is not to be set aside in deference to some consideration which overrides secondary principles and their aims. Utilitarianism at last pays attention to man in his full complexity as a developed human being, and it would have to be a very gloomy or very desiccated self-consciousness that returned the answer 'No' to the question whether the pursuit of man's happiness, when man is thus envisaged, was an end that held the promise of satisfaction.

V

However, it might now seem that utilitarianism under its second revision, or complex utilitarianism, gains, or regains, appeal, but only at the cost of scope. Let me explain.

A moral agent, we are now told, has to take ineliminable account of both his and others' secondary principles. But this is impossible unless both he and others have secondary principles, and further-more – for otherwise the account he takes of them would be eliminable – hold them not subordinately to the primary principle. He and they must have formed conceptions of their own happiness, and they must moreover have knowledge of each other's conceptions. But this is not a universally satisfied condition: it represents an achievement, first of all, in the life of the species, and then, secondly, in the life of the individual. Complex utilitarianism gains its appeal from the way in which it pays respect to the full faculties of man: but, by the same token, it appears to lose its hold when man has not entered into possession of his full faculties. In its attempt to do justice to the developmental nature of man, complex utilitarianism takes on or acquires a developmental nature. Or so it might seem. Is this so, and is this how Mill saw it?

Mill, we know, like his father and like Bentham, professed to think that any non–utilitarian morality was ultimately untenable. But did he think that utilitarian morality held in those circumstances – whether of general history or of personal biography – in which it did not hold appeal?

Explicitly, Mill never raised the question. But implicitly – or so I believe – he must have, just because he supplied the question with an answer, and an answer which, as I have already said, constitutes one of the most interesting and also most neglected aspects of his work as a moral philosopher. For what Mill did was to set complex utilitarianism within a larger structure, appropriately thought of as a three-tiered ethic, and to each tier of which he then assigned distinct conditions under which it held or in which it obliged the agent to act in conformity with it.

On one tier of this ethic, the uppermost tier, there is utilitarianism proper, by now glossed as complex utilitarianism. Complex utilitarianism enjoins the maximisation of utility, as utility is elucidated in the moral agent's conception of happiness and in the conceptions of happiness entertained by the various recipients of his action. Complex utilitarianism holds when, or in so far as, people have indeed formed their own conceptions of happiness, know of the conceptions of others, and pursue utility accordingly. It holds just when men have entered into possession of their full faculties. On the tier below this, or the middle tier, there is simple utilitarianism, where this includes both utilitarianism employing a monistic conception of utility and utilitarianism employing a conception of utility that is pluralistic but with hierarchy. Simple utilitarianism holds when, or in so far as, men have not formed conceptions of their own happiness, and pleasure rather than happiness is what they pursue for themselves and others. It is the ethic of men whose faculties are still undeveloped. Then, on the third tier, the lowermost, there is what I shall call 'preliminary utilitarianism', and I claim that it is one of the most innovative aspects of Mill's ethical thought that he identified and found a place for preliminary utilitarianism. What preliminary utilitarianism enjoins is whatever is necessary for people either to form, or having formed, to maintain, conceptions of their own happiness – or, for that matter (though I shall not pursue this aspect), envisagements of other people's conceptions of their own happiness. The conditions under which preliminary utilitarianism holds are disjunctive: that part which is concerned with the formation of people's conceptions of their own happiness holds when such conceptions are not fully formed, and that part which is concerned with the maintenance of such conceptions holds just when they are formed. Preliminary utilitarianism invariably holds. And, finally, when the injunctions of preliminary utilitarianism conflict with the injunctions of either simple or complex utilitarianism – whichever is relevant – then, unless the cost in utility is too severe, the injunctions of preliminary utilitarianism take priority. Education up to the point where happiness can be attained is more important than the attainment either of pleasure or of happiness.

I shall end by drawing attention to the three separate places

274

where Mill argues for policies or practices on the basis of preliminary utilitarianism. Two occur in the essay *On Liberty*.

The first passage is in chapter 4, where Mill, having divided the actions of the agent into the 'self-regarding' (his phrase) and the 'other-regarding' (not his phrase), exempts the former altogether from the sphere of state intervention. For this exemption might not be the verdict reached by appeal either to simple or to complex utilitarianism, and for two distinct reasons. In the first place, though it is a matter of dispute just how Mill effected the division, it seems as though self-regarding actions are not to be equated with those which in no way impinge upon others. They must be those actions which affect others, if they do, only in some discountable fashion.[11] Accordingly, there is always the possibility that a self-regarding action is in its net effect more adverse than some other action practicable for the agent. Why should not such an action, on grounds of utilitarianism, either simple or complex, be the object of state intervention? Second, self-regarding actions, however defined, have an effect upon the agent. Why should not utilitarianism decide that those with a benign effect upon him ought to be enforced by the state and those with a malign effect upon him be prohibited? Mill's counter-argument seems to be that self-regarding actions are crucial to those 'experiments of living' without which individual conceptions of happiness would either not be formed or, having been formed, would wither away (p. 74). Here we witness a case of preliminary utilitarianism overruling either simple or complex utilitarianism.

The second passage is to be found in chapter 2, where Mill discusses liberty of opinion, which once again is treated as total. Mill's argument in favour of total liberty of opinion appeals to two considerations: truth and rationality. In both cases the content of the appeal is subtle, but the question arises: why should a utilitarian, even a complex utilitarian, set such supreme value on truth and rationality? These may, of course, and almost certainly will be, amongst the ends fixed by secondary principles of the various citizens. But does this fully explain the strength of Mill's commit-ment? It seems that preliminary utilitarianism must make its contribution to the argument, in that, if it does not overrule utilitarianism proper, at least it supplements it.

The third passage is in *Considerations on Representative Government*. Mill says that representative government is the ideally best form of government in that it is 'the one which in the circumstances in which it is practicable and eligible is attended with the greatest amount of beneficial consequences, immediate and prospective'. Here, it might seem, speaks utilitarianism proper. But not so. For as Mill develops the argument, he brings forward two criteria by which the merit of political institutions is to be judged. One concerns the way in which they 'organize the moral, intellectual, and active worth already existing, so as to operate with the greatest effect in public affairs'.[12] If that sounds like the voice of utilitarianism, what are we to make of the second criterion? For this concerns the way in which political institutions 'promote the general mental advancement of the community'. If this can in part be put to utilitarianism proper – and this I do not deny – in part it attests to the influence of preliminary utilitarianism.

It is not surprising that critics are to be found who will see in these passages evidence of Mill's backslidings from utilitarianism. Given their failure to perceive the complex character of Mill's commitment to utilitarianism – more complex, it now turns out, than a mere commitment to complex utilitarianism – their criticisms are altogether understandable. However, concern for the proper interpretation of Mill requires us to reject them. Properly interpreted, Mill can be shown to concur not only with Berlin's concern for a loose pluralism in morality but also with his other, no less urgent, no less generous, and certainly related, concern for the all-important value of liberty. But that is another though not all that different a story.

NOTES

1 Mill, *On Liberty*, all references in the text are to this volume.
2 Isaiah Berlin, 'John Stuart Mill and the ends of life', this volume, (pp. 131–61).
3 Mill, *CW*, 1:139 (Autobiography, 133–4).
4 G. Himmelfarb, ed., *Essays on Politics and Culture* (New York, Doubleday, 1962); and G. Himmelfarb, *On Liberty and Liberalism* (New York, Knopf, 1974); cf. John Rees, 'The thesis of the two Mills', *Political Studies* 25 (1977), 369–82.
5 In two early essays – the 'Remarks on Bentham's philosophy' (1833), which appeared anonymously, and 'Sedgwick's discourse' (1835) – Mill sets himself against the identification of utility with selfish or self-regarding interest. In the earlier essay he uses this point as a criticism of Bentham, in the later essay he uses it in defence of Bentham against his critics. Mill, *CW*, 10.
6 For ease of exposition I write throughout as though utilitarianism were

to be construed as act-utilitarianism. I tend to believe that this is correct, but all my examples can fairly readily be converted so as to concord with rule-utilitarianism.

7 Mill, *CW*, 10:110.

8 At two different places in his edition of his father's *magnum opus* Mill seeks to forestall those who criticise the view that evolved ends derive from the pursuit of pleasure on the grounds that the two kinds of end are unresembling, by pointing out to such critics that, when the genetic derivation is lengthy, 'the resulting feeling always seems not only very unlike any one of the elements composing it, but very unlike the sum of those elements'. James Mill, *Analysis of the Phenomena of the Human Mind*, ed., John Stuart Mill (London, Longmans, Green, Reader & Dyer, 1869), 2:321; cf. 252.

9 'Of all the difficulties which impede the progress of thought, and the formation of well-grounded opinions on life and social arrangements, the greatest is now the unspeakable ignorance and inattention of mankind in respect to the influences which form human character.' John Stuart Mill, *The Subjection of Women*, *CW*, 21:277. The missing science Mill had talked about under the name 'ethology' in book 6, chapter 5 of his *System of Logic*.

10 Mill, *CW*, 10:210–13.

11 J.C. Rees, 'A re-reading of Mill on liberty', this volume, pp. 169–89. Alan Ryan, 'Mr McCloskey on Mill's liberalism', *Philosophical Quarterly* 14 (1964), 253–60; C.L. Ten, 'Mill on self-regarding actions', *Philosophy* 43 (1968), 29–37; Richard Wollheim, 'John Stuart Mill and the limits of state action', *Social Research* 40 (1973), 1–30.

12 Mill, *CW*, 19:392. Some interesting observations on the interlock between Mill's concern with the formation of character and his political views are to be found in R.J. Halliday, 'Some recent interpretations of John Stuart Mill', *Philosophy* 43 (1968), 1–17, reprinted in *Mill: A Collection of Critical Essays*, ed., J.B. Schneewind (London, Macmillan, 1968).

INDEX

INDEX

organization men, Mill's dislike of
140
originality, importance of in human
life 80–1
Orwell, George, 'Reflections on
Gandhi' 222
'other-directed' individuals 196–7
Owen, Robert 13, 14, 245–6, 250,
254, 258
Oxford Idealists 172

Paganism 66
pain, attitude of utilitarians 232–3;
and groundless antipathy 232–4
Palmerston, Lord 137
Pareto, V. 153
paternalistic government 115–16
Paul, Saint 45, 66
perfectionist theory, in criticism of
Mill 208–9, 210
Pericles 78
persecution, attempts to justify 146;
effectiveness of 142–3;
recommendation of 46–7;
success of 47–8
personal attachment 91
personal identity, Mill's theory of
249
personal preferences 223–5
pessimism, in Mill's view of human
nature 153, 256–8
Philosophic Radicals 1
Philosophical Necessity, doctrine
of 23
Plamenatz, J. 182
Plato 44, 152; dialogues 62
Platonic Guardians, Mill not
advocating 153
pleasure, and happiness 234,
270–1; principle 1; and right
acts 213; and secondary
principles 271–2; see also
hedonism
pleasures, higher 16, 190, 209–10,
272
pleasures, lower 272
pluralism of moral values 260–1
poets, expulsion of from society
152

poisons, justification for sale of
109–11
politics, need for opposing views
64–5
polygamy 106–7
Poor Law 127–8
popular opinions, limitations of 63
pork, religious objections to eating
of 99–100, 186, 213
Pound, Roscoe 182
power, of government 123–5;
justification of 30–1
preappointed evidence 111
press freedom 36
Principle of Liberty 2, 3, 6, 7, 8,
11–12, 13, 14, 15, 17–18, 239;
see also liberty
Principle of Utility 2, 3, 6, 9, 12,
16, 17; see also utility
progress, halting of 86, 87; nature
of in Europe 86–9; damage to
95
prophecy, Mill's lack of 140–1, 153
proportional representation 137
Protestantism 66; and intellectual
inquiry 54, 57; and married
clergy 100–1; persecution of 143
prudence 5–6, 7, 17, 164; and
appraisal of higher pleasures 193;
contrasted with morality 164–5
psychology, Mill's discussion of
203
public duty, and Christianity 67
public interest 186
public opinion, formers of 82
Puritanism 98, 101

qualitative hedonism, theory of
190–1

racial prejudice 228–30
rational self-direction 194, 197
rationalism, and romanticism 154,
157
rationality 133; Mill charged with
attributing too much to
mankind 152–3
Rawls, John 208, 209; A Theory of
Justice 19

284